What Critics and Professionals Say About the "Impact Guides"

THE TREASURES AND
PLEASURES OF INDONESIA

Books & CD-ROMs by Drs. Ron and Caryl Krannich

The Almanac of International Jobs and Careers
Best Jobs for the 1990s and Into the 21st Century
Change Your Job, Change Your Life
The Complete Guide to International Jobs and Careers
The Complete Guide to Public Employment
The Directory of Federal Jobs and Employers
Discover the Best Jobs for You!
Dynamite Answers to Interview Questions
Dynamite Cover Letters
Dynamite Resumes
Dynamite Salary Negotiations
Dynamite Tele-Search
The Educator's Guide to Alternative Jobs and Careers
Find a Federal Job Fast!
From Air Force Blue to Corporate Gray
From Army Green to Corporate Gray
From Navy Blue to Corporate Gray
High Impact Resumes and Letters
Interview for Success
Job Search Letters That Get Results
Job-Power Source CD-ROM
Jobs and Careers With Nonprofit Organizations
Jobs for People Who Love Computers and the Information Highway
Jobs for People Who Love Health Care and Nursing
Jobs for People Who Love Hotels, Resorts, and Cruise Ships
Jobs for People Who Love to Work From Home
Jobs for People Who Love Travel
Mayors and Managers
Moving Out of Education
Moving Out of Government
The New Network Your Way to Job and Career Success
The Politics of Family Planning Policy
Re-Careering in Turbulent Times
Resumes and Cover Letters for Transitioning Military Personnel
Shopping and Traveling in Exotic Asia
Shopping in Exciting Australia and Papua New Guinea
Shopping in Exotic Places
Shopping the Exotic South Pacific
Treasures and Pleasures of Hong Kong
Treasures and Pleasures of India
Treasures and Pleasures of Indonesia
Treasures and Pleasures of Italy
Treasures and Pleasures of Morocco
Treasures and Pleasures of Paris and the French Riviera
Treasures and Pleasures of Singapore and Malaysia
Treasures and Pleasures of Thailand
Treasures and Pleasures of the Philippines
Ultimate Job Source CD-ROM

IMPACT GUIDES

THE TREASURES AND PLEASURES OF

Indonesia

BEST OF THE BEST

RON AND CARYL KRANNICH, PH.DS

IMPACT PUBLICATIONS
MANASSAS PARK, VA

Library of Congress Cataloguing-in-Publication Data

Ronald L. Krannich.
    The treasures and pleasures of Indonesia: best of the best/ Ron and Caryl Krannich.
    p. c.m
    Revised ed. of: Shopping and traveling in exotic Indonesia. c1991.
    Includes bibliographical references and index.
    ISBN 1-57023-045-5 (alk. Paper)
        1. Shopping—Indonesia—Guidebooks. 2. Indonesia— Guidebooks. I. Krannich, Caryl Rae. II. Krannich, Ronald L. Shopping and traveling in exotic Indonesia. III. Title.
TX337.I5K74 1995
380.1'45'00025598—dc20   95-39565
                                             CIP

For information on distribution or quantity discount rates, Tel. 703/361-7300, FAX 703/335-9486, or write to: Sales Department, IMPACT PUBLICATIONS, 9104-N Manassas Drive, Manassas Park, VA 22111-5211. Distributed to the trade by National Book Network, 4720 Boston Way, Suite A, Lanham, MD 20706, Tel. 301/459-8696 or 900/462-6420.

Contents

PART I
Traveling Smart

PART II
Shopping Well

PART III
Island to Island Shopping

Liabilities and
Warranties

While the authors have attempted to provide accurate and up-to-date information in this book, please be advised that names, addresses, and phone numbers do change and shops, restaurants, and hotels do move, go out of business, or change ownership and management. Such changes are a constant fact of life in Indonesia. We regret any inconvenience such changes may cause to your travel plans.

Inclusion of shops, shippers, restaurants, hotels, tour groups, and other hospitality providers in this book in no way implies guarantees nor endorsements by either the authors or publisher. The information and recommendations appearing in this book are provided solely for your reference. The honesty and reliability of shops and shippers is best ensured by you—always ask the right questions and request proper receipts and documents.

The Treasures and Pleasures of Indonesia provides numerous tips on how you can best experience a trouble-free adventure as well as lessen the likelihood of encountering dishonesty, misrepresentation, and misunderstanding when traveling and shopping in Indonesia. As in any unfamiliar place or situation, or regardless of how trusting strangers may appear, the watchwords are always the same—watch your wallet! If it's too good to be true, it probably is.

Preface

Exotic Indonesia offers wonderful treasures and pleasures for those who know what to look for, where to go, and how to best enjoy this fascinating country. For more than 25 years we have repeatedly returned to Indonesia to further explore this ever-changing and delightful country. We've been especially intrigued by its many shopping centers, hotel shops, department stores, shophouses, factories, markets, street vendors, and peddlers. Indonesia remains one of our favorite Asian destinations. Its people and products continue to enrich our lives.

This book is really a story about what we have discovered in our varied travels to Indonesia. What we present here is a very different Indonesia largely absent in most travel guides and other literature on the country.

Indonesia offers visitors many shopping opportunities for textiles, jewelry, clothes, arts, antiques, handicrafts, and home decorative items. From each trip shoppers return home with unique and quality items to enhance their homes and wardrobes. If approached properly, we believe Indonesia may well become one of your favorite travel and shopping destinations.

What has particularly impressed us about Indonesia in recent years are the many wonderful shopping alternatives it presents to visitors. While it continues to offer interesting sightseeing and cultural opportunities, Indonesia's shopping particularly intrigues us. Indeed, we find Indonesia to be one of the best kept shopping secrets in all of Asia. Numerous shops in Jakarta, Bali, and Jogjakarta offer excellent textiles, arts, antiques, woodcarvings, ceramics, furniture, and home accessories to complement contemporary Western homes.

Shopping in Indonesia is different from shopping in Hong Kong, Tokyo, Seoul, Bangkok, Kuala Lumpur, Manila, or Singapore. If you don't know what to buy, where to go, or how to shop in Indonesia, you can easily miss some of the best shopping in Asia as you end up with only batik and a few tourist trinkets—popular items which may not integrate well with many Western wardrobes and homes. This is unfortunate for Indonesia has much more to offer you.

While Indonesia is still exotic to us, it no longer presents the mystery and confusion that often confronts first-time visitors. It is an increasingly modern, convenient, and comfortable country to visit. More and more people speak English, the transportation systems have improved, the food and hotels are often excellent, service can be exceptional, prices are still reasonable if you're careful, and the people are interesting and delightful to meet.

We wrote this book as part of a larger writing endeavor on the treasures and pleasures of exotic places with emphasis on the best of the best in travel and shopping. This volume is based on our numerous visits to Indonesia during the past 25 years. Especially during the past 15 years, we have witnessed numerous changes in traveling and shopping in Indonesia. More quality products and shops continue to appear in Jakarta, Bali, and Jogjakarta in response to growing international interest in Indonesian products. Better still, these products are becoming more and more compatible with Western design tastes. Indonesia is well on its way to becoming a shopper's paradise with its numerous unique and tasteful products.

The chapters that follow present a particular perspective on traveling in Indonesia. Like other volumes in our "Impact Guide" series, we purposefully decided to write more than just another descriptive travel guide primarily focusing on hotels, restaurants, and sightseeing and with only a few paragraphs or pages on shopping. While our primary focus is on shopping, the book had to go beyond other shopping guides that only concentrate on the "whats" and "wheres" of shopping. In addition, the book is much more than just a shopping guide to Indonesia. In many respects it is a travel guide in which shopping takes center stage in the travel process.

Our experience convinces us that there is a need for a different type of travel book on Indonesia. The book should outline the "how-tos" along with the "whats" and "wheres" of shopping in Indonesia. Such a book should both educate and guide you through Indonesia's shopping and travel mazes. Consequently, this book focuses on the **shopping process** as well as provides you with the necessary **shopping details** for making informed shopping choices in specific shopping areas, arcades, centers, department stores, markets, and shops.

Rather than just describe the "what" and "where" of travel and shopping, we include the critical "how"—what to do before you depart on your trip as well as while you are in Indonesia. We believe you and others are best served with a book that leads to both **understanding and action**. Therefore, you will find little in these pages about the general history, culture, economics, and politics of Indonesia; these topics are covered well in other types of travel books.

The perspective we develop throughout this book is based on our belief that traveling should be more than just another adventure in eating, sleeping, sightseeing, and taking pictures of unfamiliar places. Whenever possible, we attempt to bring to life the fact that Indonesia has real people and interesting products that you, the visitor, will find exciting. This is a country of talented artists, craftspeople, traders, and entrepreneurs who offer you some wonderful opportunities to participate in their society through their shopping processes. When you leave Indonesia, you will take with you not only some unique experiences and memories but also quality products that you will certainly appreciate for years to come.

We have not hesitated to make **qualitative judgments** about shopping and traveling in Indonesia, including the good, the bad, and the ugly. If we just presented you with shopping information, we would do you a disservice by not sharing our discoveries, both good and bad. Indeed, it would be irresponsible for us to just describe the "what" and "where" of shopping in Indonesia by presenting "the facts" without making judgments on what you should or should not do about Indonesia's shopping weaknesses and potential problems, such as rip-offs, touts, and commissions. Above all, we believe you could use a **good friend** when you travel to Indonesia. Hopefully this book will become your best and most trusted friend as you navigate the many promises and pitfalls of shopping and traveling in Indonesia.

While we know that our judgments may not be valid for everyone, we offer them as **reference points** from which you can make your own decisions. Our major emphasis throughout this book is on **quality shopping**. We look for shops that offer excellent quality and styles which we think are appropriate for

Western homes and wardrobes. If you share our concern for quality shopping, you will find many of our recommendations useful to your own shopping. However, we recognize that shops change. Some go out of business; others change ownership or management. So use our suggestions as a guide, but make your own decisions on "where" and "what" to buy.

Buying quality items does not mean you must spend a great deal of money on shopping. It means that you have taste, you are selective, you buy what fits into your wardrobe and home. If you shop in the right places, you will find quality products. If you understand the shopping process, you will get good value for your money. While shopping for quality may not be cheap, it need not be expensive. But most important, shopping for quality in Indonesia is fun and it results in lovely items which can be enjoyed for years to come.

Throughout this book we have included "tried and tested" shopping information. We make judgments based upon our experience and research approach: visit many shops, talk with numerous people, and simply shop.

Whatever you do, enjoy Indonesia. Its people, products, and places will charm you. While you need not "shop 'til you drop" in Indonesia, at least shop it well and with the confidence that you are getting good quality and value for your money. Don't just limit yourself to small items that will fit into your suitcase. Be adventuresome and consider acquiring larger items that can be safely and conveniently shipped home.

We wish you well in your travel and shopping adventure to Indonesia. The book is designed to be used on the roads, streets, and waters of Jakarta, Bali, Jogjakarta, Sumatra, Kalimantan, Sulawesi, and Irian Jaya. If you plan your journey according to the first four chapters, handle the shopping process according to the next two chapters, and navigate the islands, cities, and towns based on the remaining five chapters, you should have a marvelous time. You'll discover some exciting places, acquire some choice items, and return home with fond memories of exotic Indonesia. If you put this book to use, it will indeed become your best friend—and passport—to the treasures and pleasures of exotic Indonesia!

Ronald L. Krannich
Caryl Rae Krannich

THE TREASURES AND
PLEASURES OF INDONESIA

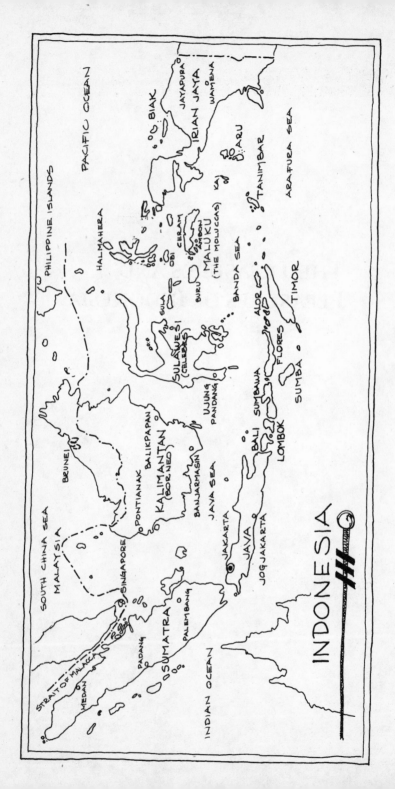

Welcome to Indonesia

Welcome to Indonesia, one of the world's most exotic, intriguing, and exciting travel destinations. A country of legendary fame, fortune, and beauty—Bali, Java Man, Spice Islands, Krakatoa, Borobudur, Batavia, Thomas Stamford Raffles, Sukarno, batik, textiles, trances, headhunters, tribes, pirates, writers, artists, exotic wildlife, and rubber, timber, and oil production—Indonesia is rich in history, culture, people, and resources. Indeed, resource-rich Indonesia is Asia's sleeping giant. For the travel industry, Indonesia has only recently become a popular destination for adventure travel and eco-tourism. However, for us, Indonesia remains one of the best kept shopping secrets in the world.

A GOOD VALUE

Within the next few years Indonesia will become Asia's fastest growing travel destination. As it develops, it may lose much of its Third World charm, seeming innocence, and price advantages for the many travelers who have repeatedly discovered the delights of Indonesia's many fascinating peoples, places, and products.

Our advice: **visit Indonesia soon** before a new wave of tourists arrives and crowds our favorite hotels, restaurants, and shops. And buy quickly before all the "good stuff" disappears or becomes too expensive. Indeed, just in the last three years have seen several signs that indicate Indonesia is heading the direction of tourism in Thailand and Malaysia—many more tourists; a better supporting tourist infrastructure of fine hotels, restaurants; and in-bound tour operators; fewer quality antiques, arts, and crafts; and, of course, higher prices.

For now, Indonesia is still one of the world's best travel secrets and values. It offers numerous inexpensive hotels, restaurants, and tours for travelers on a limited budget. At the same time, first-class and deluxe travelers will find an abundance of excellent hotels, restaurants, and tours, especially in Jakarta and Bali. Compared to many other Asian destinations, Indonesian products are a good value. You can "shop 'til you drop" in Indonesia and feel good about what you acquired and the prices you paid—our idea of the perfect trip!

An Exotic and Fascinating Place

Indonesia is a truly exotic place, completely embedded in an exotic culture, with exotic sights, smells, sounds, and people. Boasting the world's fifth largest population—dispersed over thousands of islands in an area larger than the United States— Indonesia offers a travel and shopping experience unlike anywhere else in the world.

A colorful country of great diversity and contrasts, Indonesia is many different places to many different people. And it can be approached in many different ways, from the individual backpacker and budget traveler to first-class and deluxe tours. Above all, this is a country that touches many emotions. Indonesia is as fascinating as it is frustrating, as simple as it is complex, as comprehendible as it is confusing, and as delightful as it is distressful. This is a country of conflicting images, contrasts, and complements. It will forever touch you with its images and, hopefully, its many traveling and shopping delights.

Let us share with you an unusual adventure, unlike any you may have ever experienced or are likely to encounter. We'll take you into into storybook villages, along gorgeous beaches, into colorful markets and intriguing antique shops, and through chic boutiques and air-conditioned department stores for one of the greatest travel and shopping adventures of a lifetime. When you leave Indonesia, you will take with you fond memories and unique products that you will forever cherish. And if you become addicted to the country, as we have for nearly 25 years, in another year or two you, too, may have that unexplained urge to return to experience more of the treasures and pleasures of this fascinating and exotic country.

A Unique Adventure

Largely undiscovered by Western travelers and tourists, Indonesia offers one of the world's great traveling and shopping adventures. It has everything you might want in a unique trip abroad: large cities with top international hotels, restaurants, and shops as well as a wide range of alternative budget facilities; gorgeous landscapes with rugged snowcapped mountains; active volcanos; tropical valleys and sweltering jungles; fine white and black sand beaches; interesting indigenous and colonial histories with ample museums and sites to visit; plentiful recreational facilities, including some of the world's best sailing, scuba diving, and hiking; and a splendid system of national parks and gardens exhibiting one of the world's most extensive collections of flora and fauna.

And to top this all off, Indonesia offers fine local cuisines, real dragon-lizards, and a mystical world populated by a fascinating collection of gods, demons, and spirits. It seems so unreal—a never-never land where fact and fancy become inseparable. If you stay here very long, you may become intoxicated by what you see and do. If you've just come from Hong Kong, Seoul, or Singapore, get ready for a few shocks. If you've already passed through Thailand or Malaysia, Indonesia will make these countries look like a piece of cake. You've had it easy so far. Get ready for a real challenge. Indonesia will test just how good you are with the "how," "what," "when," and "where" of shopping in exotic places!

❑ Indonesia is still one of the world's best travel values.

❑ This is an incredibly large and diverse country—nearly 190 million people; 13,667 islands, 5 main islands, 30 smaller archipelagos; 128 active volcanos; and over 300 ethnic and linguistic groups.

❑ When you shop in Indonesia, you meet artisans and shopkeepers, explore cities and villages, and see first-hand how various products are closely linked to living artistic and cultural traditions.

❑ Indonesia's living chaos, hustle and bustle, and sights and sounds are what make it such a fascinating and exotic travel adventure.

A Diverse Kaleidoscope

Indonesia is much more than just another travel and shopping destination. This is an incredibly diverse country offering some of the most unusual and exotic experiences. Above all, it can be a challenge in communication, physical stamina, patience, and perseverance. Some basic facts reveal a unique country.

Indonesia is the world's largest Muslim nation and the fifth largest country with nearly 190 million people living in an expansive east-west area the size of the United States; a country of 5 main islands and 30 smaller archipelagos; over 400 volcanos, 128 of which are active and include the famous Krakatoa among its 78 historical eruptions; 13,667 islands of which 6,000 are occupied by over 300 different ethnic and linguistic groups; fabled Bali and the Spice Islands; headhunters, pirates, seafarers, warring Stone Age tribes, missionaries, and Texas cowboy oil riggers; Muslims, Buddhists, Hindus, Christians, and animists; elegant and exotic music and dance; unique arts and crafts; intriguing primitive arts; rubber plantations and terraced rice fields; ancient schooners and sailing ships; tigers, rhinoceros, dragon-lizards, and the Bird of Paradise; 40,000 plant species including the Rafflesia, the world's largest parasitic flower; revolutions, revolts, and running amuck; and the subject of *The Year of Living Dangerously*, *Stranger at the Gate*, and other intriguing literary works.

For many travelers, Indonesia has one other attraction that makes it so appealing: one encounters few tourists outside Jakarta, Jokjakarta, and Bali. Although there are many tour operators found throughout Indonesia to assist you, in most places it's primarily you and the locals. You can still travel in many parts of this country and not see a tourist for days. In fact, fewer than 3 million people visit Indonesia each year— one-half the number that visit its neighbor Singapore, a city-state smaller than Samosir Island on Sumatra's Lake Toba!

Given the sheer size and diversity of this country, along with underdeveloped tourist facilities in the more remote islands, Indonesia presents travelers and shoppers with numerous challenges. At the very minimum, you must plan your **basics** carefully as well as be open to adventure and serendipity.

Indonesia is like no other country in the world. It is unquestionably one of the world's most interesting travel destinations, and one of its best kept shopping secrets. We highly recommend Indonesia, because it is a truly exotic country; it offers fabulous shopping opportunities centered around rich cultural traditions expressed in its arts, crafts, religions, and ceremonies. From the sophisticated, legendary, and mystical arts of Bali and Java to the more primitive artifacts of the diverse ethnic groups found in Sumatra (Batak, Nias, Minangkabau), Kalimantan (Dayak), Sulawesi (Toraja), and Irian Jaya (Asmat and Dani), Indonesia simply dazzles you with an incredible array of arts, crafts, clothes, textiles, antiques, and home decorative items.

Best of all, when you shop in Indonesia, you immerse yourself in its fascinating peoples, arts, and cultures. You will meet the artisans and shopkeepers, explore the cities and villages, and see first-hand how products are closely linked to living artistic and cultural traditions. Indeed, you may well learn more about Indonesia by shopping its many exotic places than by reading books and taking tours. If you do nothing else in Indonesia, make sure you shop it well. If you approach Indonesia right, it will not disappoint you.

Indonesia may well become your favorite destination in all of Asia. It is a very special shopping and travel experience—one you cannot find in the air-conditioned shopping malls and boutiques of Tokyo, Taipei, Hong Kong, Seoul, Bangkok, Kuala Lumpur, and Singapore. In Indonesia you go directly to the production sources—the factories, villages, homes, and street vendors. The Indonesian shopping experience involves making purchases in air-conditioned boutiques and shopping malls in Jakarta, Jogjakarta, and Bali as well as riding in speedboats, river launches, passenger ferries, and canoes, and trekking into highland villages in the tropical jungles of Irian Jaya. And wherever you go, you will encounter unique shopping opportunities. Better yet, if you travel and shop this country properly, you will return home with a treasure-trove of unique purchases. You may later get the urge to return to Indonesia to further explore its many treasures and pleasures.

GETTING TO KNOW YOU

Encountering Indonesia for the first time can be disorienting. Indonesia is a relatively poor yet rapidly developing Third World country. It exhibits many of the economic problems and promises characteristic of such countries. During the past few years, Indonesia, with its rich resources and cheap labor, has become one of Asia's booming economies. Much of the boom is centered in Jakarta and related to the export of oil, timber, and textiles.

For some travelers, Indonesia exhibits a great deal of Third World charm. For others, Indonesia can be distressing, because it looks and feels so unfamiliar; it can induce cultural shock amongst the unprepared. For example, the large cities, such as Jakarta, Surabaya, Medan, and Jogjakarta, are visually chaotic, worn, makeshift, and segments are architecturally unattractive. However, they do have a few pockets of architectural expression, symmetry, and beauty. Especially in Jakarta, the traffic can be extremely congested, disorderly, and noisy and the air polluted. Public services such as street cleaning, trash removal, and sewerage are incomplete. Being an equatorial and tropical country, much of the weather is hot and humid. On the crowded island of Java, you encounter people everywhere. The combination of visual chaos, uninspiring architecture, rudimentary public services, heat and humidity, and the masses of humanity at times takes the edge off of what is otherwise an extremely fascinating Indonesian adventure.

Other travelers see Indonesia through different lenses. Indonesia's living chaos, hustle and bustle, and sights and sounds are what make it such a fascinating and exotic travel adventure. For in the midst of all this chaos is a country incredibly rich in history and culture, one which clearly expresses diverse richness in its numerous visual and performing arts. It's a country of interesting and friendly people you should get to meet and know. For travelers who are prepared for Indonesia, this country can be a wonderful, personally rewarding, and extremely satisfying experience.

Since most tourists stay in Jakarta or Bali, most other areas of Indonesia only have basic tourist facilities at present. These facilities are primarily designed for businessmen traveling between the major islands. Understandably, these areas have a disproportionate number of inexpensive and worn second and third-class accommodations for travelers.

> ❑ Jakarta and Bali are also the centers for Indonesia's best travel amenities—fine hotels, restaurants, entertainment, and tourist sights.
>
> ❑ Travel to other areas of Indonesia is more time consuming, inconvenient, and less rewarding in terms of shopping discoveries and travel amenities.
>
> ❑ Start your shopping adventure in Jakarta or Bali.
>
> ❑ Bali produces its own unique products as well as imports a lot from the islands of Eastern Indonesia—Sulawesi, Lombok, Flores, Sumba, Timor, and Irian Jaya.
>
> ❑ The theory that goods are always cheaper at the production source is seldom true in Indonesia.
>
> ❑ You will have difficulty finding quality products and good buys outside Jakarta, Bali, and Jogjakarta.

APPROACH IT RIGHT

Very few travel agents know about travel to and within Indonesia. Most know how to get you to Tokyo, Seoul, Hong Kong, Taipei, Bangkok, or Singapore, but Indonesia and its national carrier, Garuda, are a mystery to many. Consequently, don't expect a great deal of help from the average travel agent in planning your trip to Indonesia. Most simply don't have much information about travel to this country.

To do Indonesia properly, you need to take a great deal of

initiative to ensure your trip is a truly rewarding one. You need to know which islands to visit, how to best get to each, where to go, what to look for, and how to get around from one area to another. Your approach to Indonesia will differ considerably from the travel and shopping strategies appropriate for other Asian destinations.

Whatever you do, don't miss Indonesia. It's a very special place. The shopping is marvelous and you will enjoy its wonderful people and sites. But you must approach Indonesia right, shop it properly, and give it enough time to grow on you. Like many other travelers who have discovered the delights of the many islands and peoples in this far-flung archipelago, you should leave Indonesia with a very special set of memories—and treasures—that you will cherish for years to come.

The remainder of this book is designed as a primer for making your visit to this exotic country one of your most rewarding travel and shopping adventures. If you do Indonesia right, it may well become one of your favorite destinations to which you will return many times. But a trip to Indonesia can easily go wrong for first-time visitors. Remember, do not approach Indonesia like you might approach more developed countries in Europe or elsewhere in Asia. If you do Indonesia wrong, it could very well become an unpleasant experience. This would be unfortunate, because you will have missed one of Asia's best kept travel secrets. At the very least, you need a very flexible and tolerant approach to this country.

SURPRISING ISLANDS AND COMMUNITIES

Searching for Indonesia's many treasures and pleasures primarily takes you into the shopping centers, hotel shopping arcades, department stores, street shops, factories, and markets located in and around Indonesia's major islands and cities— Jakarta, Jogjakarta, and Solo on the island of Java; Kuta Beach, Sanur Beach, Mas, and Ubud in Bali; Ujung Pandang and Toraja Land on the island of Sulawesi; Medan, Parapat, Samosir Island, Padang, Bukittinggi, and Palembang on the island of Sumatra; Balikpapan, Samarinda, and villages along the Mahakam River on the island of Kalimantan; and Jayapura on the island of Irian Jaya.

However, Jakarta, Bali, and Jogjakarta are Indonesia's three major travel and shopping areas. These are the country's centers for arts, crafts, fashion, design, production, trade, marketing, transportation, and communication. Here you will discover the finest collection of arts, crafts, and antiques which primarily come from other islands and communities in Indonesia. Jakarta, for example, draws its products primarily from the islands of Java, Sumatra, and Kalimantan. Jogjakarta is the art center for the Javanese. Bali produces numerous local products—primarily woodcarvings, jewelry, paintings, and home decorative items— as well as functions as a shopping center for products from the islands of Sulawesi, Madura, Timor, Sumba, and the remainder of Eastern Indonesia.

Jakarta and Bali are also the centers for Indonesia's best travel amenities—fine hotels, restaurants, entertainment, and tourist sights. At the same time, you will discover some unique shopping opportunities in other cities as well as in small towns and villages.

If you confine your Indonesian adventure to Jakarta, Bali, and Jogjakarta, you will have a marvelous time shopping as well as sightseeing and enjoying many of Indonesia's other travel pleasures. Visiting other islands, cities, towns, and villages can be fascinating adventures, especially in northern Sumatra (Lake Toba) and central Sulawesi (Toraja Land). However, most of these other areas will be more time consuming, inconvenient, and less rewarding in terms of shopping discoveries and travel amenities. These areas also will be less expensive compared to the higher cost of travel amenities found in Jakarta, Bali, and Jogjakarta. Visit these other areas only if you are an adventuresome traveler who has enough time, patience, and tolerance to take on many more challenging Indonesias. While you will not find many shopping treasures in these places, the pleasures may be very rewarding as you encounter fascinating cultures, gorgeous landscapes, and interesting flora and fauna.

While most of this book focuses on Indonesia's three major travel and shopping destinations, we also explore a few other areas in Indonesia that offer interesting treasures and pleasures. These include selected towns and villages on Sumatra, Sulawesi, and Irian Jaya. What lies between these major islands are hundreds and thousands of other islands and communities that are destinations for the most adventuresome travelers who are more interested in local cultures, flora, and fauna than in quality hotels, restaurants, and shopping.

A DIFFERENT APPROACH TO TRAVEL

As you will quickly discover, like other volumes in our "Impact Guide" series, this is much more than a shopping book with names and addresses of recommended shops for people who love to "shop 'til they drop." If anything, this is a book for people who generally do not like to shop. Indeed, we've specifically designed the book to be a complete travel guide, but with special emphasis on discovering unique local products and handling Indonesia's shopping process. A particular travel philosophy underlies our approach to this subject.

Shopping to us is a serious travel business rather than a frivolous or sexist activity associated with bus loads of tacky souvenir seekers. For us, shopping is the highlight of any trip to a country or community that is rich in culture as well as maintains many of its traditional arts and crafts via the activities of talented artists and craftspeople.

We approach our subject in this manner, because we believe one of the most interesting and educational travel adventures involves immersing oneself in the arts and crafts of a culture vis-a-vis its artisans, craftspeople, and shopkeepers. Such an adventure places you in direct contact with interesting and talented people who express the best of their society.

If you generally don't like to shop, you may quickly discover you love to shop in Indonesia. For what we outline in the pages that follow is much more than simple buying and selling activities that take place in the formality of department stores and shops. In Indonesia, you meet the artisans, craftspeople, and shopkeepers who teach you a great deal about themselves, their work, culture, and society.

Best of all, when you leave Indonesia with your shopping treasures, you will depart with special memories you will relive for many years to come. Approached in this manner, shopping is one of the most important activities you should engage in while visiting Indonesia.

If you fail to shop Indonesia in this manner, you will miss one of the most important aspects of traveling in Indonesia. While you may take many pictures during your trip to Indonesia, acquiring quality products while meeting local artists, craftspeople, and shopkeepers will have much more meaning in the years to come. Buy them, display them in your home, and savor again that serendipitous moment when you happened to stumble into a dusty and dimly lit shop in Jogjakarta that had a wonderful antique lantern hanging from its rafters; you bargained hard and finally got it for 50 percent less than the initial asking price. You'll forever treasure that purchase, because it was an important part of your Indonesian cross-cultural adventure. And if you probed the origin of that lantern, you might discover some fascinating aspects of Dutch colonial history in Indonesia.

This is what this book is all about—making Indonesia a very special travel adventure by discovering its many treasures and pleasures found in its numerous cities, towns, villages, and neighborhoods. If you approach Indonesia in this manner, you will get close to its people and culture. Indeed, it is shopping rather than budget travel that best puts you in contact with the locals that most interest you. While budget travel will quickly put you in contact with the lower classes, traveling for Indonesian treasures (shopping) enables you to make contacts with many different and talented classes in society.

As you seek out Indonesia's many treasures and pleasures, you may very well become addicted to this fascinating country. So beware as you turn the following pages. This may become the first of several trips you make to Indonesia in the years ahead as you discover a very special place with special people producing special products!

FOCUS ON QUALITY AND VALUE

The Treasures and Pleasures of Indonesia is a different kind of travel book for a very special type of traveler. It's not another smorgesboard of popular sites and sightseeing tours nor does it promote cheap travel or the latest travel fads. The book is designed to provide you with the necessary **knowledge and skills** to enjoy this country's many treasures. Going beyond typical sightseeing tours, we focus on how you can acquire Indonesia's many treasures by becoming an effective shopper. We especially designed the book with three major considerations in mind:

- Learn a great deal about Indonesian society and culture by meeting its many talented artists, craftspeople, and shopkeepers and exploring its cities and towns.

- Do quality shopping for items having good value.

- Discover unique items that can be integrated into your home and/or wardrobe.

As you will quickly discover, this is not a book on how to find great bargains in inexpensive Indonesia, although we do show you how to bargain and where to and how to find bargains. While you will find bargains in Indonesia and prices still seem inexpensive, this book primarily focuses on quality shopping for unique items. As such, we are less concerned with shopping to save money and to get great bargains than with shopping for local products that can be taken home, integrated into one's wardrobe and home decor, and appreciated for years to come. Rather than find a cheap textile or purchase an inexpensive piece of jewelry or art, we prefer finding the best of what there is available and selectively choose those items we both enjoy and can afford. Buying, for example, one beautiful batik shirt or blouse, a finely woven textile, a piece of exquisite jewelry, a valuable artifact or work of art that can be nicely integrated into your wardrobe and home will last much longer and you will appreciate it for many more years to come than to purchase several cheap pieces of jewelry or tourist kitsch that quickly loose their value and your interest.

Our general shopping rule is this: A "good buy" is one that results in acquring something that has good value; when in doubt, go for quality, because quality items will hold their value and you will enjoy them much more in the long run.

Indeed, some of our most prized possessions from shopping in Indonesia are those we felt we could not afford at the time, but we purchased nonetheless because we knew they were excellent quality items and we would not tire of them. In retrospect, our decisions to buy quality items were wise decisions, because these items are things we still love today.

We have learned one other important lesson from shopping abroad: good craftsmanship everywhere in the world is declining due to the increased cost of labor, lack of interest among young people in pursuing the traditional crafts, and erosion of traditional cultures. Therefore, any items that require extensive hand labor and traditional craft skills—such as woodcarvings, textiles, silver work, furniture, basketry, tribal artifacts, and handcrafted jewelry—are outstanding values today because many of these items are disappearing as fewer craftspeople are trained in producing quality arts and crafts. As elsewhere in the world, the general trend in Indonesia is to move from producing high quality arts and crafts to creating fakes and copies as well as to mass producing contemporary handicrafts for tourists and export markets.

Throughout this book we have attempted to identify the best quality shopping in Indonesia. This does not mean we have discovered the cheapest shopping nor best bargains. Our search for unique shopping and quality items that retain their value in the long run means many of our recommended shops may initially appear expensive. But they offer top value that you will not find in many other shops. When we visit specific shops in Jakarta, Bali, and Jogjakarta noted for quality, we know these shops well because we have made some of our most important purchases there. They offer both unique and quality items we will cherish for many years to come.

CHOOSING YOUR BEST PLACES TO SHOP

If you decide to include all of the shopping places outlined in this book, you may want to start your shopping adventure in Jakarta or Bali. Many visitors prefer to start in Bali. In fact, many of these people never leave Bali, because they mistakenly believe this is where all of Indonesia's shopping is found. Keep in mind that Jakarta and Bali offer very different products and shopping experiences. Jakarta, for example, is the center for items produced or collected from the island of Java and the northern and western islands of Kalimantan and Sumatra. Bali produces its own unique products as well as imports numerous products from the islands of Eastern Indonesia, especially Sulawesi, Lombok, Flores, Sumba, Timor, and Irian Jaya.

Contrary to what many others may tell you, we still prefer Jakarta to Bali for shopping, even though Jakarta still has a negative reputation amongst many travelers. Part of the reason for preferring Jakarta is that we know where to go and what to buy in Jakarta, whereas others avoid Jakarta altogether because of its reputation for being a big and ugly city. That's unfortunate because these people miss out on some of the best shopping—including prices—in all of Indonesia. That's good for us, because few tourists compete with us and Jakarta's many expatriates for the fine products found in Jakarta!

We recommend that you initially spend at least three days in Jakarta where you will have a chance to survey shops, products, prices, and shipping arrangements prior to visiting other areas of the country. Five to six days would be much better—three concentrated days for sightseeing and three days for shopping. If you plan to make many purchases that would require a sea freight shipment from Indonesia—at least one cubic meter in volume—Jakarta or Bali should become your central shipping point. It's best to begin making shipping arrangements in Jakarta before venturing on to other parts of the country which may result in large purchases that will need to be consolidated with a single sea freight shipment from Jakarta.

We recommend making Bali your second stop. This is Indonesia's major craft center, similar to Chiangmai in Thailand. Bali takes time because of its many sightseeing and shopping attractions. We recommend a minimum of four days in Bali—six to seven days for first-time visitors. While it's a small island, the shops and factories are so numerous and sightseeing is so attractive that you will want to spend some time here enjoying Bali's many pleasures.

Jogjakarta should become another one of your major destinations. This is the art and culture center for the Javanese. While lacking the many tourist amenities found in Jakarta and Bali, Jogjakarta is an interesting historical and cultural center in close proximity to the popular Borobudur and Prambanam monuments as well as the noted textile center of Solo (Surakarta). You will discover a vibrant art community here producing unique batik paintings as well as numerous arts and crafts expressive of Javanese cultural traditions.

Other areas in Indonesia also yield shopping treasures, but not like those found in Jakarta, Bali, and Jogjakarta. If we had to choose three other destinations for shopping, we would recommend northern Sumatra (Medan and Lake Toba), Sulawesi, and Jayapura. Compared to Indonesia's three major shopping destinations, these areas yield some interesting local products. However, few are of exceptional quality to justify a special trip there for shopping purposes. Shops in Jakarta and Bali still offer the best quality products from these areas. Plan to visit these areas only as part of other travel interests and to see the culture that produced items you may have acquired elsewhere.

From Jakarta and Bali you can continue on to Singapore, Malaysia, Thailand, the Philippines, Hong Kong, Australia, or New Zealand. These countries also offer wonderful shopping opportunities. Should you decide to include these countries in your trip, we recommend several other volumes in our "Impact Guide" series which cover these countries (see form at end of this book for individual titles).

COMPARE CITIES, PRODUCTS, AND PRICES

You may or may not get better buys on products found outside Jakarta, Bali, and Jogjakarta. The theory that goods are always cheaper at the production source is seldom true in Indonesia. Indeed, you will have difficulty finding quality products and good buys outside Jakarta, Bali, and Jogjakarta.

In general, we find shops in Jakarta, Bali, and Jogjakarta tend to have the best quality items; their buyers seem to pick the best of what is available in other areas of Indonesia. Considering the costs of traveling outside Jakarta, Bali, and Jogjakarta—as well as the cost of shipping items to Indonesia's two major transhipment points of Jakarta and Bali—you may do just as well confining your shopping to the many shops of Jakarta, Bali, and Jogjakarta.

Except in the case of Bali, our general rule for comparative shopping in Indonesia is this: if you see something you love, buy it now; if you wait to find it elsewhere, chances are you won't find a comparable item, and the one you left behind may be gone when you return. The copy-cat tradition in Bali is so widespread that comparative shopping makes good sense here. Except for the few true antiques, shop after shop in Bali tend to offer the same products. Consequently, take your time in Bali by comparing products and prices. You may quickly discover you can purchase the same item elsewhere for 50% less!

APPROACHING THE SUBJECT

The chapters that follow take you into the best of Indonesia's treasures and pleasures. In so doing, we've attempted to construct a complete user-friendly book that first focuses on the shopping process and then offers extensive details on the "how," "what," and "where" of shopping in Indonesia.

The chapters are organized as one would organize and implement a travel and shopping adventure to Indonesia. Each chapter incorporates sufficient details, including names and addresses, to get you started in some of the best shopping areas and shops in each city or town.

The table of contents and index provide useful details for navigating the treasures and pleasures of Indonesia. The index includes both subjects and shops, with shops printed in bold for ease of reference; the table of contents is elaborated in detail so it, too, can be used as another handy reference index for subjects and products. By using the table of contents and index together, you can access most any information from this book.

The remainder of this book is divided into three parts and 10 additional chapters which look at both the process and content of shopping and traveling in exotic Indonesia. The next three chapters in Part I—**"Traveling Smart"**—assist you in preparing for your Indonesian shopping adventure by focusing on the how-tos of traveling. Chapter 2, "Preparing for Your Adventure," examines how to best plan for your trip to Indonesia, including what best to pack as well as how to best manage your money, identify your shopping needs, and ship your purchases home with ease. Chapter 3, "Know Your Travel

Basics," takes you through the basics of getting to and enjoying your stay in Indonesia, including international and domestic transportation, language, currency, accommodations, restaurants, and useful resources. Chapter 4, "Pleasures, Pains, and Enjoying Your Stay," introduces you to both the positives and negatives of traveling in Indonesia, including local customs and approaching your first day right.

The chapters in Part II—"**Shopping Well**"—examine the how, what, and where of shopping in Indonesia. Here you will discover Indonesia's major shopping strengths and learn how and where to best shop for different products.

Part III—"**Island to Island Shopping**"—focuses on the how, what, and where of shopping in Jakarta, Bali, Jogjakarta, and other major destinations in Indonesia. Here you will take to the streets and roads to discover the best of Indonesia's shopping.

RECOMMENDED SHOPS

We hesitate to recommend specific shops since we know the pitfalls of doing so. Shops that offered excellent products and service during one of our visits, for example, may change ownership, personnel, and policies from one year to another. In addition, our shopping preferences may not be the same as your preferences.

Our major concern is to outline your shopping options in Indonesia, show you where to locate the best shopping areas, and share some useful shopping strategies that you can use anywhere in Indonesia, regardless of particular shops we or others may recommend. Armed with this knowledge and some basic shopping skills, you will be better prepared to locate your own shops and determine which ones offer the best products and service in relation to your own shopping and travel goals.

However, we also recognize the "need to know" when shopping in unfamiliar places. Therefore, throughout this book, we list the names and locations of various shops we have found to offer good quality products. In some cases we have purchased items in these shops and can also recommend them for service and reliability. But in most cases we surveyed shops to determine the quality of products offered without making purchases. To buy in every shop would be beyond our budget, as well as our home storage capabilities! Whatever you do, treat our names and addresses as **orientation points** from which to identify your own products and shops. If you rely solely on our listings, you will miss out on one of the great adventures of shopping in Indonesia—discovering your own special shops that offer unique items and exceptional value and service.

Expect a Rewarding Adventure

Whatever you do, enjoy Indonesia's many treasures and pleasures. This is a very interesting and special country that offers unique items that can be purchased and integrated well into many Western homes and wardrobes.

So arrange your flights and accommodations, pack your credit cards and traveler's checks, and head for one of Asia's most delightful shopping and travel destinations. Three weeks later you should return home with much more than a set of photos and travel brochures. You will have some wonderful purchases and shopping tales that can be enjoyed and relived for a lifetime.

Experiencing the treasures and pleasures of Indonesia only takes time, money, and a sense of adventure. Take the time, be willing to part with some of your money, and open yourself to a whole new world of exotic shopping and travel. If you are like us, your shopping adventure will introduce you to an exciting world of quality products, friendly people, and interesting places that you might have otherwise missed had you just passed through these places to eat, sleep, see sights, and take pictures. When you travel and shop in exotic Indonesia, you learn about some exciting places by way of the people, products, and places that define this country's many treasures and pleasures.

PART I

Traveling Smart

2

Prepare for
Your Adventure

While most of Indonesia is relatively convenient to travel, it nonetheless requires some basic pre-trip preparation to travel and shop this country properly. You will especially want to anticipate the most important aspects of any trip to this part of the world by budgeting overall costs, checking on Customs regulations, managing your money, gathering essential shopping information, packing right, and anticipating shipping alternatives and arrangements.

MINIMIZE UNCERTAINTY

Preparation is the key to experiencing a successful and enjoyable shopping adventure in Indonesia. But preparation involves much more than just examining maps, reading travel literature, and making airline and hotel reservations. Preparation, at the very least, is a process of minimizing uncertainty by learning how to develop a shopping plan, manage your money, determine the value of products, handle Customs, and pack for the occasion. It involves knowing what products are good deals to buy in Indonesia in comparison to similar items back home. Most important of all, preparation helps organize and ensure the success of all aspects of a travel and shopping adventure to Indonesia.

MAKE A PLAN

Time is money when traveling abroad. If you plan to include all of the shopping areas identified in this book, you will need to do some detailed planning. The better you plan and use your time, the more time you will have to enjoy your trip. If you want to use your time wisely and literally hit the ground running, you should plan a detailed, yet tentative, schedule for each day. Begin by

- Identifying each island, city, town, and shopping area you intend to visit.

- Blocking out the number of days you plan to visit in each place.

- Listing those places you feel you "must visit" during your stay.

- Leave extra time each day for unexpected discoveries.

Keep this plan with you and periodically revise it in light of new and unexpected discoveries.

At a minimum, we recommend 4-5 days in Jakarta; 4-5 days in Bali; and 2-3 days in Jogjakarta. If your plans include Sumatra, you may want to spend 7-8 days visiting Medan, Lake Toba, Padang, Bukittinggi, and Palembang. Other islands can be visited in 2-3 days each. While Sumatra and the other islands do not offer as many shopping opportunities as Jakarta, Bali, and Jogjakarta, they are interesting areas to visit and they do offer some shopping opportunities. Local government tourist offices as well as several private tour companies can provide you with information on these areas.

CREATE YOUR OWN GOOD LUCK

Indonesia is a very special place where you are likely to encounter a great deal of good luck. It's a great place for dashing well designed plans, altering expectations, and experiencing serendipity. The funniest and most unexpected events usually arise in Indonesia to make any travel and shopping adventure to this country a most rewarding and memorable one.

But just how much pre-trip planning should you do? Our experience has taught us that planning is fine, but don't overdo it and thus ruin your trip by accumulating a list of unfulfilled expectations. Planning needs to be adapted to certain realities which often become the major highlights of one's travel and shopping experiences.

Good luck is a function of good planning: you place yourself in many different places to take advantage of new opportunities. You should be open to unexpected events which may well become the major highlights of your travel and shopping experiences.

If you want to have good luck and experience a truly rewarding shopping adventure, plan to visit many different shopping centers, hotel shopping arcades, street shops, factories, and villages in and around Jakarta, Bali, and Jogjakarta. Expect to alter your initial plans once you begin discovering new and unexpected realities. Serendipity—those chance occurrences that often evolve into memorable and rewarding experiences—frequently interferes with the best-laid travel and shopping plans. Welcome serendipity by altering your plans to accommodate the unexpected. You can do this by revising your plans each day as you go. A good time to summarize the day's events and accomplishments and plan tomorrow's schedule is just before you go to bed each night.

Keep in mind that your plan should be a means to an end—experiencing exciting travel and shopping—and not the end itself. If you plan well, you will surely experience good luck on the road to a successful adventure in Indonesia!

CONDUCT RESEARCH AND NETWORK

Do as much research as possible before you depart on your Indonesian adventure. A good starting place is the periodical section of your local library. Here you may find a few magazine and newspaper articles on travel and shopping in Indonesia. Several travel magazines and newspapers as well as the travel sections of major newspapers, such as the **New York Times** and the **Los Angeles Times**, run special sections on shopping around the world. Occasionally an article will appear on shopping in Indonesia.

You also might want to subscribe to a travel newsletter that specializes in travel to exotic locations. One of the most useful such publications is the **International Travel News**. Published monthly, each issue includes over 125 pages of articles, testimonials, networking opportunities, reviews, and ads relevant to exotic locations in the developing world. Each issue also includes several ads from travel companies specializing in travel to Indonesia. In fact, most companies that focus on Indonesia will have ads in this publication. In preparation for your Indonesian adventure, it's well worth contacting several of these companies for their brochures which outline their Indonesian itineraries. For an annual subscription or a sample copy, contact: International Travel News, P.O. Box 189490, Sacramento, CA 95818-9490, Tel. 1-800-366-9192.

We also recommend **networking for information and advice**. You'll find many people, including relatives, friends, and acquaintances, who have traveled to Indonesia and are eager to share their experiences and discoveries with you. They may recommend certain shops where you will find excellent products, service, and prices. Ask them basic "who," "what," "where," "why," and "how" questions:

- **Where** (islands) did you find the best shopping?
- **What** shops did you particularly like?
- **What** do they sell?
- **How** much discount could I expect?
- **Whom** should I talk to?
- **Where** is the shop located?
- **Is** bargaining expected?
- **Do** they pack and ship?

Once you arrive in-country, you may want to contact the local tourist offices. Unfortunately, the tourist offices in Jakarta, Bali, and Jogjakarta only provide basic information on local attractions, accommodations, and restaurants. If you want information on other islands and communities, you will either have to contact a nationwide tour company, such as Pacto, or travel directly to the other places where provincial tourist offices have information on their local areas. You should also contact your hotel concierge for information on local travel and shopping opportunities.

CHECK CUSTOMS REGULATIONS

It's always good to know Customs regulations **before** leaving home. If you are a U.S. citizen planning to return to the U.S. from Indonesia, the United States Customs Service provides several helpful publications which are available free of charge from your nearest U.S. Customs Office, or write P.O. Box 7407, Washington, DC 20044.

- *Know Before You Go* (Publication #512): outlines facts about exemptions, mailing gifts, duty-free articles, as well as prohibited and restricted articles.

- *Trademark Information for Travelers* (Publication #508): deals with unauthorized importation of trade-marked goods. Since you will find some copies of trade-marked items in Indonesia, especially clothes, this publication will alert you to potential problems with Custom inspectors prior to returning home.

- *International Mail Imports* answers many travelers' questions regarding mailing items back to the U.S. The U.S. Postal Service sends all packages to Customs for examination and assessment of duty before they are delivered to the addressee. Some items are free of duty while others are dutiable. The rules have recently changed on mail imports, so do check on this before you leave the U.S.

- *GSP and the Traveler* itemizes goods from particular countries that can enter the U.S. duty-free. GSP regulations, designed to promote the economic development of certain Third World countries, permit many products, especially arts and handicrafts, to enter the United States duty-free. Most items purchased in Indonesia will be allowed to enter duty-free. However, many items from Indonesia—especially some jewelry and textiles—will be dutiable if they are not part of your US$400 exemption.

MANAGE YOUR MONEY WELL

It is best to carry traveler's checks, two or more major credit cards with sufficient credit limits, U.S. dollars, and a few personal checks. Our basic money rule is to take enough money and sufficient credit limits so you don't run short. How much you take is entirely up to you, but it's better to have too much than not enough when shopping in Indonesia.

We increasingly find **credit cards** to be very convenient when traveling in Indonesia. We prefer using credit cards to pay for hotels and restaurants and for major purchases as well as for unanticipated expenses incurred when shopping. Most major hotels and shops honor MasterCard, Visa, American Express, and Diner's cards. It is a good idea to take one or two bank cards and an American Express card. Take plenty of **traveler's checks** in US$100 denominations. Smaller denominations are often more trouble than they are worth, and some places impose a small fee per check cashed. Most major banks, hotels, restaurants, and shops accept traveler's checks.

Personal checks can be used to obtain traveler's checks with an American Express card or to pay for goods to be shipped later—after the check clears your bank. Consider keeping one personal check aside to pay Customs should you have dutiable goods when you return home.

Use you own judgment concerning how much **cash** you should carry with you. Contrary to some fearful ads, cash is awfully nice to have in moderate amounts —especially in smaller bills—to supplement your traveler's checks and credit cards. But of course you must be very careful where and how you carry cash. Consider carrying an "emergency cash reserve" primarily in US$50 and US$100 denominations, but also a few US$20's for small currency exchanges. These cash reserves will come in handy in many places you shop in Indonesia.

❑ Use credit cards to pay for hotels and restaurants and for major purchases.

❑ Carry one or two bank cards and an American Express card.

❑ Consider requesting a higher credit limit on your bank cards.

❑ Take plenty of $50 and $100 traveler's checks.

❑ Keep one personal check aside to pay Customs should you have dutiable goods when you return home.

❑ Carry an "emergency cash reserve" primarily in $50 and $100 denominations.

❑ Keep a good record of all charges in local currency— and at official exchange rates.

USE CREDIT CARDS WISELY

Credit cards can be a shopper's blessing. They are your tickets to serendipity, convenience, good exchange rates, and a useful form of insurance. Accepted in many places throughout Indonesia, they enable you to draw on credit reserves for purchasing many wonderful items you did not anticipate finding when you initially planned your adventure. In addition to being convenient, you usually will get good exchange rates once the local currency amount appearing on your credit slip is converted by the bank at the official rate into your home currency. Credit cards also allow you to float your expenses into the following month or two without paying interest charges. Most important, should you have a problem with a purchase—such as buying a piece of jewelry or an antique which you later discover was misrepresented—your credit card company can assist you in recovering your money and returning the goods. Once you discover your problem, contact the credit card company with your complaint and refuse to pay the amount while the matter is in dispute. Businesses accepting these cards must maintain a certain standard of honesty and integrity. In this sense, credit cards are an excellent and inexpensive form of insurance against possible fraud and damaged goods when shopping abroad. If you rely only on cash or traveler's checks, you have no such institutional recourse for recovering your money.

The down-side to using credit cards is that some businesses will charge you a "commission" for using your card, or simply not go as low in the bargaining process as they would for cash or traveler's checks. Commissions will range from 2 to 6%. This practice is discouraged by credit card companies; nonetheless, shops do this because they must pay a 4-6% commission to the credit card companies. They merely pass this charge on to you. When bargaining, keep in mind that shopkeepers usually consider a final bargained price to be a "cash only" price. If you wish to use your credit card at this point, you will probably be assessed the additional 2 to 6% to cover the credit card commission or lose your bargained price altogether. Frequently in the bargaining process, when you near the seller's low price, you will be asked whether you intend to pay cash. It is at this point that cash and traveler's checks come in handy to avoid a slightly higher price. However, don't be **"penny wise but pound foolish."** You may still want to use your credit card if you suspect you might have any problems with your purchase.

A few other tips on the use and abuse of credit cards may be useful in planning your trip. **Use your credit cards for the things that will cost you the same amount no matter how you pay,** such as accommodations and meals in the better hotels and restaurants or purchases in most department stores. Consider requesting a higher credit limit on your bank cards if you think you may wish to charge more than your current limit allows.

Be extremely careful with your credit cards. Some restaurants and shops have been known to alter credit card amounts as well as make duplicate cards. Be sure merchants write the correct amount and indicate clearly whether this is U.S. dollars or Indonesian rupiah on the credit card slip you sign. It is always a good practice to write the local currency symbol before the total amount so that additional figures cannot be added or the amount mistaken for your own currency. For example, 18,000 Rupiah are roughly equivalent to US$100 dollars. It should appear as "R18,000" on your credit card slip.

Forging credit cards is more difficult today given present

credit card company attempts to make the perfect forge-proof card. Nonetheless, it still happens, and you could become a victim of such an attempt. Should any restaurant, hotel, or shop keep your credit card for more than five minutes, we recommend that you ask for it back immediately. Someone could be in a back room making impressions of your card, or running it through the card machine several times in an attempt to create several blank forms with your card number to be filled out later with phony purchases and a forged signature.

And keep a good record of all charges in local currency—and at official exchange rates—so you don't have any surprises once you return home!

SECURE YOUR VALUABLES

Indonesia is a relatively safe country to travel in if you take the normal precautions of not inviting potential trouble. We have never had a problem with thieves or pickpockets but neither have we encouraged such individuals to meet us. You are more likely to be cheated or charged exorbitant commissions on purchases than to encounter a simple thief. If you take a few basic precautions in securing your valuables, you should have a worry-free trip.

Be sure to keep your traveler's checks, credit cards, and cash in a safe place along with your travel documents and other valuables. While money belts do provide good security for valuables, the typical 4" x 8" nylon belts can be uncomfortable in Indonesia's hot and humid weather. Our best advice is for women to carry money and documents in a leather shoulder bag that can be held firmly and which should be kept with you at all times, however inconvenient, even when passing through buffet lines. Choose a purse with a strap long enough to sling around your neck bandolier style. Purse snatching is not a common occurrence in Indonesia, but it is best to err on the side of caution than to leave yourself open to problems that could quickly ruin your vacation.

For men, keep your money and credit cards in your wallet, but always carry your wallet in a front pocket. If you keep it in a rear pocket, as you may do at home, you invite pickpockets to demonstrate their varied talents in relieving you of your money, and possibly venting your trousers in the process. If your front pocket is an uncomfortable location, you probably need to clean out your wallet so it will fit better.

You may also want to use the free hotel safety deposit boxes for your cash and other valuables. If one is not provided in your room, ask the cashier to assign you a private box in their vault. Under no circumstances should you leave money and valuables unattended in a hotel room, at restaurant tables, or in dressing rooms. You may want to leave your expensive jewelry at home so as not to be a likely target for theft. If you get robbed, chances are it will be in part your own fault, because you invited someone to take advantage of you by not being more cautious in securing your valuables.

TAKE ALL NECESSARY SHOPPING INFORMATION

We recommend that you take more than just a copy of this book to Indonesia. At the very least you should take:

- A prioritized "wish list" of items you think would make nice additions to your wardrobe, home decor, collections, and for gift giving.

- Measurements of floor space, walls, tables, and beds in your home in anticipation of purchasing some lovely home furnishings, tablecloths, bedspreads, or pictures.

- Photographs of particular rooms that could become candidates for home decorative items. These come in handy when you find something you think—but are not sure—may fit into your color schemes, furnishings, and decorating patterns.

- An inventory of your closets, with particular colors, fabrics, and designs you wish to acquire to complement and enlarge your present wardrobe.

DO COMPARATIVE SHOPPING

You should also do comparative shopping before arriving in Indonesia. This is particularly important in the case of jewelry which is available elsewhere in the world and which can be easily appraised for its international market value. Other Indonesian products tend to be unique and thus difficult to compare with shops in other countries. However, the general rule of thumb we discovered is that most unique Indonesian items, such as antiques and home decorative items found in shops outside Indonesia cost at least five times what they would cost in the shops of Jakarta, Bali, and Jogjakarta.

Within Indonesia, prices will vary from area to area and from shop to shop. But don't plan to do a great deal of comparative shopping within Indonesia other than in Bali where many factories and shops offer similar products and where prices can vary by as much as 500%. Do expect shops where tour buses stop to charge at least 50% to 100% more than shops in town. The idea that products are always cheapest at the production source is not always true. In many cases shopkeepers may charge exorbitant prices depending on their assessment of a potential buyer's ability to pay. Except in the case of Bali, comparative shopping amongst most Indonesian shops is often difficult, because many Indonesian products are truly unique. Consequently, it's often better to have an eye for quality and learn to bargain effectively than to spend precious shopping time doing comparison shopping.

KEEP TRACK OF ALL RECEIPTS

Be sure to ask for receipts and keep them in a safe place. You will need them later for providing accurate pricing information on your Customs declaration form. Take a large envelope to be used only for depositing receipts. Organize it periodically by the type of items purchased. List on a separate sheet of paper what you bought and how much you paid for each item. If you are also visiting other countries, list your purchases separately by country. When you go through Customs with your purchases organized in this manner, you should sail through more quickly since you have good records of all your transactions.

PACK RIGHT AND LIGHT

Packing and unpacking are two great travel challenges. Trying to get everything you think you need into one or two bags can be frustrating. You either take too much with you, and thus transport unnecessary weight around the world, or you find you took too little.

We've learned over the years to err on the side of taking too little with us. If we start with less, we will have room for more. Your goal should be to avoid lugging an extensive wardrobe, cosmetics, household goods, and library around the world! Make this your guiding principle for deciding how and what to pack: **"When in doubt, leave it out."**

Above all, you want to return home loaded down with wonderful new purchases without paying extra weight charges.

Hence, pack for the future rather than load yourself down with the past. To do this you need to wisely select the proper mix of colors, fabrics, styles, and accessories.

You should initially pack as lightly as possible. Remember, except in a few mountainous areas in Sulawesi and Sumatra, Indonesia's climate is usually hot and humid. Take only lightweight clothes made primarily of natural fibers. Avoid garments made of polyester or wool. Since dress in Indonesia is very casual, you need not take suits and coats.

Items you are likely to pack but are also readily and inexpensively available in Indonesia include clothes, suitcases, bags, stationery, and audio cassettes. Consequently, you may want to limit the number of such items you take with you since you can always buy more along the way. But do take all the shoes, specific medications, film, and makeup you will need on the trip. These items may be difficult to find in the brands and prices you desire.

Since you will do a great deal of walking in Indonesia, take at least one pair of comfortable walking shoes and one pair of dress shoes. Break these shoes in before you take them on this trip. Wearing new shoes for lengthy periods of time can be very uncomfortable.

CHOOSE SENSIBLE LUGGAGE

Whatever you do, avoid being a slave to your luggage. Luggage should be both **expandable and expendable**. Flexibility is the key to making it work. Get ready to pack and repack, acquire new bags along the way, and replace luggage if necessary.

Your choice of luggage is very important for enjoying your shopping experience and for managing airports, airplanes, and Customs. While you may normally travel with two suitcases and a carry-on, your specific choice of luggage for shopping purposes may be different. We recommend taking two large suitcases with wheels—it's best when one can fit into another; one large carry-on bag; one nylon backpack; and one collapsible nylon bag.

If you decide to take hard-sided luggage, make sure it has no middle divider. With no divider you can pack some of your bulkier purchases. This type of luggage may appear safer than soft-sided luggage, but it is heavy, limited in space, and not necessarily more secure. A good soft-sided piece should be adequately reinforced.

Your **carry-on bag** should be convenient—lightweight and

with separate compartments and pockets—for taking short trips outside major cities. For example, you may want to visit Bogor and Bandung when staying in Jakarta; take a trip to Solo or Semarang when staying in Jogjakarta; travel to Lake Toba or Nias Island in Northern Sumatra while based in Medan; adventure into Toraja Land from your base in Ujung Pandang in Sulawesi; or travel up the Mahakam River when visiting Balikpapan in Kalimantan. When visiting these areas, plan to store your big pieces of luggage at your hotel in your base city and travel lightly to these other areas with just your carry-on bag.

❏ Since Indonesia's climate is usually hot and humid, take only light-weight clothes made primarily of natural fibers.

❏ Take at least one pair of comfortable walking shoes.

❏ We recommend taking two large suitcases with wheels.

❏ Your carry-on bag should be convenient for taking short trips outside major cities.

We also recommend taking a small nylon **backpack** in lieu of a camera bag. This is a wonderfully convenient bag, because it can be used as a comfortable shoulder bag as well as a backpack. It holds our cameras, film, travel books, windbreakers, umbrella, drinks and snacks and still has room for carrying small purchases. We take this bag with us everywhere. When we find our hands filled with purchases, our versatile backpack goes on our back so our hands are free for other items.

It's useful to pack a collapsible **nylon bag**. Many such bags fold into a small 6" x 8" zippered pouch. You may wish to keep this bag in your backpack or carry-on for use when shopping.

SHIP WITH EASE

One of the worst nightmares of shopping abroad is to return home after a wonderful trip to find your goods have been lost, stolen, or damaged in transit. This happens frequently to people who neglect to ensure against such problems. Failing to pack properly or pick the right shipper, they suffer accordingly.

On the other hand, you should not pass up buying lovely items, such as art, antiques, and furniture, because you feel reluctant to ship them home. Indeed, some travelers only buy small items that will fit into their suitcases, because they are reluctant to ship large items or they don't know how to go about making shipping arrangements.

You can easily ship from Indonesia, especially from Jakarta, Jokjakarta, and Bali, with the expectation of receiving your goods in excellent condition within four to eight weeks by sea or two to four days by air. We do not hesitate to make large purchases because of shipping considerations. We know we can always get our purchases home with little difficulty. Indeed, over the years we have received several large shipments from Indonesia with little or no difficulty.

For us, shipping is one of those things that must be arranged. We have numerous alternatives from which to choose, from hiring a professional shipping company to hand carrying our goods on board the plane. Shipping may or may not be costly, depending on how much you plan to ship and by which means. Over the years we have shipped numerous times from Indonesia and seldom has it been a hassle. Overall the shipping services have been excellent.

Before leaving home you should identify the best point of entry for goods arriving by air or sea. Once you are in Indonesia, you generally have five alternatives for shipping goods home:

- Take everything with you.

- Do your own packing and shipping through the local post office (for small packages only).

- Have each shop ship your purchases.

- Arrange to have one shop consolidate all of your purchases into a single shipment.

- Hire a local shipper to make all shipping arrangements.

Taking everything with you is fine if you don't have much and you don't mind absorbing excess baggage charges. If your bags are overweight, ask about the difference between "Excess Baggage" and "Unaccompanied Baggage." Excess baggage is very expensive while unaccompanied baggage is much less expensive, although by no means cheap.

Many shops that are used to dealing with international travelers and dealers are skilled at shipping goods abroad for customers. They often pack the items free and only charge you for the actual postage or freight. Many of these shops use excellent shippers who are known for reasonable charges, good packing, and reliability. Other shops do their own packing and then arrange shipping through a reputable shipper. However, many small shops in Indonesia, especially those outside Jakarta and Bali, do not ship and thus you will need to make your own arrangements through another shop (consolidate) or contact a shipper directly in these situations. If you choose to have a shop ship for you, insist on a receipt specifying they will ship the item and that the shipment is insured against both loss and damage.

If you have several large purchases—at least one cubic meter—check with local shippers since it is cheaper and safer to consolidate many separate purchases into one shipment which is well packed and insured. Choose a local company which has an excellent reputation among expatriates for shipping goods. Consult the Yellow Pages under the headings "Shipping" or "Removers." Do some quick research. If you are staying at a good hotel, ask the concierge about reliable shippers. He should be able to help you. Personnel at the local embassy, consulate, or international school know which companies are best. Contact a few expatriates (start with your hotel) and ask for their best recommendations.

❑ Shipping is one of those things that must be arranged.

❑ Before leaving home, identify the best point of entry for goods arriving by air or sea.

❑ The two best shipping points in Indonesia are Jakarta and Bali.

❑ Shops in Indonesia generally do not pack your items: they merely cover them with one thin layer of newspaper. Be sure to take bubble-wrap with you so you can protect your delicate purchases.

❑ Be sure to insure your shipments against both loss and damage.

The two best shipping points in Indonesia are Jakarta and Bali. If you purchase large items, you may want to consolidate your purchases with a single shipper in either Jakarta or Bali. Shipping is not particularly reliable outside these areas. It is best to take all of your purchases with you and consolidate them for shipment from either Jakarta or Bali. And be sure to repack your purchases so they travel safely to Jakarta or Bali. Shops generally do not pack your items: they merely cover them with one thin layer of newspaper. Our suggestion: take bubble-wrap with you or find a local carpet and flooring shop from which you should purchase carpet padding—preferably foam— to secure your delicate purchases. In addition, insist on hand-carrying on the airplanes as many items as you can. The Indonesian airline baggage handlers are not careful with fragile items. Your purchases will get damaged if you are not extra careful in securing them from rough and careless handling.

In Jakarta you should be able to find a reliable international shipper. Our approach again is to ask for recommendations from expatriates. Call embassy personnel in Jakarta and ask them which international shippers expatriates are currently using and are noted for reliability. You should get three or four recommendations. During the past few years, the following movers, packers, and shippers have been recommended by the American expatriate community:

- **Crown Pacific Jaya**: Jl. Matraman Raya 79, Jatinegara (Tel. 884923 or 881742). Agents for North American Van Lines.

- **Four Winds Worldwide Movers:** Jl. Daan Mogot Raya 73, Grogol (Tel. 594370 or 593747).

- **Global Forwarding, Inc.:** Jl. Pintu Satu, Senayan, Asri Hotel (Tel. 582376 or 582654).

- **International Mover and Storage:** Jl. Raya Warung Buncit 81, Manpang (Tel. 793389). Agents for Atlas Van Lines, American Vanpac Carriers, and Interconex Inc.

- **Lang-Lang Buana Worldwide Move:** Jl. Daan Mogot 151 (Tel. 497463-5 or 591621).

You may also want to contact shippers with offices in the major hotels as well as major airlines that handle air freight shipments. **United Airlines**, for example, has an air cargo office at Jl. Veteran 1, #1 (Tel. 3846989). The people at this office are very experienced and extremely reliable.

Sea freight charges are usually figured by volume—either by the cubic meter or a container. **Air freight** charges are based on a combination of size and weight. For a sea shipment there is a minimum charge—usually for one cubic meter—you will pay even if your shipment is of less volume. There are also port fees to be paid, a broker fee to get the shipment through Customs, and trucking fees to move your shipment from the port of entry to your home. On air freight you pay for the actual amount you ship—there is no minimum charge. You can usually have it flown to the international airport nearest your home and avoid port fees altogether. However, there will be a small Customs fee.

If you buy any items that are less than three feet in length, and you don't wish to hand-carry them home, consider sending them by **parcel post**. This is the cheapest way to ship. Parcel post tends to be reliable, although it may take three to six months for final delivery. Most shops will take care of the packing and shipping for parcel post. Small and light weight items can be reliably and inexpensively shipped by **Express Mail** or through one of the major international delivery services, such as DHL, with the expectation of arriving within three to four days.

If you have items that are too large for parcel post, but nonetheless are small and relatively lightweight, air freight may be a viable option. Consider air freight if the package is too large to be sent parcel post, but much smaller than the minimum of one cubic meter, and does not weigh an excessive amount relative to its size. Air freight is the transportation of choice if you must have your purchase arrive right away. Sea freight is the better choice if your purchase is large and heavy and you are willing to wait several weeks for its arrival. When using air freight, contact a well established and reliable airline. It will be most cost effective if you can select one airline, i.e., the same carrier flies between your shipment point and the international airport nearest you.

When you use a shipper, be sure to examine alternative shipping arrangements and prices and play an active and critical role in the decision-making process. If you don't, you may be overcharged and literally taken for a ride. Unfortunately, shipping is not one of our more highly regarded businesses. Remember, these are very competitive businesses which some-times want you to think they are the only game in town. For example, the type of delivery you specify at your end can make a significant difference in the overall shipping price. If you don't specify the type of delivery you want, you may be charged the all-inclusive first-class rate. If you choose door-to-door delivery, you will pay a premium to have your shipment clear Customs, moved through the port, transported to your door, and un-packed by local movers. On the other hand, it is cheaper for you to have the shipment arrive at your door; you do your own unpacking and you cart away the trash. For US$100 to US$125 a local broker will save you the hassle of clearing Customs and moving your shipment out of the port and onto a truck for transport to your home. But you may want to do this yourself if you are conveniently located near the port of entry. With shipping charges added to the broker's fees, you can easily save yourself $300-400 by picking up your shipment, and the process is relatively easy although time consuming. Once home, if you use a broker, be sure to compare prices of brokers and request that they shop around for reasonably priced truckers. Prices can vary from 100 to 200%! If you ask questions from three or four shippers, brokers, and truckers, you will learn a great deal about how to best ship your goods and save money at the same time. Please don't rely on shipping information provided by a single source.

We simply cannot over-stress the importance of finding and establishing a personal relationship with a good shipper who will provide you with services which may go beyond your immediate shipping needs. A good local shipping contact will enable you to continue shopping in Indonesia even after returning home!

3

Know Your Travel Basics

The more you know about the details of traveling and shopping in Indonesia, the better prepared you should be to enjoy your Indonesian adventure. If you do not adequately prepare for Indonesia, you may waste a great deal of your precious travel time attending to the basics, such as getting from airports to hotels, finding local transportation and restaurants, locating shops, and arranging shipment of your purchases.

While this chapter focuses on the basics of traveling in Indonesia, Chapters 4 and 5 provide numerous helpful hints on how to best approach the travel and shopping processes. Other chapters provide details on the "what" and "where" of shopping in Indonesia's major shopping areas.

LOCATION

Indonesia occupies the largest portion of island Southeast Asia. Linking Asia to Australia with a string of lush volcanic and barren tropical islands, Indonesia is the world's largest archipelago. Extending 3,200 miles from east to west and 1,100 miles from north to south, Indonesia's 2,027,076 square kilometers (1,266,905 square miles) of land is scattered over an area approximately the size of the United States.

Indonesia is the world's major island nation, claiming five of the world's 10 largest islands. A unique communication and transportation challenge, Indonesia consists of 13,677 islands. Most of Indonesia's 190 million people reside on the five major islands: Sumatra, Java, Kalimantan (the southern 2/3 of Borneo), Sulawesi, and Irian Jaya (the western half of New Guinea). Nearly 60% of the population is crowded on Java, an island approximately the size of California and constituting only 8 percent of Indonesia's total land area. Java also is Indonesia's political, social, communication, cul-tural, and artistic center.

❑ Most of Indonesia's 190 million people reside on the five major islands: Sumatra, Java, Kalimantan, Sulawesi, and Irian Jaya.

❑ Nearly 60% of the population is crowded on Java, an island approximately the size of California or 8% of Indonesia's total land area.

❑ Sumatra is an adventuresome shopping area for textiles, embroidery, primitive wood-carving, panels, and silver.

❑ Java is a convenient and exciting shopping area for all types of "refined" Javanese arts, crafts, textiles, antiques, gold, and silver.

❑ Bali is a fabulous shopping area but somewhat overwhelmed with copycat tourist items and tourist kitsch, especially in Kuta Beach.

❑ Irian Jaya is one of the world's last frontiers with more than 250 ethnic and linguistic groups living primitive lifestyles.

THE EIGHT INDONESIAS

The Indonesian government's continuing attempts to create "Unity in Diversity" recognizes the existence of at least eight Indonesias. These, in turn, further unravel into a few hundred more Indonesias. Indeed, the more you think you understand this country and its culture, the more you find it is many countries with many cultures. Somehow it hangs together with its communication systems, evolving national language, common religion, national ideology, and symbols of unity. For travelers, these many different Indonesias offer numerous alternative travel adventures.

Generalizing about the "real" Indonesia is at best difficult given the existence of so many different islands, peoples, cultures, and languages that make up the nation of Indonesia. Indeed, you can return again and again to Indonesia to experience still another unique adventure, depending on where you go and how you travel.

You will find at least eight Indonesias among the major islands and island groupings in this diverse archipelago of more than 300 different ethnic and linguistic groups living in cities, towns, villages, and tribal settlements. Each unravels into several other regional Indonesias:

- **Sumatra:** The world's fifth largest island situated at the western end of Indonesia. It includes beautiful volcanic

mountain ranges, lakes, jungles, rainforests, and mangrove swamps filled with wonderful flora and fauna. A
culturally rich area, it is the home of the Achenese,
Batak, Nias, Minangkabau, and several other distinct
cultural groups producing an exciting array of textiles
and primitive arts and crafts. Major towns include Aceh,
Medan, Padang, Bukittinggi, Jambi, and Palembang.
Ethnic, linguistic, and cultural divisions follow a north,
west, and south regional pattern. An adventuresome
shopping area for textiles, embroidery, primitive woodcarvings, panels, and silver. Best shopping items relate to
the arts and crafts produced by the Batak and Nias
peoples in the north. The major shops are found in
Medan as well as in and around Lake Toba. While
interesting for some visitors, the remainder of Sumatra
offers limited shopping opportunities. Most communities
have a decided worn and makeshift look to them, limited
travel amenities, and are not particularly interesting to
most visitors who have limited time to visit Indonesia.

- **Java:** In many respects Java is Indonesia. This is the
  political, administrative, and communication center for
  Indonesia and the cultural center for the Javanese. A
  beautiful volcanic island with smoking craters, terraced
  rice fields, and sandy beaches. Terribly overpopulated,
  Java encompasses the largest population concentration
  in the country. Major cities include Jakarta, Bandung,
  Semarang, Surakarta, Jogjakarta, Surabaya, and Malang.
  Ethnic, linguistic, and cultural subdivisions follow a west,
  central, and east regional pattern. A convenient and
  exciting shopping area for all types of "refined" Javanese
  arts, crafts, textiles, antiques, gold, and silver as well as
  for numerous products from the Outer Islands, especially
  the more "primitive" arts and crafts of northern Sumatra
  and Kalimantan. Best shopping is found in Jakarta,
  Jogjakarta, and Surakarta (Solo). Somewhat overrun by
  copycat arts and crafts made especially for tourists. A
  cultural, travel, and shopping tour de force.

- **Bali:** A relatively self-contained social and cultural entity
  just off the east coast of Java. The major Indonesian
  tourist destination for international travelers. Especially
  noted for its natural beauty (mountains, beaches, terraced rice fields), unusual architecture, delightful people,
  and exotic and mystical Hindu culture centering around
  village and temple ceremonies, dance and musical per-

formances, and mythical gods and demons. Balinese exhibit linguistic and cultural subdivisions following a central, east, north, and west pattern. Tourism is primarily confined to the southern region of this entrancing island around Nusa Dua, Kuta Beach, Sanur Beach, and Ubud. Fabulous shopping area, but somewhat overwhelmed with copycat tourist items and tourist kitsch, especially in the highly congested Kuta Beach area. A great place to experience one of the world's most exotic cultures.

- **Kalimantan:** Occupies the southern two-thirds of the world's third largest island—Borneo. An underdeveloped and frontier area, it is home to the river and interior Dayak tribespeople–formerly headhunters and the coastal Bangerese, Chinese, and international oil and timber companies. Major coastal cities include Pontianak (west), Banjarmasin (south), and Balikpapan (east). Ethnic, linguistic, and cultural subdivisions follow two patterns: west, south, and east regions; and coastal and river interior communities. Offers interesting Dayak arts and crafts as well as semi-precious stones and diamonds. A difficult area to shop. A great place for adventuresome travelers who have lots of time, patience, and perseverance to explore what are essentially worn and makeshift frontier communities.

- **Sulawesi:** Located east of Kalimantan and north of Flores (Nusa Tenggara), this is one of the most beautiful and intriguing islands in all of Indonesia. Major ethnic, linguistic, and cultural groups are found in the distinct north, central, south, and southeast coastal and mountain regions: Manadonese (north), Toraja (central), and Buginese (south). Major cities central to these regions are Manado, Rantepao, Ujung Pandang (formerly Makassar), and Kendari. Offers unique but limited shopping opportunities for textiles, woodcarvings, and silver. Major shops found in the towns of Ujung Pandang and Rantepao.

- **Irian Jaya:** One of the world's last frontiers and most primitive and underdeveloped areas. Located on the western half the world's second largest island—New Guinea. Its black-skinned, Melanesian peoples occupy small river and upland tribal settlements. More than 250 ethnic and linguistic groups live here and some still practice primitive and Stone Age lifestyles. Most cities and towns are found on the northern coast (Biak and Jayapura) or in the remote interior (Wamena and Meranke). This area yields numerous primitive arts and crafts, especially from the highly artistic Asmat on the southern coast and among the Stone Age Dani tribespeople in the central highlands. Major shops found in the capital city of Jayapura and on the island of Biak.

- **Lesser Sunda Islands (Nusa Tenggara):** A chain of islands located immediately to the east and south of Java, Bali, and Sulawesi. Major islands include Lombok, Sumbawa, Flores, Alor, Timor, Roti, Sawu, and Sumba. Most islands have internal ethnic and linguistic subdivisions following an east-west pattern. Includes some of the most beautiful (Flores) and barren Indonesian islands as well as several famous islands for fabulous textiles (Sumba, Flores, Timor). More low lying, arid islands with savannah grasslands than the tropical islands to the east and west. Famous area for unique ikat textiles and some woodcarvings.

- **Molucca Islands:** Thousands of islands lying between the Greater and Lesser Sunda Islands and Irian Jaya. Historically known as the Spice Islands. Includes such major islands as Ambon, Ceram, Obi, Halmahera, Buru, Banda (Nutmeg Island), Ternate and Tidore (Clove Islands), and the Tanimbars. Each island has its own distinct ethnic, linguistic, and cultural groups. Islands follow north, central and southeast divisions. These islands are off the beaten travel path and are of more interest to adventuresome budget travelers in search of a cultural experience. Some islands offer interesting textiles and woodcarvings, but this is not a noted shopping area.

Indonesia has several large cities which attract travelers and shoppers. Jakarta, with a population of nearly 8 million, is located on the northwestern coast of Java. It is Indonesia's, as well as Southeast Asia's, largest city. Other large cities, with a population of over 500,000, include Surabaya, Jogjakarta, Semarang, and Bandung on the island of Java and Medan on the island of Sumatra. The fabled island and favorite tourist destination of Bali lies a few miles off the east coast of Java.

Indonesia's climate, flora, and fauna follow a distinct east-west pattern. The western portion—also known as the

Greater Sunda Islands—includes the four large islands of Sumatra, Java, Kalimantan, and Sulawesi as well as Bali. Most of this section has similar climate, typography, flora, and fauna as the rest of tropical Southeast Asia. But the eastern portion —consisting of the Lesser Sundas, Moluccas, and Irian Jaya—are more closely associated with the climate, typography, flora, and fauna of Australia.

Another useful way to approach Indonesia is to look at Java and Bali versus the rest of the country. Historically, Java has been the political, cultural, and intellectual center of Indonesia, with Jogjakarta and Jakarta vying for dominance. The Javanese, with their own distinct culture and style of communication (indirect and elusive), dominate the key institutions in this country—the military and bureaucracy. Java also has the best developed transportation and communication facilities and provides relatively convenient tourist accommodations and attractions. Jogjakarta in Central Java still remains the cultural center of the Javanese people. Bali maintains its own distinct culture and traditions based on a mixture of Hinduism and animism. This contrasts sharply with the Islamic and animistic traditions on Java.

Outside Java and Bali live the remaining 40% of the population. Representing over 300 ethnic and linguistic groups, these 75 million people primarily reside in small villages and towns. They include the fascinating Achenese, Nias, Batak, and Minangkabau peoples of Sumatra; the Dayak of Kalimantan; the Buginese and Toraja of Sulawesi; and the Asmat and Dani of Irian Jaya—peoples with very distinct cultures and who produce a very attractive array of arts and crafts. Once outside Java and Bali, it is these Outer Island areas and ethnic groups that make Indonesia such a fascinating travel and shopping adventure. And it is in these areas where you will find the least developed tourist facilities.

Parts of Indonesia are incredibly beautiful. The islands of Sumatra and Java alone have over 70 active volcanos, 10 of which erupt each year and are the centers for daily earthquakes. Irian Jaya boasts a snowcapped mountain of more than 15,000 feet. Many of the beaches and clear waters of Bali, Java, and smaller islands are splendid for swimming, surfing, scuba diving, and boating. The multi-tiered rice fields of Java and Bali are truly picturesque. Add to this natural beauty the exotic Hindu and Buddhist cultures of Java and Bali overlaid with orthodox Muslim culture and a heavy dose of animism, you have a recipe for one of the world's most exciting travel adventures.

CLIMATE, SEASONS, WHEN TO GO

Quite frankly, you will sweat a lot in Indonesia. Indonesia's equatorial climate is generally hot and humid year-round. Temperatures range from 78°F to 95°F and humidity averages 75%. Daily temperatures do reach the high 90°s, and the humidity is often in the 90°s. Seasonal variations are slight, normally more or less hot and humid. Nonetheless, at certain times of the year the climate is more pleasant than others.

Indonesia basically has two seasons—wet and dry. The wet season occurs between October and April, with January and February being the wettest months. During this time many parts of Indonesia, especially Sumatra, are mired in mud as rains constantly pour. In other parts of Indonesia the rains are mainly a nuisance for travelers.

The dry season occurs between May and September. Temperatures are hot, but the humidity is less than during the wet season.

- ❑ You will sweat a lot in Indonesia with temperatures ranging from 75°F to 95°F and humidity averaging 75%.

- ❑ The best time to visit Indonesia is during the May to August dry season.

- ❑ You can dress casually in Indonesia; formal attire is seldom required.

- ❑ Take sunglasses and a hat for the bright equatorial light and intense sunshine.

- ❑ Garuda Indonesia Airways offers a "Visit Indonesia Air Pass" which is one of the best air travel deals you will find anywhere.

Climates do vary from one island to another. For example, the islands east of Java tend to have a more pronounced dry season. Some islands, such as Timor and Lombok, experience lengthy droughts. The islands to the west experience rain year-round, but in lesser amounts during the dry season. The highland and mountainous areas in northern and central Sumatra, Sulawesi, and Irian Jaya tend to have very pleasant temperate climates. In these areas temperatures often drop dramatically in the evenings and can be cold.

The best time to visit Indonesia is during the May to August dry season. Temperatures are relatively pleasant, and the humidity is less oppressive than during other times of the year. July is an especially good time to visit Sumatra, Java, Kalimantan, Sulawesi, and Bali.

Given the equatorial climate of Indonesia, you need only pack lightweight clothes for your trip. Stay with thin cottons. If you plan to venture into the hill and mountain areas, be sure to take some extra clothes, such as a sweater or jacket, for the cool evenings.

You can dress casually in Indonesia; formal attire is seldom required. For men, shirts and trousers are perfectly acceptable for most occasions. For women, dresses, blouses, and skirts and slacks are adequate. In fact, you may wish to pack fewer clothes for Indonesia since you can purchase plenty of attractive batik shirts, dresses, and blouses in the major cities on Java and in Bali. These Indonesian clothes are relatively inexpensive and comfortable to wear in the tropical climate.

It also is wise to take sunglasses and a hat for the bright equatorial light and intense sunshine. Your photos will turn out better if you take a light filter for your camera.

GETTING THERE

Indonesia still remains off the beaten path for most airlines and ships. The national Indonesia airline, Garuda, has limited direct connections from the United States or Europe. You can enter Indonesia by air or sea. However, you will most likely enter by air via one of Asia's major cities.

Garuda offers the most direct flights to Indonesia. It flies from the United States to Indonesia on a Los Angeles-Honolulu-Biak-Bali-Jakarta run. Most airlines originating in the United States and Canada first fly to Tokyo, Hong Kong, Bangkok, or Singapore before proceeding on to Jakarta or Bali. If you come via Europe, you can connect with a Garuda flight in Paris, Amsterdam, Zurich, Frankfort, or Rome. A few international airlines—Cathy Pacific, China Airlines, Japan Air Lines, KLM, Lufthansa, MAS, Philippine Airlines, Qantas, Singapore Airlines, Swiss Air, Thai International, and UTA—service the two major international gateway cities in Indonesia—Jakarta and Denpasar (Bali).

The normal round-trip airfare from New York City to Jakarta is over $2,000. But many "bucket shops" sell discounted tickets for as low as $945 round-trip. These tickets are normally with Korean Air or China Airlines. These airlines also offer the option of stopping at other major Asian cities for $50 per additional stopover. A few airlines have special packages to Bali. Korean Air, for example, offers a special five-day all inclusive "Bali Holiday" from Los Angeles for $1,159.

However, Garuda remains the most convenient international air carrier to Indonesia. In addition, Garuda offers special domestic airfares in conjunction with their international airfares. When combining both the international and domestic airfares with Garuda, you may find that Garuda offers the best prices. Indeed, when planning your flights to Indonesia, be sure to calculate both international and domestic airfares. Only Garuda can combine the two into a special savings package.

Before you schedule an international flight to Indonesia, you need to decide exactly where you plan to visit within Indonesia. For your international air ticket may affect how much you will pay for domestic air fares. The cheapest international air ticket into Jakarta, for example, could cost you more in the long run, because you will have to pay a premium for your domestic flights. Domestic air travel can be expensive if you buy separate air tickets for each city you wish to visit. But there is one trick to the international-domestic airfare you need to know before purchasing your international and domestic tickets. Few travel agents know that Indonesia's special domestic airpass constitutes one of the world's best travel bargains.

Garuda Indonesian offers a **"Visit Indonesia Decade Pass"** which is one of the best air travel deals you will find anywhere. It is the least expensive and most convenient way to visit 10 Indonesian cities throughout the archipelago. The pass enables you to develop several flexible itineraries for a base three-city price of US$300. Each additional stopover costs US$100. Therefore, if you want to visit only three cities, your cost is US$300. If you plan to visit five cities, your cost is $500, and so forth. For $1,000, you can make all 10 permitted stopovers.

However, there are certain restrictions on this pass. For example, you must:

- Purchase the pass outside Indonesia as part of your international ticketing. If, for example, you are arriving from the U.S., you must enter on Garuda Indonesia flight GA801. Alternatively, you can arrive on a Garuda Indonesia flight from all cities in Europe, Japan, and Australia as well as from the cities of Seoul, Auck-land, and Taipei.

- Enter and leave Indonesia via its eight gateway cities: Jakarta, Denpasar (Bali), Pontianak, Medan, Biak, Pekanbaru, Padang, and Balikpapan.

- Stay a minimum of five days but no more than 60 days. An unused pass is fully refundable, but unused portions of the pass are not refundable.

- Make only one stopover per city. In other words, you may not visit a single city more than once. However, routing can be made twice in the same city for transfers and connecting flights taking no longer than 4 hours.

- Identify the order of the cities you plan to visit.

- Book all of your flights once you arrive in Indonesia by presenting a coupon book issued by Garuda.

This is a very good bargain. For example, if you purchased separate tickets for flights into four cities, it could cost you over $800 rather than the bargain "pass" price $400. Similarly, if you want to visit eight cities ($800 with the pass,) it could cost you more than $1,500 by booking each flight separately.

The major inconvenience with this pass is having to book your flights upon arrival in Indonesia. You arrive in Indonesia with a coupon book and a tentative itinerary of the cities you wish to visit. You cannot alter this itinerary by your choice, yet you may have to because of certain local problems with booking each flight. While there are frequent flights between the major cities in Indonesia, many of these flights may be fully booked before your arrival. Consequently, the exact itinerary you choose when purchasing your pass may have to change in light of local flight realities.

If you can be flexible and alter the order of your cities, the pass should work well for you. Indeed, during one of our visits, we were forced to change our plans. Instead of doing Medan first, Balikpapan second, and Ujung Pandang third, we had to reverse the order. In addition, we were unable to get a direct connection from Ujung Pandang in Sulawesi to Balikpapan in Kalimantan. As a result, we were forced to spend the night in Surabaya, a city we had not planned to visit. Turning a potential negative into a positive, we spent a delightful evening dining at a fine restaurant in Surabaya as well as shopping for antiques and gorgeous Dayak and Asmat artifacts which we had not seen elsewhere in Indonesia. Surabaya turned out to be one of our best serendipitous shopping experiences. Had it not been for the scheduling of flights, today we would not have some lovely additions to our ethnographic art collection from Kalimantan and Irian Jaya! We confirmed, again, the need to be flexible and the importance of keeping yourself open to serendipity.

Since many travel agents do not know about this special pass or Garuda Indonesia Airways, you may wish to first contact Garuda for information. Ask them for their brochure which outlines the options and cities. Once you pick your option and decide on the order of your cities, give this information to your travel agent so he or she can coordinate your international air tickets with this pass. For information on the "Visit Indonesia Decade Pass," write or call:

Garuda Indonesia Airways
3457 Wilshire Blvd.
Los Angeles, CA 90010
Tel.   800/342-7832 (reservation center, Los Angeles)
         310/348-9577 (Los Angeles office)
         800/876-2254 (New York office)
         212/370-0707 (New York sales office)

You should get this information at least two months before departing for Indonesia.

If you primarily plan to visit Jakarta and Bali, it may be best to book a round-trip ticket to either Jakarta or Bali. If your plans also include stops in Hong Kong, Bangkok, Kuala Lumpur, and Singapore, you can be able to add these cities to your round-trip ticket for a minimal additional cost.

If you plan to continue on to Papua New Guinea, Australia, or New Zealand, be prepared for some inconvenience. Papua New Guinea offers some outstanding shopping opportunities for primitive art, especially along the Sepik River and in the capital city of Port Moresby (see one of our other two books—***Shopping in Exciting Australia and Papua New Guinea*** or ***Shopping the Exotic South Pacific***). However, due to continuing border conflicts between Indonesia and Papua New Guinea, you may have difficulty flying back and forth across this border. At present the border conflicts have subsided and flights are proceeding according to the regular schedule. The national Papua New Guinea airline, Air Niugini, does have one flight a week (Flight PX 049 on Wednesday, 9am departure) from Jayapura in Irian Jaya to Vanimo, Wewak, Mt. Hagen, and Port Moresby in Papua New Guinea.

The return flight from Papua New Guinea into Indonesia is the ultimate exercise in uncertainty. You may or may not be able to return, depending on how the Indonesian authorities feel on any particular Wednesday when the only flight into Irian Jaya from Papua New Guinea is supposed to take off (Flight PX 048). If fighting along the border flares up, the plane will probably be prohibited entry until the following Wednesday. In the meantime, you will have to re-route to Cairns or Sydney, Australia, or arrange a direct flight to Singapore—both of which are extremely expensive ways to go. Alternatively, you can return to Singapore and take a flight to Sydney, Australia and then back-track into Papua New Guinea. However, this too can be very expensive.

In the meantime, it is more predictable and you will have greater peace of mind if you enter Papua New Guinea via the South Pacific run from Honolulu to New Zealand and Australia. But for a true adventure in flying, try to go from Irian Jaya to Papua New Guinea and then back into Indonesia. Good luck. May the gods, spirits, and serendipity be with you!

Documents

Entry into and exit from Indonesia is relatively easy in terms of documentation as long as you plan a normal trip. A normal trip is to enter and exit from one of the gateway airports: Jakarta, Denpasar (Bali), Pontianak, Medan, Biak, Pekanbaru, Padang, and Balikpapan. You are not required to have a visa if you enter at these points, and if you are a citizen of the United States, Canada, or most European and Asian countries. You only need a passport valid for at least six months beyond the date you enter Indonesia. Upon arrival you are issued a tourist pass valid for a two-month stay.

If you are uncertain about your entry or exit points, or wish to attempt an entry or exit from Irian Jaya, play it safe by getting a visa before arriving in Indonesia. You cannot enter or exit Indonesia at other than the eight gateway cities without one of these visas. A visa is good for 30 days and can be extended for 15 additional days.

Health documents are not required except in certain situations. If you arrive within six days from an area infected with smallpox, yellow fever, or cholera, you must produce international certificates showing that you have received the appropriate vaccinations. Also, be aware that some areas in Indonesia do have occasional outbreaks of these infectious diseases. If you visit these areas, you may have to be inoculated before visiting other countries.

Arrival and Connecting to Hotels

Because of the numerous entry points into Indonesia, we hesitate to generalize about a typical arrival experience. Nonetheless, in most cases you should be able to retrieve your baggage and pass through Immigration and Customs within an hour.

During the past 10 years Indonesia has made major progress in improving the overall efficiency of its airport operations. It has done this by greatly improving its air terminals and transportation services. Most airports are air-conditioned and have basic services expected by international travelers. Airport personnel are generally courteous and helpful. Our major complaint is the poor ventilation found in the arrival and departure lounges. These areas are often choking with heavy smoke from smokers who burn the popular but deadly Indonesia clove cigarettes. In many airports the porters in yellow jump suits descend on you like a swarm of bees, but they are convenient and inexpensive to use.

Airport shops are often nice surprises. If you look carefully through some of the airport shops, you may discover unique items not available in shops elsewhere. Indeed, you may want to arrive an hour early just to visit the airport shops. The shops at the Biak, Jayapura, and Ujung Pandang airports, for example, offer some nice ethnographic artifacts, such as drums and war shields from Irian Jaya. The shops at the international airport in Jakarta and Jogjakarta offer excellent quality jewelry, textiles, clothes, and woodcarvings. One shop in the departure lounge of the Jogjakarta airport even puts on a classy batik fashion show for most departing flights!

Most visitors enter Indonesia by way of Jakarta's impressive new **Cengkareng (Sukarno-Hatta) International Airport**, located 13 miles west of Jakarta near the town of Tangerang. This is one of the world's most creatively designed and experimental airports. Combining the best of traditional Indonesian architecture and Javanese symbolism with France's most advanced airport technology, Cengkareng is laid out as a series of attractive terminal buildings connected by air-conditioned corridors and mobile walkways surrounded by nicely landscaped gardens. It is a pleasant introduction to Indonesia. Once you pass through Immigration and Customs, you can make hotel reservations and arrange for transportation into Jakarta at the appropriate counters adjacent to the baggage claim area. Services here are very efficient and convenient.

The airport to city transportation is relatively well organized. The Blue Bird transport company controls most of the airport transportation. You can take a metered taxi or an air-conditioned chauffeured car from the airport to the city for $17 to $21. You will be expected to pay the $3.00 toll road fee. You also will encounter a few freelance drivers who will offer you a "bargain fare" into the city. However, at best you may save $2 to $4 which may not be worth the hassle. The airport also offers a shuttle bus service.

The ride from Cengkareng International Airport to Jakarta is relatively pleasant as you travel mostly on the new expressway. But as you come closer to the city you begin seeing glimpses of what will become daily urban sights—major gaps between the rich and poor. Indonesia is a poor country with several pockets of wealth dotting its crowded urban land-scapes. Much of the wealth is most recently symbolized by numerous television satellite dishes dotting the city's landscape.

Like many other Third World capitals, Jakarta is an extreme-ly large and overcrowded city populated by thousands of squatters who attempt to eke out a living in this sweltering capital. It also is the country's financial, commercial, political, administrative, and communication center. As you travel the streets of Jakarta, you will see poor people and unsanitary conditions normally associated with overcrowded cities experi-encing the double-whammy of strained city services and a less than efficient city administration operating on a shoestring budget. At the same time, you will see impressive modern office, hotel, and government buildings which grew up in response to the glut of oil money which flowed into Jakarta during the late '70s and early '80s.

Entrance into other Indonesian cities is similarly convenient. Most airports have a hotel reservation desk which will book hotel reservations for you. Many of the hotels also offer tran-sportation from the airport to their hotel. The airport to city transportation is well organized with fixed-fare taxis. Most airports have a taxi counter where you purchase a taxi ticket and then present it to the driver in the nearby taxi queue. You also can find bus transportation as well as freelance drivers with all types of vehicles willing to give you a "bargain" fare to your hotel. The airport taxis will cost you 30% more, but in terms of comfort and convenience, they are well worth the extra.

CUSTOMS

Indonesian Customs regulations are similar to Custom regula-tions in other Asian countries. You are permitted to enter with no more than two liters of alcohol, 200 cigarettes or 50 cigars or 100 grams of tobacco, and a reasonable amount of per-fume. You are prohibited from bringing into Indonesia arms and ammunition, TV sets, tape/radio cassette recorders, porno-graphic objects and publications, printed matter in Chinese characters, and Chinese medicine. You need prior approval to carry transceivers. And you need to have any developed movie film or video cassettes censored by the Film Censor Board. You go directly to jail for drugs.

Indonesian Customs normally go through the motions of checking your baggage. Unless you are Chinese, chances are your baggage check will be pro forma. If you normally travel with a small radio and cassette player as part of your travel gear, chances are it will go through customs with no difficulty. In fact, you are permitted to bring in photographic equipment, typewriters, and radios as long as you take them out with you.

AIRPORT TAX

Each airport levies an airport tax on departing passengers, even on domestic flights. The airport tax on international flights is about $10.00. Airport taxes on domestic flights vary depending on the airport. Most range from $2.50 to $5.50.

CURRENCY AND CREDIT CARDS

You will feel rich in Indonesia since you will be carrying literally thousands of the local currency. The Indonesian currency is called the rupiah (Rp). The banknotes come in denominations of 20,000, 10,000, 5,000, 1,000, 500, and 100. Coins are issued in denominations of 100, 50, 25, 10, and 5. Since at present 2,267 rupiah (Rp. 2,267) equals US$1, you must carry a great deal of Indonesian cash when shopping. Indeed, the largest bill is only equivalent to U.S. $8.82!

The best places to exchange your money are at banks and with money-changers; both give similar rates. The airport branch banks give the same rates as the banks in the city. In most major cities you should have no problem exchanging money. But outside these cities you may have problems cashing traveler's checks or using credit cards. In addition to carrying a pile of Indonesian rupiah, you should carry U.S. dollars into these areas. The $10, $20, and $50 banknotes are good choices. Everyone seems to recognize the U.S. dollar and will honor it similarly to the local currency. In very remote areas, take only Indonesia rupiah, and especially coins and numerous small bills.

Credit cards are widely accepted in major hotels, restaurants, and shops. However, outside the major cities and resort areas, you will have difficulty using your plastic money. In addition to the local currency, expect to use traveler's checks and U.S. dollars to get you through Indonesia. A money belt may be a wise investment, but you may find it uncomfortable to wear in Indonesia's heat and humidity. Bargained prices in Indonesia are generally cash only prices—not credit card prices.

Getting change is a constant problem in Indonesia. Be sure to stock up on small change, especially Rp. 100 coins and Rp. 500, 1,000, and 2,000 banknotes. This small change comes in handy for telephones and tips for taxi drivers, porters,

bellhops, and waiters. Few people will have change for your
Rp. 5,000 and 10,000 banknotes and hardly anyone will change
a Rp. 20,000 banknote. Yes, this means weighing yourself down
with a great deal of cash!

SECURITY AND SAFETY

Indonesia's airport security system involves hand checks and
X-rays of carry-on luggage. Security personnel go through this
ritual relatively quickly. We normally do not put our film
through the X-ray machines, even though security officials claim
their machines are film-safe.

Indonesia is a relatively safe country for travel. Like many
other countries, it has its share of pickpockets and thieves.
Remember, this is a poor country where all foreigners appear
rich; thus you may become a target for petty thievery. Take the
normal precautions you would elsewhere—keep valuables out
of sight, watch where you carry your purse or wallet, and don't
wander off the beaten path at night.

TIPPING

Tipping is gradually becoming an acceptable practice in Indonesia. Most major hotels and restaurants add a 10% service
charge to your bill. Where no service is added, a 5 to 10% tip
would be adequate. Taxi drivers, even though they have metered
cabs, like to receive tips. Leave them some loose change of no
more than Rp. 1,000. Hotel and airport porters expect to receive
Rp. 800-1,000 per bag. In many cases airport porters will also
take care of your baggage and ticket and thus save you the
hassle of having to push and shove your way through the masses
that converge at counters. This additional service should be
rewarded with Rp. 3,000 to 4,000.

Be sure to carry plenty of small change for tips. The Rp. 100
coins and Rp. 500 and 1,000 banknotes often come in handy.

LANGUAGE AND COMMUNICATION

The national language is Bahasa Indonesia, one of the world's
easiest languages to learn. However, not everyone speaks this
language within Indonesia. Indonesia is a diverse country where
more than 300 languages are spoken. Even if you learn Bahasa
Indonesia, you will have trouble communicating in many parts
of the country.

English is widely spoken and understood in the major hotels, restaurants, and shopping areas. Few taxi drivers understand or speak English, but cabs are metered in Jakarta; you should have no problem using them. Other modes of transportation—becaks, bemos, colts— pose communication problems. You will have to bargain for these rides. Do this by using a form of sign language which combines pointing to your destination on a map, writing on a piece of paper the number of rupiah you are willing to pay, and reconfirming the price by showing the exact number of rupiah you will pay with your fingers (each finger will represent Rp. 1,000) and banknotes. In many cases you may think you have a language problem, because the driver takes you to the wrong place, you get bad directions, or you receive the wrong restaurant order. This may not be the case.

There is a general communication problem in Indonesia which is related more to education and culture than to language. When asked for information, many drivers and waiters, for example, are simply confused, lack information, or are uneducated to begin with, regardless of whether you speak the local language or not. They may be polite in giving what may appear to be knowledgeable infor-

❏ Airport shops are often nice suprises. You may discover unique items not available in shops elsewhere.

❏ Most Indonesian airports have a hotel reservation desk which will book a hotel for you.

❏ Getting change is a constant problem in Indonesia. Be sure to stock up on small change, especially Rp. 100 coins and Rp. 500 and 1,000 bank- notes.

❏ Bargained prices in Indonesia are generally cash only prices —not credit card prices.

❏ While English is widely spo- ken and understood in the major hotels, restaurants, and shopping areas, expect to frequently encounter commu- nication problems in Indone- sia which may test your pa- tience and tolerance.

❏ Air is the fastest and most convenient way to get around Indonesia.

mation, but more often than not, they will give you incorrect information! Expect to get lost several times in Indonesia, because of incorrect information you receive from well-meaning people.

Expect to frequently encounter communication problems in Indonesia which may test your patience and tolerance. While frustrating, most are minor problems and somewhat amusing. The problem is that most Indonesians are very polite and accommodating, but they often lack accurate information. Rather than tell you "I don't know" in response to your ques- tions and thus disappoint you, they proceed to give you an answer which is inaccurate. When they say "yes," they some- times mean "no." Consequently, you frequently get wrong directions, and communication can become very frustrating at times. Keep in mind that this is not a problem just for foreign- ers. Indonesians in general, and Javanese in particular, have problems communicating with each other. They may say "yes" when they mean "no," and they give and get confusing directions and instructions. You must be tolerant to survive this seemingly irrational element in Indonesia. Better still, get answers to your questions from three different sources before venturing off in any direction.

Business Hours and Time

Most shops are more or less open from 8am to 9pm. Many close on Sunday, or are open only part of the day, since Sunday is a public holiday. Shopping centers and department stores are usually open from 8:30am to 8pm seven days a week.

Banking hours are usually from 8am to 2pm, Monday through Friday, and from 8am to 11am on Saturday. Some banks remain open until 3pm. However, banks in hotels and money-changers have longer hours. Post offices have similar hours as banks.

Government offices are open 8am to 3pm Monday through Thursday, from 8am to 11:30am on Friday, and from 8am to 2pm or 3pm on Saturday.

But be prepared for the ubiquitous *jam burapa*, or "rubber time," as well as "day-lighting." Indonesia does not operate according to a Western clock, and punctuality is not a national virtue. Shops which are supposed to be open are sometimes closed with no explanation. Consequently, you may have to visit some shops several times to find them open. This is particularly irritating, especially if you traveled a long distance to get to a shop or when the shop is located in a major tourist complex, such as Taman Mini Indonesia Indah (Beautiful Indonesia in Miniature Park) and Ancol Art Center. And even if a shop or office is open, you may enter to find no one around to help you. If you wait awhile, someone eventually will show up to announce whether or not they are doing business. At other times you may visit an office or shop to see a particular person; or a bank or government office may require you to wait for the signature of their boss. If the person is not in, you may be told he or she will be back in a few minutes or "soon." The person may be out doing personal business or "day-lighting"—working a second job on official time. If so, you will probably have to wait, wait, and wait. The longer you wait, the more irritated you may get. Unfortunately, there is little you can do other than wait, wait, and wait. Take a good book with you so you are adequately equipped to kill time. Welcome to the land of *jam barapa* and "day-lighting."

Much of the inefficiency and inertia you encounter in Indonesia is directly related to this sense of time.

TRANSPORTATION AND TAXIS

Indonesia has a well organized network of airlines connecting the major islands and cities throughout the Indonesia archipelago. **Air** is the fastest and most convenient way to get around Indonesia. The airlines fly everything from jumbo jets to small prop planes. The national airline, Garuda, three major domestic airlines—Merpati, Bouraq, and Pelita—and several small airlines service all of Indonesia. Merpati flies into much of eastern Indonesia and its services are coordinated with Garuda for scheduling convenience. Garuda is a little more expensive than the other domestic airlines, but it does offer the bargain "Visit Indonesia Decade Pass." Each airline publishes a nationwide timetable. If you do not use the bargain airpass but plan to do some air travel in Indonesia, you should pick up these time tables as soon as you arrive at an airport in Indonesia.

In some of the more adventuresome regions of Indonesia, such as Irian Jaya and Kalimantan, you may be able to arrange flights into the remote interiors by contacting some of the missionary groups which regularly fly prop planes into these areas. Similar arrangements can be made through foreign oil companies that fly helicopters and small aircraft into Kalimantan. This is truly an adventurous way to go. Allow yourself plenty of time and flexibility since such flights are unpredictable. You can get on them only if there is extra room, which is often uncertain until the plane is ready to leave.

Land transportation between cities will vary from one island to another. **Rail** transportation is only found on Sumatra and Java. The most developed rail system is on Java. Two lines—a north and south track—run west to east beginning in Jakarta and joining again at Surabaya. One line runs from Surabaya to the east coast, at which point you can take a ferry to Bali. The train is a good way to see the island of Java. But even the fast train is slow, and you may find them uncomfortable unless you go first-class. The stations and trains tend to be very crowded.

The rail line on Sumatra is very limited, confined to the less interesting southern part of the island. Transportation within Sumatra is primarily by air, bus, or car.

The best developed **road** systems are on Java, Sumatra, Sulawesi, and Bali. Buses, minivans, cars, taxis, and motorcycles are the primary modes of transportation connecting cities on these islands. While much improved over the past 15 years, the quality of roads varies. Expect to encounter narrow, winding, potholed, and muddy roads in many parts of the country. Distances between cities can be great. Taking a bus or car can become a full-day adventure and an uncomfortable one after just two hours. If you decide to travel between cities by road, we recommend hiring a car and driver rather than taking a bus or minivan. Buses and minivans, while inexpensive, tend to be very crowded and uncomfortable. If you are looking for a cultural experience—complete with goats, chickens, and local produce—the public transportation may be just what you need!

Road transportation on Kalimantan and Irian Jaya is very limited, confined primarily within a 100 mile radius of the major cities of Pontianak, Banjamasin, and Balikpapan on Kalimantan and Jayapura on Irian Jaya. On Kalimantan, the major mode of transportation in addition to air is the **riverboat**. Long, narrow, lumbering riverboats, reminiscent of the *African Queen*, connect the numerous towns and villages on the major rivers of Kalimantan. These are slow and uncomfortable, but a cultural experience nonetheless. They come complete with goats, chickens, fresh fruits, and vegetables, and motorcycles tied to their roofs. In the dry season you may need to take a small canoe into some areas, because the water level may be too low for the larger boats. On the other hand, if you have limited time and want greater comfort, you can charter your own **speedboat**—usually a 15 to 18 foot motorboat—to take the same river trip. This is an expensive way to go, but three hours in the speedboat may be preferable to 14 hours on a slow riverboat which stops at every little town and village along the way.

The road system on Irian Jaya is largely non-existent except in and around the major cities and towns. You must fly from one town and village to another. Regularly scheduled airlines do fly into a few towns, such as Wamena, Sorong, Timika, Meranke, and Nabire from Biak Island and Jayapura. You can also arrange missionary or charter flights into the remoter areas of this island.

A bewildering variety of transportation conveyances await you in Indonesia. Most are used within cities and towns and for short distances outside urban areas. The major conveyances are becaks, helicaks, bajaj, bemos, colts, dokar (horse carts), minibuses, buses, trucks, taxi cabs, and private cars. **Becaks**, three-wheeled pedicabs, are found everywhere in Indonesia, although they are gradually disappearing in Jakarta. These are inexpensive ways to go short distances within a city or town. You must bargain for each fare.

Helicaks are an interesting way of living dangerously for 15 minutes. These motorized scooters carry two passengers under a covered bulb with a driver sitting in the rear steering the vehicle. What a thrill to be up front where you can see all the traffic unobstructed by your driver who weaves in and out of the chaotic traffic. Just hope he steers in the right direction and doesn't abandon you in a tight moment! The **bajaj** are small three-wheeled enclosed motorized vehicles. They carry two passengers. They are primarily found in Jakarta and are a hot, dirty, but cheap way of traveling. Not our idea of a good time.

Bemos are small scooter-steered minivans with two rows of bench seats capable of carrying seven passengers. These vehicles follow specific routes and operate similarly to buses. They can be crowded, hot, and dirty. Many passengers use them to haul goods short distances, such as produce, baskets, birds, and bicycles. They can be slow since the driver takes his time stopping along the way to find passengers. They also tend to over-charge if they can get away with it. You can arrange to charter a helicak or bemo by the hour, half day, or day. Except for the cultural experience, we do not recommend a steady diet of bemos for doing your shopping. However, in some towns bemos may be the most practical way to get around.

Colts, also called **oplets** in some parts of the country, are small minibuses or vans with a sliding side door or one that opens directly. They are more comfortable than helicaks and bemos, and they operate similarly—follow a set route, stop frequently to find passengers, and can be crowded and hot. Colts can be rented for US$35 a day. They are one of the most comfortable ways of traveling when it is just you and the driver. In some parts of the country, such as southern Sumatra and Irian Jaya, they are the major means of public transportation. In these areas you will find few if any becaks, bemos, or helicaks.

Buses are the least expensive mode of transportation, but they also are the most crowded, hot, dirty, and dilapidated ways of traveling within and between cities. They follow set routes with set fares. Not recommended unless you want another cultural experience.

Metered taxis are plentiful in Jakarta but less so elsewhere. Your choices are air-conditioned or regular taxis. Both are relatively comfortable, inexpensive, and the price differences between the two are minimal. Always try to get an air-conditioned cab, which are plentiful. Air-conditioned taxis have an "AC" sign on their front windshield. As you see one coming down the street, just wave your hand for the driver to stop. All you need to do is get in, tell the driver where you want to go, and make sure he puts the meter on. At the end of the trip, leave a little extra change over the metered price—Rp. 700-1000 is plenty. You will find taxis outside Jakarta, but most are not metered nor do they have air-conditioning. Airports have a transportation counter at which you can get a fixed price taxi.

Air-conditioned and regular **private cars with driver** can be rented by the hour, half-day, or day. They are the most convenient and comfortable way to travel within and between cities. Expect to pay around US$60 a day for a car with driver in the city. The cost will be more if you require long distance traveling which consumes more gasoline. You can arrange for these cars at your hotel or through a car rental or travel agent. Many freelance drivers are found at hotels. Be sure to bargain for the price—expect a 20 to 50% discount from the initial asking price.

You can rent **motorbikes** on most of the islands. But we do not recommend doing so for transportation within most large and crowded cities. Motorbikes are best rented on the island of Bali. This, too, is the only place we recommend you even consider renting a **self-drive car**. You will need an international drivers license.

You will enjoy your stay and shop much better if you confine your transportation to air-conditioned taxis or rent private cars or colts, depending on what is available in a particular locale. In Jakarta, stay with the air-conditioned taxis or private cars. Elsewhere air-conditioned vehicles may be difficult to find. In these areas it may be best to rent a colt for a half or full day. Such rentals are relatively inexpensive—ranging from $40 to $55 a day with driver—given the comfort and convenience and compared with your alternatives. Stay near the major hotels to charter these vehicles. Be sure to bargain for the price.

Given the heat and humidity in most parts of Indonesia, it is not wise to do much walking during the heat of the day or use crowded public transportation. Unless you are well adapted to equatorial climates, walking more than a mile in the heat and humidity can well ruin your day. And taking a bus, bajaj, or bemo long distances may also ruin your day. Take taxis or colts for even short distances. Your goals are to enjoy shopping and your stay—not experience the worst aspects of the local transportation systems and climate.

TOURS AND TRAVEL AGENTS

Before you depart for Indonesia, you may want to contact several travel agencies that specialize on travel to Indonesia. Most of these agencies offer a complete group tour package. Some of them can arrange individualized tours or arrange for specialized local tours. Call a few of these companies and ask for their brochures on Indonesia: **Bolder Adventures** (800-642-

2742), **Innovasian Travel** (800-553-4665), **Natrabu** (800-628-7228), **The Pacific Explorers** (800-972-6632), **Passport to Indonesia** (800-303-9646), **Select Tours International** (800-356-6680), **Sita World Travel** (800-421-5643), **Vayatour** (800-999-8292), and **Zegrahm Expeditions** (800-628-8747). Your local travel agent should have information on tours to Indonesia sponsored by many of the large international tour groups, such as **Abercrombie and Kent**, **American Express**, **Globus**, and **Travcao**.

If you arrive in Indonesia on your own, you may want to visit part of Indonesia with the assistance of professional tour groups. You will find several reputable Indonesian firms able to assist you. Most can be contacted in Jakarta, and many have branch offices in several cities throughout Indonesia. You can arrange all your travel needs—including air tickets, cruises, travel documents, hotels, and guides—through these firms prior to arriving in or leaving Jakarta. However, unless you prefer setting your schedule in advance, you can usually arrange your tours and travel needs once you arrive in a particular city. Just contact your hotel for information, and you will be directed to a travel agent who has regularly scheduled group tours or can custom-design a tour to meet your particular needs. The firms have English-speaking guides and drivers. These are good resources to use for arranging a shopping tour when you have limited time.

Some of the better known and most reliable firms are **Pacto** (Borobudur Hotel, 3rd Floor, Tel. 370108, 356952, or Jl. Surabaya 8, Tel. 351534, 343007, 320309), **P.T. Vayatour** (Jl. Batutulis, Tel. 354457, 365008), **Panorama** (Jl. Balikpapan 22-B, Tel. 350438, 376718, 376782), **Satriavi** (Jl. Prapatan 32, Tel. 353543, 355438, 370385), **Tunas Indonesia** (Jl. Abdul Muis 37, Tel. 341085, 355167, 355168), and **Natrabu Tours & Travel** (Hotel Kartika Plaza Arcade, Jl. M. H. Thamrin, Tel. 322-978). More than 100 additional travel agencies are found in Jakarta, and more than 10 agencies are found in each major city.

FOOD, DRINK, AND RESTAURANTS

Indonesia is another one of our favorite destinations for food. The Indonesian cuisine is somewhat similar to Malay and Thai cuisine, although regional varieties are quite diverse. Indonesian food tends to be very spicy. Peanuts, coconut milk, curries, and coriander are used generously in much of Indonesian cooking.

Some favorite **Indonesian dishes** for Western travelers are *sate* (grilled skewered beef, chicken, or lamb dipped in a spicy peanut sauce), *gado gado* (a special Indonesia salad with a peanut dressing), *rendang* (curried beef with coriander in coconut milk), *ayam goreng* (fried chicken), and *nasi goreng* (fried rice). The *rijstaffel*, or Dutch "rice table," is a mini-buffet consisting of various Indonesian foods served at your table. Padang food, from western Sumatra, is also popular, especially the mini-buffet served with numerous small dishes. Many Padang restaurants are found in Jakarta and Sumatra and are well worth a visit just for the cultural experience. The Indonesia *sate* is served by numerous vendors along the streets. When in doubt what to order, you seldom can go wrong by ordering *nasi goreng* and *sate*.

Chinese and western **restaurants** are found in most large cities. For one of the most memorable treats in all of Asia, dine at the **Oasis Restaurant** in Jakarta. The ambience, service, entertainment, and food are outstanding. It is relatively expensive, but well worth at least one visit. Go there also to see how one can decorate rooms using primitive art, antiques, and stained glass—one of the best examples of eclectic interior decorating using local arts and crafts. You will find several fast food establishments in Jakarta—Pizza Hut, Shakey's, Kentucky Fried Chicken, and Swensens. The popular Hard Rock Cafe and Planet Hollywood also operate in Jakarta.

Indonesia offers a great variety of tempting **fruits**, similar to those found in Thailand and Malaysia. Our favorites include *pisang* (bananas), *nanas* (pineapple), *mangga* (mango), *manggis* (mangosteen), *nangka* (jackfruit), and oranges. You will find numerous fruit stalls throughout Indonesia where you can conveniently buy these fruits.

Indonesia also offers a wide variety of **drinks**. Tap water is not safe to drink, but you can buy bottled water in small plastic containers. These are convenient to carry and are found in most grocery stores and small shops in large cities. You also will find a large variety of soft drinks, such as Coca Cola, 7-Up, Sprite, and Fanta, in bottles and cans. Local beers—Bintang and Anker—are very good although they are expensive and often served warm or diluted with ice. Beer production has definitely been influenced by the Dutch. Fruit juices are a real treat in Indonesia. You can buy several varieties of fruit juices in small paper cartons or cans which can be conveniently carried. The Indonesian guava and orange juices are very good.

You must acquire a taste for Indonesian coffee and tea. The coffee is served sweet and the granules are included in your cup or glass—most often floating on top! Many westerners prefer not drinking everything in the cup or glass. If you let the granules settle and leave the final 1/4 inch behind, the coffee is not bad. Most major hotels and restaurants also serve western varieties of coffee—both brewed and instant. You might want to pack your own instant coffee, additives, cup, and heating element to make your own coffee.

Indonesian tea is very different from teas elsewhere. Many visitors love it whereas others find it too unique. Much of the tea is served strong and sweet.

As in most other Third World countries, you need to be careful about where you eat and the local ice. You will find small restaurants and food stalls everywhere you go in Indonesia. Much of the food is safe, especially the *sate* and *nasi goreng* which are made before your eyes. But be careful about many of the other dishes which may sit out in the open all day absorbing the heat, dust, and flies.

One of the real treats in Indonesia are the many **buffets**, usually found in hotels, which offer numerous Indonesian and international cuisines. Try the **Bogor Brasserie** coffee shop at the Borobudur Hotel, the **Peacock** at the Hilton Hotel, or **Vic's Viking** at Jl. M.H. Thamrin 31 for some of the better buffets in Jakarta.

ACCOMMODATIONS

Indonesia offers a wide variety of alternative accommodations from expensive deluxe hotels to inexpensive *wisman* and *losmen* (Indonesia's version of bed and breakfast accommodations). Such hotels as the Grand Hyatt, Borobudur, Hilton, Regent, and Mandarin in Jakarta are outstanding in terms of service, ambiance, convenience, and comfort. They also have shopping complexes on their premises. These hotels cost $180 and up per night, double occupancy. Other hotels in the first-class and deluxe range cost $100 to $150 a night.

Indonesia has one of the largest concentration of inexpensive accommodations anywhere in the world. At the bottom end, you can find many guest houses (*wisman* and *losmen*) which cost anywhere from $6 to $25 a night. However, many lack such amenities as air-conditioning and private baths. You also will find several middle-bracket hotels in the $35 to $60 a night range.

Accommodations outside Jakarta vary considerably. Bali offers an excellent range of accommodations from the top end to the bottom. Smaller cities and towns offer first-class accommodations, but these may be somewhat basic, worn, and a bit short on maintenance. Accommodations on such islands as Kalimantan and West Irian can be very expensive for what you get in terms of quality and service.

Many of the Indonesian deluxe and first-class hotels are expensive compared to their counterparts in Kuala Lumpur or Manila. This is in part due to the business orientation of these hotels. Their prices have been influenced more by the influx of easy oil money than by the more competitive international tourist trade. Nonetheless, you can offset the high prices by getting discounts at deluxe and first-class hotels in Indonesia. You can do this by either booking your hotel reservation through a local travel agent (10 to 20% discount) or asking for a special discount at the front desk (20 to 40% discount). If you book the reservation yourself without asking for a discount, you may be one of the few to pay the full room rate. You may, for example, be able to stay in a $180 a night room at a deluxe hotel for only $120 by asking for a special business or government discount. Since oil prices have dropped and Indonesia is in a recession, hotel occupancy rates are not as high as expected. The hotels are more willing to do this type of discounting.

If you stay in inexpensive hotels or guest houses, keep your valuables close to you and be prepared to rough it. Security in many of these places is lax, and doors are easy to open even when locked. Be prepared for gloomy rooms. Rooms may lack hot water and adequate water pressure but include an ample supply of ants, water bugs, and cockroaches. You may be without an air-conditioner or have one that only makes noise. Many of these places also are located in a noisy section of town. For a few dollars more with a discount, you may wish to treat yourself to a nice hotel where you can concentrate on shopping rather than hassle with daily living. The better hotels also can help you with your local transportation, packing, and shipping needs.

ELECTRICITY AND WATER

Electricity in Indonesia is both 220 and 110 volts. Most hotels use 220 volts 50 cycles. Some of the smaller, older hotels still use 110 volts. Be sure to check the electrical current with your hotel before plugging in any appliances. You also may need an adapter for the Indonesian configured outlets as well as an extension cord to reach the limited number of outlets.

Tap water is unsafe to drink, as is ice made from tap water. Most hotels provide bottled water in plastic bottles or in a thermos. Also use this water to brush your teeth. Given the heat and humidity of Indonesia, you may dehydrate quickly or frequently want to quench your thirst. For these occasions, carry a small plastic container of bottled water, purchase fruit juices in cans or cartons, or stop at a restaurant for a soft drink (without ice), coffee, or tea. Bottled water and fruit juices packaged in such containers are readily available at most grocery stores throughout Indonesia. You may want to occasionally shop at these stores to replenish your supply of drinks.

USEFUL RESOURCES

While a great deal has been written on Indonesia, resources on this country are not widely distributed either within Indonesia nor in other countries. Indeed, you may have difficulty finding useful information to plan many of the details for your trip. Nonetheless, you should be able to find a few key resources for planning your trip.

Several excellent travel guides are available on Indonesia. Most of these are primarily designed for budget travelers and backpackers who have little money but a great deal of time on their hands to experience the local cultures, mingle with the lower classes, and tolerate the inconveniences in Indonesia. Most of these guides are also preoccupied with "understanding" the history, anthropology, culture, and religion of this country.

The best travel guide on Indonesia remains Bill Dalton's monumental *Indonesia Handbook* (Chico, CA: Moon Publications). Banned in Indonesia because of its uncomplimentary view of Indonesian politics, the military, and corruption, this is the most thorough examination of every nook and cranny in Indonesia. Encyclopedic in nature, this book will take you to every imaginable island and town in Indonesia. It may overwhelm you with information, details, and tidbits you may or may not wish to know. If you have six months and limited money, and don't mind living close to the land, this book will show you how to travel inexpensively through all the islands. It's a useful introduction and insightful view of how budget travelers try to make ends meet and enjoy their stay at the same time. The book also provides some information on shopping. Regardless of what style you choose to travel in, this book provides a goldmine of information on Indonesia. It's a "must read" for any traveler to Indonesia as long as you keep in mind that it is targeted for a particular type of traveler who expects to "rough it" on $15 to $25 a day rather than for first-class and deluxe travelers who expect to have things at least equivalent or better than back home. This book also includes a useful annotated bibliography. Shoppers interested in Indonesian arts and crafts will find these sections especially useful.

The Lonely Planet's *Indonesia—A Travel Survival Kit* (Berkeley, CA) is another good budget travel guide. In the encyclopedic tradition of Dalton's book, it tries to cover all of Indonesia, from ethnology to sightseeing to accommodations. Somewhat preoccupied with history and anthropology, take this one with you if you plan to do Indonesia on a shoestring. Otherwise, look at it for information on history, culture, geography, and tips on getting around. Lonely Planet also publishes two other volumes—*Lombok and Bali* and *Southeast Asia on a Shoestring*—which cover parts of Indonesia from a similar perspective.

APA produces an excellent volume on Indonesia—*APA Insight Guide: Indonesia*. Similar to other volumes in the series, this is perhaps the best of the APA Insight Guides. In fact, this wonderful series was initially conceived because of the creator's love of Indonesia. And his fascination with Indonesia shows through in this well conceived volume. Beautifully illustrated in the tradition of National Geographic Society publications, *Indonesia* covers the history, culture, regions, islands, and cities of this island nation. Like other books in this series, it's long on history, culture, and anthropology which help one "understand" and "appreciate" the country, but short on useful information for navigating the country. However, this particular volume does include a useful travel section which gives basic information on travel, accommodations, dining, shopping, and entertainment for the major islands and cities. If you choose only one book to read on Indonesia, make sure you read this one. But do so **before** arriving in Indonesia, and leave the book at home. It's big and heavy and somewhat limited on travel information.

One of the best series of regional guides on Indonesia is published by Passport Books (National Textbook Company, Lincolnwood, Illinois): *Bali, Indonesian New Guinea, Spice Islands, Java, Indonesian Borneo, Sulawesi, Sumatra, East of Bali,* and *Underwater Indonesia.* Authored and beautifully photographed in the tradition of the National Geographic by one of today's top photo journalists specializing on Indonesia—Dr. Kal Muller—these books provide an excellent introduction to each of the major islands. They also include some travel information as well as suggestions for further reading. Read these books before you go and leave them at home.

Times Editions in Singapore publishes a series of books on Indonesia's major travel destinations—*Jakarta, Bali, Yogyakarta,* and *Borneo.* While primarily photo books also in the tradition of The National Geographic and the APA series, these volumes include some text that you may find useful in planning your trip. Like the APA books, they are big and heavy; they should be read before you arrive in Indonesia.

Papineau publishes two general volumes on Indonesia—*Jakarta* and *Bali*. Both are somewhat dated. The Jakarta volume includes a good map of the city. Nice pictures, but these books won't take you far into Indonesia. Nonetheless, they give a good overview of the two major tourist destinations in Indonesia. These hard-to-find books are best purchased in Singapore and Hong Kong.

Indonesia's Directorate General of Tourism also publishes numerous books, brochures, and maps for tourists and businessmen. However, few of these are available through the embassies or representatives outside Indonesia. This is unfortunate, because some of the information would be useful for preplanning one's trip. In fact, this information is not widely distributed even in Indonesia. For example, on arriving in Jakarta you can visit the Visitor Information Center at the airport or on Jl. MH. Thamrin (#9 and #51) to get maps and brochures on Jakarta. Some of the travel agents have guide books on all of Indonesia, but these books tend to be very general. No one in Jakarta seems to have information on the rest of the country. Instead, you are advised to just go to the particular area where everything should work out okay. Well, many people in strange places would like more travel information on an area before arriving. However, unless you go to a tour company, such as Pacto, which can arrange tours with their local representatives on the Outer Islands, you will probably remain in the dark until you arrive.

Part of the problem is that the national government has only recently begun to promote tourism in Indonesia. In the meantime, each of the 27 provinces is supposed to develop its own literature to promote tourism. Indeed, once you arrive in an area, the local tourist development board or provincial tourism office more or less have booklets, brochures, and maps on their areas. This information and local travel services will vary greatly in quality from one province to another. But ironically it is just like they tell you in Jakarta—"no problem once you get there." In most provinces you can conveniently join tours or arrange your own private tour, rent a car with driver, and enjoy your stay relatively trouble-free. It is the **lack of prior information** and the **uncertainty** of what lies ahead that may deter many people from venturing beyond the well trodden tourist paths of Jakarta and Bali. Given this state of travel information on Indonesia, both abroad and within the country, don't expect your local travel agent, who is probably used to booking European tours, to give you **any** information on Indonesia other than a colorful brochure promoting Indonesia as part of a package tour option for Southeast Asia.

A great deal of academic literature is available on the politics, arts, and culture of Indonesia. For a good introduction to Indonesian society, take a look at Clifford Geertz's *The Religion of Java* and Claire Holt's (ed.) *Culture and Politics in Indonesia*.

In preparation for shopping in Indonesia, you will find several excellent books on Indonesian arts and crafts. One of the best treatments of Javanese and Balinese art, for example, is Claire Holt's *Art in Indonesia*. Information on the primitive arts and crafts of Sumatra, Kalimantan, West Irian, and several other islands is difficult to find. But one of the best sources is the special September-October 1980 *Arts of Asia* issue on "Primitive Art in Indonesia." Three of our favorite books include Jerome Feldman's *The Eloquent Dead: Ancestral Sculpture of Indonesia and Southeast Asia*, Bernard Sellato's *Hornbill and Dragon*, and Barbier and Newton's *Islands and Ancestors: Indigenous Styles of Southeast Asia*. One of the best books on Indonesia crafts is Seni Kriya's *The Crafts of Indonesia*. If your interests include traditional Indonesian jewelry, you'll enjoy reading Susan Rogers' *Power and Gold*. For Indonesian textiles, the definitive book is Mattiebelle Gittinger's *Splendid Symbols: Textiles and Tradition in Indonesia*. For understanding Indonesian batik, see *Contemporary Batik and Tie-Dye: Methods, Inspiration, Dyes* and Sylvia Fraser-Lu's *Indonesian Batik*.

While many of these books are difficult to find, the major Times and MPH bookstores in Singapore as well as the bookstore in the New York Metropolitan Museum stock several of these titles. You also may be able to get copies by contacting one of the large superstores in the U.S., such as **Borders** or **Barnes and Noble**. The **Tattered Cover Book Store** in Denver (2955 East First Avenue, Denver, CO 80206, Tel. 303/322-7727 or 800/833-9327), for example, has excellent travel and art sections. Considered by many users to be one of the best bookstores in the country for selections and service, the Tattered Cover Book Store occasionally carries some of these books, or they can special order them for you. Three of the finest travel bookstores in the U.S. are **Travel Books and Language Center** (4931 Cordell Ave., Bethesda, MD 20814, Tel. 800/220-2665 or 301/951-8533), **Traveller's Bookstore** (22 W. 52nd St., New York, NY 10019, Tel. 212/664-0995), and **Book Passage** (51 Tamal Vista Boulevard, Corte Madera, CA 94925, Tel. 800/321-9785). You may want to get copies of their exhaustive direct-mail catalogs of travel resources while should include several books on Indonesia. Specialty catalog booksellers, such as **Oceanie-Afrique Noire** (9 East 38th Street, New York, NY

10016, Tel. 212/779-0486), may also be able to assist you in finding these and other Indonesian titles.

Once you arrive in Indonesia you might want to pick up a volume published by the American Women's Association, *Introducing Indonesia*. Designed for expatriates living in Indonesia, the book has a great deal of useful information on getting around Indonesia; it also outlines major shopping areas in Jakarta and lists reliable shippers. This book is found in most major hotel book shops.

You will find three English-language newspapers published in Jakarta: *The Indonesian Times*, the *Indonesian Observer*, and the *Jakarta Post*. Most major hotels throughout the country stock international newspapers and magazines, such as the *New York-Herald Tribune, USA Today, Time, Newsweek,* and the *Economist*. English-language paperback book selections are limited, so bring your own reading material.

Whatever you do, we strongly recommend that you do some background reading on Indonesia and its rich arts and crafts traditions. The problem many visitors to this fascinating country immediately experience is being overwhelmed with so many new, intriguing, and attractive arts and crafts that are not part of their own traditions and previous travel experiences. One of their first responses is to want to know more about particular arts and crafts that they are unprepared to fully appreciate. For example, many visitors become fascinated with the traditional and mystical Indonesia dagger, the kris, or the beautiful gold and silver jewelry from Java, Sumatra, Sumba, and the Moluccas; the traditional batik and ikat textiles from Java, Bali, Sumba, Flores, and Timor; and the primitive woodcarvings and panels from Sumatra, Kalimantan, Sulawesi, Timor, and Irian Jaya. But their non-Southeast Asian background leaves them unprepared for the onslaught of such stimulating arts and crafts traditions. A little background reading will help prepare you for what may well become one of the most intriguing travel and shopping experiences of a lifetime!

4

Pleasures, Pains, and Enjoying Your Stay

Travel in Indonesia is exciting, because it results in new, unexpected, and positive experiences as well as many shopping treasures. But like any country, Indonesia also has its share of unpleasantries and discomforts. Fortunately, Indonesia's positives outweigh its negatives.

We have experienced numerous positives and negatives in our travels throughout Indonesia. We've stayed at fabulous and friendly hotels, discovered outstanding restaurants, observed some of the world's most beautiful scenery, met fascinating peoples, visited awe inspiring monuments, attended exotic and colorful cultural events, and purchased some of our favorite textiles and ethnographic art pieces in Indonesia. But we've also stayed in depressing hotels, eaten in dreadful restaurants, been given wrong directions on numerous occasions, been overcharged for tours and meals, become ill and sunburned, and experienced the discomforts of excessive heat and humidity.

With repeated visits, we have learned how to best minimize the unpleasantries and discomforts. You may experience some of these pleasures and pains, depending on how you approach travel in Indonesia. We share several of these with you so you can best prepare yourself to more fully enjoy your adventure. None should dissuade you from visiting this intriguing land.

EXPERIENCE THE PLEASURES

On the positive side, Indonesia offers a great deal to international travelers. It is especially noted for its varied sights, exotic settings, excellent hotels, unique foods, warm and friendly people, and wonderful shopping opportunities. If you know where to go in Indonesia and approach it right, you should have a marvelous time. Better still, you'll want to return again and again.

VARIED SIGHTS

Few places in the world offer such a variety of things to see and do as a country with over 300 ethnic and linguistic groups. Its 13,677 islands include lush rain forests, idyllic beaches, towering volcanos and snowcapped mountains, intriguing wildlife, deep sea adventures, storybook villages, picturesque terraced rice fields, and exotic Hindu ceremonies. It's an ideal country for individuals wishing to experience unique outdoor adventures, learn about other cultures, and meet interesting peoples. You can literally spend months experiencing many different Indonesias—wildlife, horticulture, music, textiles, arts, crafts, history, trekking, beachcombing, sailing, scuba diving, and shopping. If you like to take pictures, colorful Indonesia is a photographer's paradise.

> ❑ The hotel situation outside Jakarta and Bali is much different with greater emphasis on second-class and budget accommodations for local business travelers.
>
> ❑ Dinner at the Oasis in Jakarta is one of Asia's finest dining experiences.
>
> ❑ Indonesians tend to be very polite, friendly, and accommodating. Even when they don't deliver with expected service, which frequently occurs, they at least try and do so with a smile!
>
> ❑ Indonesia is unpredictable and full of serendipity. Visitors are continually surprised by what they discover.

EXCELLENT HOTELS

Hotel accommodations in Indonesia are improving as more and more business people and tourists visit this country. While it has few hotels on the par with Hong Kong's Mandarin, Regent, and Peninsula, Bangkok's Oriental, Regent, and Sukhothai, or Singapore's Shangri-La, Raffles, and Oriental, Indonesia does have several excellent first-class and deluxe hotels. Most are found in Jakarta and Bali, the two major destinations for business people and tourists. In Jakarta, the best hotels are the Mandarin Oriental, Grand Hyatt, Regent, Hilton, Borobudur, and Mandarin. In Bali, the Four Seasons, Amandari, Oberoi, and Tanjung Sari stand in a class of their own. In addition to their excellent accommodations, these hotels offer good service and a pleasant ambience. Especially in Jakarta, these hotels are also the centers for Indonesia's top restaurants, entertainment, and shopping arcades. The hotel situation outside Jakarta and Bali is much different with greater emphasis on second-class and budget accommodations for local business travelers. Often poorly maintained and operated with untrained staffs, most of these hotels offer facilities and service that are at best well intentioned and tolerable. Many also offer comfortable accommodations operated by friendly and helpful people.

Unique Foods and Restaurants

If one judges a country by its foods and restaurants, then Indonesia should rank among Asia's best. Indeed, Indonesia is a gourmet's delight. The local and international cuisines, as well as fruits and vegetables, are both excellent and exotic. You'll discover such wonderful dishes as *rendang* (curried beef with coriander in coconut milk), *sate* (grilled skewered beef, chicken, or lamb dipped in a spicy peanut sauce), *gado gado* (salad with peanut sauce), *ayam goreng* (fried chicken), and *nasi goreng* (fried rice). Local varieties of foods, such as Padang dishes or the unique *Rijstaffel* (mini-buffet), make dining in Indonesia a very special experience. Indeed, you could well spend several weeks in Indonesia visiting its kitchens and sampling its many regional foods.

Your choice of eating establishments includes colorful street vendors and food stalls (*warang*), plush hotel restaurants, and pleasant local dining spots. Dinner at the **Oasis** in Jakarta, for example, is one of Asia's finest dining experiences. Restaurants in most deluxe and first-class hotels are of international standard, and many serve excellent breakfast and luncheon buffets (our favorite is breakfast at the **Bogor Brasserie** coffee shop in Jakarta's Borobudur Hotel). Although dining in Bali is not particularly noteworthy since it has few good restaurants compared to Jakarta and other places in Indonesia, we have enjoyed a few good restaurants in Bali such as **Kul Kul** in Sanur, the **Lotus Cafe** in Ubud as well as outstanding restaurants at the Four Seasons Resort in Jimbaran and the Amandari in Ubud.

Exceptional Service

Service is often excellent to simply outstanding in Jakarta, Bali, and Jogjakarta. Indonesians tend to be very polite, friendly, and accommodating. Even when they don't deliver with expected services, they at least try and do so with a smile. The trained staffs found in most deluxe and first-class hotels and restaurants of international standard often pamper you, making your visit pleasant, convenient, and comfortable. Be it laundry, haircuts, repairs, or arranging tours and shipping, you will often experience outstanding service. Indeed, you may well miss such services once you return home to the drudgeries of everyday life. Unfortunately, such service is not uniform nor widespread in Indonesia.

WARM AND FRIENDLY PEOPLES

Most Indonesians tend to be a very warm, friendly, humorous, helpful, and courteous people, even though they may not speak your language. Many love to look, smile, wave, joke, and ask innocent but sometimes shocking questions (*"How much money do you make?"*). Many are gracious and thoughtful, always appearing to be concerned about your well-being, and helpful. The children are delightful, usually well-mannered and curious about you. Some of your fondest memories of Indonesia will be the many nice, friendly, and hospitable people you meet.

UNPREDICTABLE AND EXCITING EXPERIENCES

Indonesia, like much of Asia and other Third World countries, is unpredictable and full of serendipity. Visitors are continually surprised by what they discover—the chance meeting of old acquaintances; the discovery of wonderful shops and goods; an unparalleled view of a harbor, skyline, or city lights; a memorable ride on the harbor or up a river; and exotic nightlife in crowded markets and along the streets.

SHOPPING PARADISES

Few, if any, places in the world can compare to the unique and varied shopping available in Indonesia. You will discover a wonderful and exciting array of textiles, home furnishings, antiques, arts, and crafts found from throughout the archipelago. Best of all, you'll have numerous opportunities to meet wonderful artists, craftspeople, and shopkeepers in villages, factories, studios, street shops, shopping centers, and markets who will forever enrich your visit to Indonesia. You'll leave Indonesia with many quality products which should integrate well into your home and wardrobe. We love shopping in Indonesia, and we believe you will too.

PREPARE FOR INCONVENIENCES

Indonesia can be an inconvenient and difficult country to get around in if you do not organize yourself for many of its inconveniences and discomforts. In fact, you may encounter some irritants that could possibly spoil your trip. These are in part due to the lack of Western tourist and business facilities which are so well developed in many other countries. It's also in part due to the geography, climate, and economy of Indonesia. Some are cultural in nature; others are based on class differences; many are basic organization and management weaknesses; some are inherent to the tourist trade; and still others are a function of social problems commonly found in many Third World countries.

DISORDERLINESS

Like many other Third World countries, Indonesia is visually disorienting. Architectural designs, public works, settlement patterns, and orderliness commonly associated with zoned communities in developed Western countries are somewhat foreign to Indonesia. Except for the main business sections of Jakarta and the major hotel complexes in Bali, in most cities buildings look worn, architecture is uninspired, traffic seldom flows neatly, neighborhoods are largely unzoned, and there is a certain makeshift quality to the place. Much of Indonesia looks and feels chaotic, inconvenient, and uncomfortable. Once you descend into its streets, Indonesia can become inconvenient.

What do you do in such a situation? You simply need to be tolerant and adjust. Keep in mind that this is not home. You're here to learn and experience the positives of Indonesia. Therefore, you should not approach Indonesia like you would your own country.

HEAT AND HUMIDITY

Much of lowland and coastal Indonesia is really hot and humid. Consequently, prepare for this climate by confining your high energy activities to the early mornings and evenings. The late mornings and afternoons can be trying. Don't expect to get much done outdoors at these times. Assuming you will feel Indonesia's heat and humidity more than back home, you can best prepare yourself for this climate by following a few of these basic rules:

- Wear lightweight clothes made from natural fibers.

- Carry a hand fan and use it when necessary.

- Wear a hat on sunny days.

- Plan to be indoors, especially in air-conditioned areas, during the heat of the day.

- Plan to do very few things that require a great deal of walking.

- Use public transportation—preferably air-conditioned —for even short distances.

- Slow down your walking pace—shorter stride at one-half your normal walking speed.

- Drink plenty of liquids.

By making a few of these adjustments in your lifestyle, you should be able to take the heat and humidity with little difficulty. The climate may even seem pleasant after a while. But if you insist on walking everywhere at a frantic pace, the heat and humidity will seem oppressive and will quickly run you down.

TRAFFIC PATTERNS AND HABITS

The traffic in many parts of Indonesia can be bewildering. Traffic patterns tend to be chaotic, public transportation is often overcrowded and uncomfortable, routes and pricing practices are difficult to understand, and tourists are frequently overcharged for rides. The variety of vehicles plying the streets in Indonesia —bemos, colts, helicaks, becaks, buses, taxis—are much greater than in most other Asian cities and countries.

Unless you want to repeatedly punish yourself, we do not recommend using buses in Jakarta. They are cheap, but they are terribly over-crowded, hot, slow, and occasionally serviced by your local pickpocket. Pay a little more for a relatively inexpensive air-conditioned taxi.

POVERTY AND SANITATION

You will encounter some poverty and sanitation problems, especially off the beaten tourist paths, which may at times disturb your sensibilities. City sewer systems are often over-taxed, and you will see litter and garbage strewn in many public areas. Many parts of cities, especially large squatter settlements, are unsanitary breeding grounds for public health problems. Occasionally you will be aghast as you see people bathing and washing clothes in canals that are basically sewers. Yuk! Nothing you can do about this other than be very careful about where you stay, what and where you eat, and then keep moving on to better sights.

Jakarta is a good case in point. It functions as an economic magnet attracting poor rural and landless peasants from the countryside who migrate to the city in search of better opportunities. Large sec-tions of this city are occupied by squatters and slum dwellers. The local government has yet to deal effectively with the problems of urban poverty which further tax the already inadequate, decrepit, and over-burdened water, sewer, and electrical systems. Consequently, if you arrive in Jakarta from home—or from squeaky-clean, middle-class Singapore—you may encounter many sights that disturb your sensibilities.

❑ If you insist on walking everywhere at a frantic pace, the heat and humidity will seem oppressive and will quickly run you down.

❑ We do not recommend using buses in Jakarta. They are cheap, but they are terribly over-crowded, hot, slow, and occasionally serviced by your local pickpocket.

❑ When approached by touts, do not start a conversation. Keep walking and say *"jalan jalan"* which means you are just out strolling. Everyone suddenly leaves you alone when you say these words!

❑ Be very cautious in trusting anyone in Indonesia when it comes to money matters.

❑ If you stay at such impressive resorts as the Four Seasons or and Amandari in Bali, you may think you have gone to heaven! These places represent Indonesia at its very best.

While much improved since the poverty stricken 1960s and 1970s—and by no means as bad as parts of India, Pakistan, or Bangladesh—major sections of Jakarta as well as other Indonesia cities are dirty and dilapidated. Most Indonesian cities display unimaginative architecture, and buildings look worn, beaten by a combination of tropical decay and the failure to adequately maintain them. In many parts of cities, sidewalks and street curbs are either nonexistent or in serious disrepair. You must watch where you walk or you could fall and twist an ankle or break a leg!

Nonetheless, Indonesian cities have impressive pockets of wealth and promises of an exciting future. In the midst of negative conditions, you see modern growth centering around new hotels, banks, housing estates, and shopping centers—evidence of rapidly growing middle and upper classes which are destined to reshape the future of this fascinating though somewhat mysterious, confusing, and at times frustrating place. And you will even discover some very imaginative architecture amongst Jakarta's rapidly changing skyline of high-rise buildings. If you stay at such impressive resorts as the Four Seasons or Amandari in Bali, you may think you have gone to heaven! No doubt about it. These places represent Indonesia at its very best.

TOUTS AND CHEATING

In some places—especially Bali—you will encounter local touts who prey on tourists. These are the "10 to 30 percent men"— you are potentially worth 10 to 30 percent to them if you buy where they take you. They often function as a guide or driver or they approach you along the street. Avoid these people if you can. They only take you to places which give them a 10 to 30 percent commission. This is no deal when you have paid their commission by purchasing an item for 20 to 50 percent more than you could have on your own without the tout.

When approached by such people, do not start a conversation since you will merely encourage them to further pester you. Keep walking or say *"jalan jalan"* which means you are just out strolling. For some reason, everyone suddenly leaves you alone, not wishing to bother someone who is enjoying a private moment, when you say these words!

You should also beware of tour guides and drivers who want to end your tour or journey by giving you one "extra"—an unscheduled trip to a local factory or shop where they will give you a "very special deal." The so-called "special" is most likely you getting ripped-off and the guide getting a 10 to 30 percent commission on any of your purchases. The pattern is always the same. If you are being taken to a special shop, you are indeed being "taken."

You may also encounter cheating, mostly petty, on occasion. The cheating will range from misrepresentation of goods to giving you the wrong change or over-charging you for hotels, meals, and transportation. Big cheating may occasionally be related to the sell of antiques and jewelry. However, it's petty cheating that you are likely to encounter. Petty cheating is found everywhere. The bemo driver may charge you three or four times the going rate for a short ride. Vendors may purposefully give you the wrong change. A merchant may double or triple the price on an item because you are a foreigner. Your guide may take you to a restaurant where he handles the bill—charging you twice the standard rate and pocketing his half. Indeed, there is a certain culture of corruption permeating much of Indonesia society. Underlying this is a general lack of trust in people, which is probably justified since it is easy to get cheated in Indonesia, even by a family member. Many people are literally "on-the-take," trying to squeeze an extra rupiah or dime whenever possible. In some areas, piracy still seems alive and well! This mentality of petty corruption tends to view tourists as stupid suckers who can be ripped off at ease and who are rich enough to afford it. At times cheating is conducted very subtly; at times it is very blatant. And it is the blatant petty corruption that will disturb you the most. It seems so unnecessary and can possibly sour you on what is otherwise a wonderful trip.

If you are lucky, you will not knowingly encounter this aspect of Indonesia society. If you are unlucky and seek recourse through confrontation or by reporting the incident to authorities, you may be disappointed by the response. The best thing to do is to be very cautious in trusting anyone in Indonesia when it comes to money matters. Stay at good hotels, frequent good restaurants, and use reputable tour companies and shipping services.

CROWDS

You will indeed experience the teeming masses wherever you go. Indonesia cities tend to be very crowded and congested. Everywhere you go on the island of Java in Indonesia there are people, people, people. To best enjoy your shopping experience, don't spend long hours in these crowds. Occasionally retreat to your hotel room or an uncongested restaurant to experience an hour or so of personal space.

Weekends are a good time to avoid shopping centers and markets as well as take tours outside the city. On Saturdays and Sundays sidewalks and shopping centers are very crowded with children and office workers who have the weekend off.

POOR ACCOMMODATIONS AND FACILITIES

If you choose to stay at less than first-class or deluxe hotels, you may experience unique accommodations with poor facil-ities. Most of the problems center around the lack of adequate maintenance. Among the most frequent problems you can expect are:

- Air-conditioned rooms without cool air. Sometimes it's better to turn off the air-conditioner and open the windows, but then the mosquitos may get you!

- Leaking faucets and dripping pipes which keep your bathroom floor wet and you awake at night.

- Cold rooms without a blanket or top sheet, or ones with a dirty blanket but no top sheet.

- If you pack a sheet, you can eliminate the problem as well as have a sheet for packing your valuables!

Your shower may or may not work at full capacity, depending on the varied water pressure. Many inexpensive hotels only have cold water. In some hotels hot water is only available during certain hours. And when you do get hot water, it may be difficult to regulate. We have been scalded more than once in the middle of our showers!

Since many Indonesia hotels use small wattage bulbs and have few lights, your room may be dark and hard to read in. Furthermore, rooms may only have one electrical outlet for plugging in your appliances. Since this electrical outlet is usually inconveniently located behind a bed or dresser, it is essential that you carry a long extension cord for these occasions.

INSECTS, BUGS, AND MOSQUITOS

Indonesia's tropical climate generates a great many flying and crawling insects you may encounter in your hotel room, restaurants, and unexpected places. Most will not harm you, but they are annoying for people not used to living in such environments. If you have problems in your hotel room—most likely with ants, roaches, waterbugs, and mosquitos—ask the hotel to spray your room when you are out. Many hotels do so everyday while others only do so upon request. If you are particularly susceptible to mosquito bites, be sure to take with you a mosquito repellant at all times. Spray before going out at night. While you do not need to take malaria pills if you are planning to stay in the cities, you may need to if you plan to rough it in remote village areas. Consult a doctor, but only one who is familiar with tropical medicine; others may give you inappropriate or bad advice. Malaria pills, especially Fansidar, can kill you and thus may be worst than the disease! Indeed, we have been generally surprised with the level of misinformation among medical professionals concerning tropical diseases, medical conditions, inoculations, and medications appropriate for Asia.

SURPRISING RESTROOMS

Should you choose inexpensive hotels or find yourself outside major cities, be prepared for the Third World toilet experience.

The waterseal toilet is the standard fixture found outside most western hotels and restaurants. Built of porcelain and nearly level with the floor, it requires squatting skills most Westerners find discomforting. Be prepared to encounter a few of these.

Also, toilet paper is usually absent in such places. Be advised to always travel with an emergency supply of paper or tissues. You may also encounter restrooms which seem dirty and smelly. It is best to use your hotel room facilities before going out. If you later need a restroom, try to find a deluxe hotel which should have familiar and clean public facilities.

SMOKERS

If you are a nonsmoker, many places in Indonesia may bother you. Indonesians tend to be heavy smokers, and they disregard the presence of nonsmokers as well as ignore no smoking signs. Waiting areas in airports are filled with smokers and polluted air. Many restaurants have yet to reserve nonsmoking areas. The airlines have poorly ventilated nonsmoking sections and are very lax in enforcing the no smoking rule in the no smoking section. They let people smoke everywhere unless someone complains and then they ask the smoker to move to the smoking section. This will irritate you if you hate smoking and specifically reserved a seat to avoid the pollution.

If you are a non-smoker and encounter these problems, it is best to take preventive action or nicely complain. In public waiting areas, such as airports, which do not set aside no smoking areas, try to seat yourself as far away from crowds as possible or near a ventilated door or window. Use your hand fan for ventilation. Move somewhere else if someone begins smoking near you. If the smoke gets too oppressive, which it often does, ask airline personnel for assistance in getting relief. They usually are very helpful in satisfying your needs. In restaurants without no smoking sections, ask to be seated by a window or near a ventilated area. If you are in the middle of your meal and smoke begins to bother you ask to be moved to another table and nicely complain that *"the smoke is terrible in your restaurant."* The restaurant will usually accommodate.

❑ Indonesians tend to be heavy smokers. Many airport waiting areas and restaurants are filled with smoke.

❑ Tap water is not safe to drink. It's best to drink bottled water, soft drinks, and fruit juices.

❑ There is no faster way to drive up your restaurant bill than to order a bottle of imported wine.

❑ Airport departure times can be unpredictable—both late and early. Occasionally flights depart 20 minutes early!

❑ Parts of Indonesia still operate according to "rubber time" and few Indonesians observe Western queuing behavior.

❑ You should not try to arrange everything yourself. You can't afford it mentally, and financially it may not be a savings.

If you are sitting in a no smoking section on an airplane and someone lights up, by all means nicely point out this fact to the airline personnel who will then ask the person to either extinguish their cigarette or move to the smoking section. Do this rather than complain directly to the violator. Indonesian passengers usually do not take such initiative. Therefore, it may be up to you to point out the problem.

QUESTIONABLE WATER, DRINKS, AND FOODS

Tap water is not safe to drink in Indonesia. It is best to drink bottled water or bottled soft drinks and fruit juices which are readily available throughout the country. Also, watch the ice which may be made from tap water. Most major hotels serve bottled water and safe ice. You can buy bottled water in convenient small plastic containers. Familiar soft drinks, such as Coke, Pepsi, 7-Up, and Sprite, are readily available. A special treat are the numerous and exotic fruit juices, packaged in small paper cartons, which make wonderful drinks and are convenient to carry when traveling. Local beers are good, rivaling the best of the European beers. Indonesian coffee is difficult for many people to drink since it is very sweet, includes the grounds, and is often served steaming hot in a glass without a handle. Not only is it difficult to drink from a glass rather than a cup, but the grounds are a little difficult to swallow and may stain your teeth! Other than that, Indonesian coffee is not bad, although it will not win any awards with visitors.

A word of caution about wines. There is no faster way to drive up your restaurant bill than to order a bottle of imported wine. Since wines are subject to heavy import duties, a bottle of wine worth $20 may cost you $50 in a restaurant. Unaware of this, when handed the wine list, many people routinely order a wine with dinner and then are shocked by the final bill—the wine may cost more than dinner! You may want to forego wine.

While many of the foods in Indonesia are wonderful, be careful with what you eat. Avoid raw and undercooked meats, vegetables, and fruits that have not been cleaned. Many of the beautiful looking dishes are fiery hot with heavy doses of chili peppers. For the initiated, these dishes can wreak havoc with one's system. If you do eat something too hot, you can partially alleviate the pain by eating sugar.

Regardless of how careful you are with the local foods and drinks, you may still have stomach and intestinal problems. This usually lasts a day or two. Take some medications with you for upset stomach and diarrhea. If you eat lightly, take it easy, and use some medication, the problem should go away shortly.

AIRPORT TAXES AND FLIGHT DEPARTURES

Each domestic airport collects an airport tax. The procedure involves going from one chaotic counter to another and back. You usually pay the tax when you check in at the airport for your departure flight. You may want to tip your porter 3,000 rupiah to fight the crowds.

Departure times can be unpredictable—both late and early. Make sure you arrive at the airport at least one hour before departure time. While flights normally depart near the stated departure time, occasionally a flight takes off 20 minutes **early** to the surprise of foreign travelers who are accustomed to late departures. You can easily miss your flight even though you arrived on time!

SCHEDULING AND QUEUING

Parts of Indonesia still operate according to "rubber time," and few Indonesians observe Western queuing behavior. Schedules are often changed, or you must waste time booking flights and arranging transportation. This often means spending hours in crowds which converge on counters where everyone pushes and shoves to become first. There are few orderly lines in Indonesia —mainly masses of humanity converging on counters and desks for less than efficient service. The best you can do is (1) hire someone to take care of your scheduling needs, such as a travel agent, (2) push and shove like everyone else, and/or (3) take a good book with you to kill time. In the end, somehow it all works. You will not get lost and stay in Indonesia the rest of your life!

COMMUNICATION

Communication in Indonesia is often confusing for those unfamiliar with Indonesia's many cultures. Contrary to what may visitors may think, this confusion has little to do with language problems. Indonesians, especially the Javanese, are generally noted for their indirect and often Byzantine approach to interpersonal communication. They often mean *"no"* when they say *"yes,"* and they give wrong information instead of telling you *"I don't know."* Indeed, you may ask an Indonesian for directions, but he or she knowingly gives you wrong information rather than disappoint you by not giving you any information at all! If you rely on information from only one source, you may frequently find yourself lost and confused. Our rule of thumb is to ask the same question from two or three different people in the hopes of getting correct information. And even this approach doesn't always work well! On the other hand, the Batak and Minangkabau in Sumatra can be very aggressive, direct, and frank in their communication. You may feel more comfortable conversing with these people.

UNCERTAINTY

The best laid plans tend to go awry in Indonesia. Shops that are supposed to be open are often closed; your flight booked to Ujung Pandang may now be canceled, or you get bumped; the hotel that you had reservations with somehow cannot find your reservation; you are given wrong information; and you're never quite sure what's up next. Take, for example, travel information on areas outside Java and Bali. Even once you arrive on Java or Bali, you will find little travel information on the other islands. While you may be hesitant to plan a trip to Sumatra, Kalimantan, Sulawesi, Timor, or Irian Jaya without information, you will be told it's *"no problem—you can arrange everything once you arrive there."* Our experience is that this is generally true; you can indeed arrange local tours and transportation with relative ease. But, still, this general lack of travel information on most of Indonesia prior to visiting an area is problematic for many people who are used to doing some minimum pre-travel planning. Such uncertainty is a way of life in Indonesia. For tourists and travelers, Indonesia is one great serendipitous experience. Your visit to Indonesia will be one discovery after another. While this environment of uncertainty and serendipity at times can be irritating and stressful, if you are patient and take life as it comes your way—go with the flow—the relatively disorganized Indonesian way of doing things may grow on you after a while. It also leads to many humorous stories about visiting Indonesia.

COPING BETTER

You need to be prepared to respond to potential problems as well as avoid certain situations which inevitably lead to disappointments. Indeed, many of the problems of travel in Indonesia can be avoided by taking a few precautions and preparing accordingly. We find that many tourists bring the problems on themselves, because they act naive or are looking for that proverbial "free lunch."

Remember, this is not home; you may or may not have it as good or better as home, depending on how you position yourself for traveling in Indonesia. Since complaining and confrontation will not help you much in getting your way, you are always better off practicing a certain degree of "avoidance behavior" to most enjoy your trip. Like many Indonesians, you must **create your own private space** when handling daily problems. By all means avoid the touts and the "good deal" merchants; none have anything special to offer you other than getting you to pay exorbitant prices. If you shop for quality goods at quality shops, you will most likely avoid many disappointments and enjoy your purchases more.

Keep in mind, especially in poor Third World countries, you are seen as a rich tourist, ripe for possible plucking, especially by locals who hang around areas frequented by tourists. People who tell you they can give you a "good deal" are about to help themselves to your wealth. More often than not, they are touts who will take advantage of you. Know the signals and avoid these people. There is no such thing as a free lunch, so don't let people convince you they have a special deal for you. It may sound trite, but you usually get what you pay for. Therefore, stay close to quality hotels, quality restaurants, and quality shops. You may pay a little more, but you will save yourself a great deal of grief which comes with being a little greedy in trying to get a super bargain or save a few dollars.

You also need to develop a certain degree of patience, tolerance, flexibility, and humor. At times you may become irritated by traffic problems, poor facilities, smokers, crowds, lack of queues, and restrooms without toilet paper. When many of these problems occur together in the heat and humidity of the day, life may seem miserable. If and when this happens, it is best to keep your cool and shift gears. Stop what you are doing and change your environment by retreating to an air-conditioned taxi or a nice hotel, restaurant, or coffee shop for some comfort and privacy from the chaos of the streets. Indonesian cities tend to be chaotic; they test your sensibilities, and at times stretch your level of tolerance. Take it easy. Don't take yourself too seriously. A good sense of humor will get you through the difficulties. After all, tomorrow will be another and, hopefully, more exciting and rewarding day. You will be home shortly, and these difficult experiences will become part of your interesting travel tales.

PRACTICE TOLERANCE AND PATIENCE

The many inconveniences of Indonesia can be lessened by observing a few rules on how to best cope with this country and its people. The major rule is this: **be patient and never show**

your anger or frustrations. Most Indonesians are a very warm and accommodating people, although the Javanese may frustrate you more with their indirectness, and the Batak may shock you with their aggressiveness. This is a very complex society. You are not about to learn all its nuances and idiosyncrasies, even if you live there for years.

You should also minimize many of the basic living and traveling inconveniences by hiring, whenever possible, someone to take care of the more irritating travel and scheduling matters. You can travel Indonesia on the cheap—$20 a day for everything—if you want to. But unless you have a great deal of time to experience inertia and inefficiency, want a cultural experience with the lower classes, and can afford to piddle away your time, don't be too cheap. Time and inconvenience are money. Remember, Indonesia is not yet a do-it-yourself or self-service society. Since labor is cheap and locals are looking for additional income, use them whenever you can. At airports pay $3.00 or $4.00 extra to have a porter take your bags and ticket to the counter and check you through. He's good at it, and he appreciates the extra income. Read your book while he—rather than you—pushes and shoves through the masses to get everything checked through properly. At your hotel use the concierge service for confirming your air tickets, making reservations, arranging a car, and shipping your goods. Tip him a few dollars for this service.

Believe us when we say you should not try to arrange everything yourself in Indonesia. You can't afford it mentally, and financially it may not be a savings. In fact, you may quickly find that it is much cheaper in the long run to stay at a $120 a night hotel which provides all these services than to save $40 by staying an another hotel without such services.

The same is true for getting around in Indonesia. It is much more convenient to take air-conditioned taxis, hire a car, or charter a colt for a half day or day than to hassle with buses, bajajs, helicaks, or bemos just to save a few bucks.

If you prefer not experiencing poor service, leaky plumbing, cold showers, bugs, uncomfortable beds, and dimly lit rooms, then stay at the better hotels; you tend to get what you pay for —cheap hotels can very well ruin your whole visit. If you want to avoid stomach problems, then be careful what and where you eat. If poverty and sanitation bother you, then don't visit the beggars, slums, or local markets. If you want to experience good food, then frequent those restaurants with reputations for good food. If you hate crowds, then retreat from them whenever you feel the urge to get "away from it all" or be alone. If the heat and traffic bother you, take air-conditioned taxis. Don't punish yourself by walking long distances in the heat of the day or by riding crowded buses. If smokers bother you, then avoid them. And if you don't want any surprises in restrooms, then stay close to major hotels and carry sufficient paper with you.

Our point is that Indonesia can be a wonderful experience if you let it be by approaching it properly and by using common sense. Indonesia will not adapt to your needs, but it is remarkably tolerant, flexible, and filled with options enabling the visitor to make adjustments and shift gears when necessary. You will need to adapt to Indonesia by seeking alternatives which, in the end, will more than meet your needs. The alternatives are there and they can exceed your expectations. Your task is to discover appropriate alternatives to make your visit a wonderful and rewarding experience.

DON'T WORRY MUCH ABOUT CULTURE AND CUSTOMS

Contrary to what many people may tell you, or what others may write about cross-cultural problems, as a tourist you need not worry a great deal about how you should behave in Indonesia. Many of the so-called cultural taboos are most relevant to traditional rural village communities—places which do not offer many shopping opportunities and most likely will not be on your travel itinerary. Furthermore, you are not expected to go native. Many urban Indonesians are fairly cosmopolitan in their own behavior. Except in some conservative Muslim communities in Sumatra, Indonesian tend to be very tolerant of Western behaviors, including occasional faux pas. Most genuinely try to please visitors and find their faux pas somewhat amusing.

However, you should use common sense and observe a few basic rules of decent middle to upper class behavior. Among the most important rules are to:

- **Dress properly:** Do not wear shorts, sleeveless T-shirts, and low-cut blouses outside your hotel recreation areas and the beach. While most Indonesians are not conservative dressers, they do have a sense of what constitutes decent dress. Colorful sport shirts, slacks, and dresses are perfectly acceptable apparel for sightseeing, shopping, and restaurants. Too much skin showing is simply low class and impolite. But even if you dress improperly, you probably won't create serious problems. People may stare a little more, laugh, and rationalize that you are having one of your "private moments" in public.

- **Pass items with your right hand:** The left hand still has negative connotations associated with the lack of paper in those interesting restrooms. However, if you forget to do this, you will not create serious problems. This taboo seems to be disappearing in many areas.

- **Be patient, tolerant, and easy going:** Indonesians do not appreciate loud, pushy, and impatient people who verbally express their impatience in public. The quickest way to get no cooperation from a Javanese is to display your impatience in public through verbal confrontation. This does not mean you must be meek and non-assertive. Rather, you should be persistent in a non-aggressive and friendly manner. Instead of making demands, complaining, and being brutally frank about your feelings, try to be indirect by asking polite, friendly, humorous, yet leading questions.

  For example, when bargaining in shops, don't respond to what appears to be an unreasonable price by saying *"That's highway robbery!"* Rather, look a little disappointed and then respond with a statement and a question: *"That's a little more than I had planned to spend. Is it possible to do any better on this price?"* Anything is possible in Indonesia. If your hotel forgets to put towels in your room, don't call room service and say: *"I want some towels right now."* Instead, *"I've looked all over my room and can't find any towels. Could someone help us? We would like to have some towels in about five minutes. Thank you."* Someone will usually come to your assistance if you ask for or look like you need help.

  Informal, polite, and low-keyed interpersonal relationships will resolve many problems as Indonesians generally seek to avoid conflict, confrontation, and anxiety. Their primary concern is to please you so that relationships will remain smooth, workable, and pleasant.

- **Be friendly and smile a lot:** While there are differences amongst the many ethnic groups, on the whole Indonesians tend to be spontaneous, colorful, friendly, helpful, smile a great deal, spread good will, and are fun to converse with. They are often the source of your serendipity experiences in Asia. You can easily talk and joke with them. You may be overwhelmed with their kindness and graciousness. Try to be responsive by also being spontaneous with these people—smiling, waving, and thanking them for their assistance.

BALANCE YOUR SCHEDULE

There is no need to "shop 'til you drop," although this is both tempting and easy to do in Jakarta and Bali. If you are not careful, you may experience "shoppers' burnout." To best prevent this from happening to you, do what many Asians do—they **balance** their daily lives with complementary opposites. In Indonesia you should work hard and play hard. Shopping is hard work. But all shopping and no touring and recreation will turn you into a dull and exhausted traveler. Keep in mind that you will have a great deal of time to shop since most shops are open from 8am to 9pm.

Therefore, we recommend that you set aside some time each day for sightseeing, people watching, strolling, entertainment, eating, drinking, and using your hotel recreational facilities. These other activities will nicely complement your shopping activities. If you are an early riser, you may wish to enjoy a nice breakfast buffet and take an early morning tour or stroll before shopping. After doing a few hours of shopping, you may wish to rest for two hours in the afternoon, resume your shopping around 6pm, and then end your day with a late evening dinner in a nice restaurant. If you balance work with play, take life easy, and don't run around trying to squeeze all your plans into a tight time schedule, you will experience the unique subtleties and serendipity which make travel to Indonesia such an enjoyable experience.

APPROACH YOUR FIRST DAY RIGHT

It is tempting to get off your plane, rush to your hotel, and immerse yourself in a shopping orgy on your first day. Your detailed action plan will guide you in the right direction. However, we have learned to put each city or island into a proper first-day perspective which includes only limited shopping.

Upon arriving at the airport, be sure to **confirm any flights** you will be taking within 72 hours. Pick up any travel literature available. If you do not have hotel reservations, many airports have a tourist information desk that can assist you.

After arriving at your hotel, **contact the hotel concierge service** to answer questions or resolve any problems you may have concerning tours, restaurants, entertainment, transportation, repairs, etc. If, for example, you wish to rent a car with an English speaking driver, make reservations at a good restaurant, arrange a party or contact shippers, the concierge will help you. Unfamiliar to many travelers, this imported European hotel service has been nicely adapted to most major Indonesian hotels. Using this service will greatly assist you in navigating through an unfamiliar and chaotic community. In fact, a good concierge service may more than pay for the extra expense of a deluxe hotel.

If you arrive late in the day, you may want to **survey the shops** in your hotel or in a nearby shopping arcade to get some idea of the range of goods, prices, and the local bargaining culture. This is a good time to do window shopping and get a feel for shopping at night.

On your first day we recommend that you **take a morning city tour**. Several alternative city tours can be arranged through your hotel. A three-hour morning tour should give you a good overview of the city, including historical sites, shopping areas, and transportation. In addition, the tour guide should be able to answer any of your general questions concerning shopping areas. We find it is important to start with such a tour in order to place our shopping adventure into proper geographic and cultural contexts.

After a pleasant lunch, **begin your shopping adventure in earnest**. Select one or two major shopping areas and work from one end to another. In the evening review your detailed plan and make the necessary adjustments based upon this first-day overview of options. The remaining time should be spent on targeting particular shopping areas and specialty shops.

But do balance your daily shopping routine with other normal types of travel activities. As you look back at your adventure on your last day in a community, you should have enjoyed the place along with acquiring some wonderful purchases. For we often find the true enjoyment of our trip is not so much in having saved a great deal of money on purchases but in the adventure of discovering new things, in the process of bargaining for the right price, and in combining our primary shopping activities with ample time for excellent tours, restaurants, and entertainment. In the end, we return home with both wonderful purchases and memories of a trip that was primarily pleasure!

PART II

Shopping Well

5

Shopping Rules, Bargaining Skills, and Potential Problems

Shopping in Indonesia is as much a cultural experience as it is a set of buying and selling transactions in unique commercial settings. While many of the shops, department stores, and markets may look similar to ones you shop in back home, they do have important differences you should know about prior to starting your Indonesia shopping adventure. Most of these differences relate to certain shopping and pricing traditions that constitute an important set of shopping rules and bargaining skills you can and should learn before you begin making purchases in Indonesia.

BEWARE OF UNWANTED ADVICE

One problem visitors to Indonesia encounter is in communicating their shopping desires and standards to Indonesians, many of whom do not understand Western tastes. Many Indonesians seek to please you, put their best foot forward, and show you where a "good deal" can be made. Often overly obsessed with getting a bargain, many Indonesians shop for the cheapest price rather than the best quality. Consequently, they frequently help you get products at a very cheap price, but the designs and quality also may look cheap.

When asked where is the best place to shop, Indonesians often recommend places where they shop, because they believe you must have a personal relationship with a shopkeeper in order to get the best buy. They're convinced tourists cannot get a good deal by merely walking into a shop and negotiating a price; it's best that you know someone who is a friend or relative of the shopkeeper to get the best buy. Our experience is that this belief is largely a myth on the part of many Indonesians who are obsessed in using personal relationships and connections in getting their way. Tourists can often do just as well —and sometimes better—on their own without the assistance of well-meaning locals who believe they are doing you a favor by loaning you their connections. Time and again we have received better buys on quality items than Indonesian friends because when we walked unannounced into a shop by ourselves, shopkeepers were more willing to give deep discounts precisely because we were **not** from the area; they knew we would be here today and gone tomorrow. They were less likely to do so with a local Indonesian who would be back tomorrow expecting the same discount! Consequently, if someone tells you it is best to go shopping with an Indonesian who can get you better prices, don't take them too seriously. At best, consider them naive in their own shopping culture. Ironically, you may pay more in the long run by believing this myth.

When asked where is the best place to shop, many Indonesians also recommend a typical tourist shop filled with trinkets —many items you neither need nor want in your wardrobe or home. But this is their idea of a "good time" for tourists. After all, you are a tourist and they feel this is what tourists want to shop for when visiting Indonesia. They feel they are helping you by showing you where to buy items real cheap rather than send you to places that are very expensive. Their concepts of design, color, and quality will seldom be the same as yours. As a result, many visitors to Indonesia leave disappointed with their shopping experience and purchases.

AVOID THE COMMISSION GAME

Another shopping problem many visitors to Indonesia encounter is with tour guides and drivers who take them to particular "recommended" shops. Invariably the tour guide or driver takes you to a place which gives him or her a 10 to 20% commission on everything you buy—the universal tout problem. The problem is especially pronounced in Bali where some tour guides and drivers demand a 30% commission from shops, especially from the silver shops in Celuk. Not surprisingly, prices in these shops will be inflated and the quality of goods usually will be mediocre. We recommend avoiding such shops by asking the tour guide or driver to take you back to your hotel or put you in a taxi—say you feel ill. If this doesn't work, ask for your money back. There is nothing worse than wasting time in such a shop and knowing full well you are about to be "taken."

At the same time, a driver or guide may ask the shopkeeper for a commission, even though you had the driver or guide take you to a shop recommended in this book and you have expressively told him that he is not to ask for commissions. The usual approach is for the guide or driver to accompany you to the shop for the ostensible purpose of "helping" you with your purchase. Once he goes into the shop with you, the shopkeeper is likely to automatically add 10 to 30% to your prices, because that's what the shopkeeper expects the guide will demand once you complete your transaction. If he doesn't go in the shop with you, he will probably ask you what appears to be three innocent questions—*"Where did you go, what did you buy, and how much did you pay?"*—once you return to the vehicle. If you reveal information on your purchases, he will usually return to the shop and ask for a 10 to 30% commission. The best approach here is to tell your guide or driver **before** you go shopping that you will only hire his services if he agrees not to take commissions. While he will probably agree to this stipulation but still take commissions, you at least put him on notice that your rules are different. When you arrive at your destination, tell your guide or driver to wait at the car while you're gone. Once in a shop and before you discuss prices, tell the shopkeeper three things:

- ❑ It is simply a myth that tourists can't do as well on prices as the locals.

- ❑ The tout problem is especially pronounced in Bali where some tour guides and drivers demand a 30% commission from shops.

- ❑ Good detailed city maps are very difficult to find in Indonesia.

- ❑ Since most shops only wrap purchases in a thin layer of newspaper to disguise the item, you'll have to repack your purchases to prevent damage. Your packing kit, which should include bubble-wrap, will come in handy on such occasions.

- ❑ Be careful you don't get cheated when shopping. Expect some merchants to inflate prices, refuse to bargain, and sell "new antiques" at old antique prices.

- ❑ Expert shoppers from fixed-price cultures may feel lost when shopping in Indonesia's variable price culture.

"I came to this shop on my own without the assistance of any guide or driver."

"I've told my driver that he does not receive commissions when we go shopping. If he comes back and asks, tell him I told you he is forbidden to ask for any commissions."

*"I will not tell him what I bought here or how much I paid
for any items."*

By doing this, you give notice to the shopkeeper that you
expect to be given the best "non-commission" price. When you
return to your guide or driver and he asks you where you
shopped, what you bought, and how much you paid, tell him:

*"A place down the street. I didn't pay much at all since I
told the shopkeeper he's not supposed to give commissions."*

Remember, if a guide or driver takes you to one of his or her
recommended shops or walks in the shop with you, at least
10%—and possibly as much as 30%—of the price you pay will
go directly into the pocket of this "helpful" individual. You will
do everyone a favor, including yourself, if you tell your driver
and shopkeepers that the prices you pay should not include
commissions.

KNOW AND PRACTICE
21 KEY SHOPPING RULES

In many other countries you can be assured of good shopping
by staying close to the major hotels, shopping arcades, and
department stores. Good to excellent tourist infrastructures are
in place and well organized to put you conveniently and
comfortably in these places. Fixed prices, as well as bargaining
cultures with relatively well understood rules, make shopping
both a predictable and enjoyable experience.

But Indonesia is different. Indonesia has an incredible
amount of arts and crafts to overwhelm the international
shopper. These are more difficult to find and purchase than in
most other Asian countries. A basic tourist infrastructure puts
you conveniently in the major cities and enables you to visit
most of the major islands. Deluxe and first-class hotels make for
a relatively comfortable visit in these areas. But once you leave
your hotel, you are largely on your own. You may lack a basic
map to navigate the streets and roads. You must go hunting for
particular shops and factories which may or may not be
conveniently located near your hotel, and which may or may
not be open according to their stated hours. At best you will
find shops selling similar goods located near each other along a
particular stretch of road.

Nonetheless, there are a few shopping rules emerging in
Indonesia to help you navigate through what appears to be a

helter-skelter shopping culture. These rules apply to most of Indonesia, although the structure of shopping in the most highly touristed areas—Jakarta, Jogjakarta, and Bali—will differ somewhat.

The basic rules on where to shop appear to be these:

1. **Indonesia's geographic and cultural diversity requires choosing one of two shopping strategies:**

   ■ **Identify what it is you wish to buy and then develop your travel itinerary around this plan.** For example, if you are particularly interested in batik, then book your flights and hotels for Jakarta, Jogjakarta, Solo, Cirebon, Pekalongan, and Bali. If you are interested in ethnographic arts and crafts—want to experience the cultures that produced them—plan trips to Medan, Lake Toba, Nias, Padang, and Bukittinggi on Sumatra; Balikpapan on Kalimantan; Ujung Padang and Rantepao on Sulawesi; and Jayapura in Irian Jaya. In the case of batik, you can fly into Jakarta and take the train from there or fly to the other cities on Java and then fly from Jogjakarta to Bali. In the case of ethnographic art shopping, you should consider purchasing the "Visit Indonesia Decade Pass" ($300 for 3 cities) to complete this shopping tour. The batik shopping trip will also put you in the major areas for purchasing Javanese and Balinese textiles, woodcarvings, paintings, puppets, silver, Dutch and Chinese antiques, and a host of other arts and crafts. But remember, this is the road to the sophisticated cultures of the Javanese and Balinese—only two of more than 300 cultural and ethnic groups in Indonesia. The ethnographic art route is more adventuresome, and it puts you into contact with the ancient Dong-Son cultures of more than 80 million Indonesians who live in some of the world's most beautiful and fascinating areas. The ethnographic art trip is less comfortable and convenient than the batik tour, but you need not rough it. However, you may find that traveling to the "source" for "ethnographic" crafts only uncovers newly made or poor quality pieces. In general, we have found the best quality available in the major commercial centers of Jakarta, Bali, and Jogjakarta.

- **Wander around Indonesia to discover its multitude of shopping pleasures.** This is the normal approach of most tourists and travelers who know little about Indonesia. They start in Jakarta for two or three days and then fly to Bali for four or more days. In the process of absorbing museums, gardens, and beaches, they do some shopping. The result of this approach is a sampling of Indonesia's copy-cat arts and crafts—some batik clothes and a batik painting, a wood carving or two, a mask, a wayang puppet, and a kris. Much of their shopping is confined to the tourist shops and stalls in Jakarta and Bali.

Your major choice is whether to confine your visit to Java and Bali or venture to the outer islands which are relatively untouched by the average tourist and traveler to Indonesia. You may want to wander initially and then later return for a more focused shopping experience.

2. **Two "where to shop" theories compete with each other in Indonesia, neither of which is always applicable.**

The distribution of arts and crafts from one island to another is influenced by a network of middlemen who supply the major shops in Jakarta and Bali. If you talk to shopowners in Jakarta and Bali, they will tell you not to waste your time visiting the Outer Islands to buy arts and crafts similar to those found in their shops. The reasons they give seem sensible. The local producers inflate prices for both tourists and residents from Jakarta and Bali. They are viewed as "rich Jakartians" or "rich foreigners." Given the logic of pricing in much of Indonesia, you may well pay more for an item on Kalimantan or Irian Jaya than if you brought the same item in Jakarta. As a result, many of the dealers in Jakarta and Bali only buy through local middlemen. They avoid traveling to the Outer Islands, because they know their presence will drive up the prices. As a foreign tourist, you may have to pay an even higher premium for your presence. Indeed, if you observe many of the well established antique shops in Jakarta, you will see this buying and selling structure. Individuals come to the front and back doors with items to sell. These are often from families who need cash and thus are willing to settle for the price set by the buyer. If the shopkeeper went out looking for these items, he would pay a premium. In other words, many well established shops play a passive buying role—wait for sellers to come to them, and then wait for the buyers to come to get a better deal than if they went to the Outer Islands on their own.

The second shopping theory is that prices in Jakarta and Bali are inflated due to the presence of tourists and monopolized markets. Therefore, if you want to get a good deal, you should avoid these shops and head for the factories and shops outside Jakarta and Bali.

Our shopping experience in Indonesia neither confirms nor denies these two competing theories. There is some truth to both. If you confine your shopping only to Jakarta, Bali, and Jogjakarta, you will find some very nice items, but your selections will be limited. In addition, in many cases you will pay more than in other areas of Indonesia. But this is not always true. For example, if you shop for antiques along Jl. Surabaya, the price may fluctuate greatly from one day to another, from one hour to another, and from one stall to another. If you arrive early in the morning and the vendor is in need of cash that day, he may let you purchase a $200 item for $50. It depends on timing, the cash flow needs of the vendor, and your bargaining skills. On the other hand, just around the corner from the Jl. Surabaya antique market is the famous antique shop/home of Alex and Caecil Papadimitriou. Here, quality is excellent and prices are high. The Papadimitriou's have little incentive to discount since they are well established, sellers come to them with good quality antiques and textiles, they regularly service foreign buyers who pay the asking prices, and they are financially stable. Considering the cost of traveling to the Outer Islands and the likelihood of not finding the family heirlooms which automatically come to the Papadimitriou's front door due to their reputation, you are probably better off visiting Alex and Caecil rather than running around the country in hopes of buying similar goods. What Alex and Caecil have in their shop/home are extremely difficult for tourists and short-term travelers to find on their own since they are not plugged into this highly personalized supply and demand network which links many of the shops in Jakarta and Bali to factories, shops, and homes elsewhere.

On the other hand, selections are always limited in Jakarta and Bali. For example, if you are interested in shopping for Batak house gables, panels, staffs, containers, and wood carvings, a trip to Medan and Lake Toba may well be worth it. Shops in Jakarta and Bali do carry Batak items, but the selections are limited and the prices are high. You will do much better on selections, quality, and prices by visiting the shops along Jl. Jend A Yani in Medan and in Parapat and a few villages on Samosir Island of Lake Toba. The same is true for Dayak artifacts. The selection of such noted Dayak items as masks and baby carriers is very limited outside Kalimantan. On the other hand, a trip to Kalimantan may not be worth it since the selections there are also limited and the prices are the most inflated of any we found in Indonesia. Arts and crafts from Sulawesi are nearly nonexistent in Jakarta and Bali. You will have to make this lovely trip to shop for Toraja artifacts. In the case of Irian Jaya, shops in Jakarta and Bali seem to be well supplied with Asmat arts and crafts. This is in part due to the government's promotion of Asmat arts and crafts. The Asmat are producing many arts and crafts which appear in several antique shops on Java, Bali, and Sulawesi. Older pieces are hard to find and extremely expensive. But the newer pieces, which imitate the older ones, are increasingly available at reasonable prices. Consequently, you may not wish to make a special trip to Irian Jaya for shopping purposes. If you do, you may pay more there than in the shops on Bali, Java, and Sulawesi for the same quality goods.

3. **Shopping is best done by taxi or private car.** Since Indonesian shops and shopping are not con-

centrated around hotels and shopping centers and within convenient walking distance of each other, you need to be as mobile as possible. In Jakarta this means taking taxis or hiring a car with driver to take you to the various hotel shops, Jl. Kebon Sirih Timur Dalam, Jl. Surabaya, various Sarinah department stores, the National Museum, Beautiful Indonesia in Miniature, and the Ancol Art Center. Since taxis are plentiful, comfortable, convenient, and inexpensive in Jakarta, you may wish to just use the taxis rather than hire a car with driver. However, in Jogjakarta and Bali, you may wish to hire a car with driver or rent a motorbike to get around to the various shopping areas and galleries. Bargaining for a *becak* is no fun after the novelty wears off about your third ride! On the Outer Islands we recommend a car with driver and an English speaking guide. These options can be easily arranged through your hotel and they are not expensive.

4. **Be prepared to pack and repack your purchases many times.**

Most shops will wrap your purchases in a thin layer of newspaper—covering just enough to disguise what you bought. Your purchases also are wrapped with colorful plastic twine which can serve as a convenient handle. Unfortunately, you cannot travel far without damaging such purchases. You will need to find an appropriate packing material to safely pack your purchases for flights elsewhere. If you don't take packing material with you, look for a carpet shop which sells foam carpet padding. Several such shops are found in most cities and towns. These shops will sell you carpet padding in meter lengths ($3-4 a meter). The foam carpet padding makes a good packing material in lieu of other alternatives. Better still, take one suitcase filled only with bubble-wrap, cord, and tape with you or pick it up in Hong Kong or Singapore. If you don't repack your purchases securely, expect some damage. Indonesian baggage handlers are not always careful even when the airlines paste the big red "Fragile" signs on your baggage. Hand-carry your most valuable and fragile purchases.

5. **Expect to encounter a great deal of seemingly "irrational" business logic and behavior in many parts of Indonesia.**

    Unless you are dealing with Chinese, Batak, or Padang shopkeepers, who seem to understand supply and demand pricing logic, other business people in Indonesia often defy Western pricing, bargaining, and purchasing logic. The Chinese merchants are similar to Chinese merchants in Hong Kong, Singapore, and Bangkok—they appear to want to sell and make a profit. They will bargain. Padang merchants, who dominate the antique stalls along Jl. Surabaya in Jakarta, are downright aggressive and are willing to strike bargains to sell their goods. And the Batak women, who dominate trade in northern Sumatra, are very aggressive and will strike bargains to sell and are probably the most delightful people in Asia to buy from; you will feel comfortable dealing with these merchants. They will give you the standard 20 to 50% discounts you are used to getting elsewhere in Asia.

    But doing business elsewhere in Indonesia is often perplexing and problematic. Other groups do not appear to be good business people. Some might say "piracy is well and alive" among these groups! They poorly display their goods, often close their shops whenever they feel like it, make you feel uncomfortable when you enter to browse, state ridiculously inflated prices which can double or triple on your second or third visit, are unwilling to bargain, and are generally uncooperative. In Kalimantan and Sulawesi many of the shopkeepers are simply lethargic; many make you feel you are inconveniencing them from what they are doing— which is nothing more than sitting and eating. Some will even complain if you want to have them take an item down for you to examine. The complaint is often that you may not buy it and thus the person will have to put it back! When you get to the pricing stage, get ready to take a bath.

    The problem of business in Indonesia is serious. There is a certain exploitative mentality among some Indonesian merchants that is self-destructive to the Indonesian tourist trade. This mentality has been around for centuries and is not about to change. The logic goes something like this: *"You are rich, I am poor; therefore, I can take you for whatever I can get."* This logic is not aimed just at foreign tourists. Fellow Indonesians also are targets of this logic and potential exploitation. This is what Jakarta merchants mean when they say they don't travel to the Outer Islands to buy because they are seen as "rich Jakartians" ripe for the plucking. Many Indonesians do not trust each other, because they know they will be taken advantage of if they are not careful. Remember to always be on your guard against cheating. This tendency permeates much of Indonesian society and makes what is otherwise a delightful country and people less than appealing for repeat business.

What you will often encounter is a merchant who is more interested in playing the power game of taking advantage of you for a quick windfall than in selling their goods for incremental profits. This makes for some interesting bargaining scenarios which defy our "rational" bargaining logic.

Unfortunately, this is one of the major reasons many importers from Hong Kong, Bangkok, and Singapore refuse to deal with Indonesians. The business culture in Indonesia is seen as one of corruption, distrust, and petty gamesmanship. We say this not to discourage you from shopping in Indonesia. Rather, we want to warn you against potential problems when dealing with different types of merchants. Be careful you don't get cheated. Expect some merchants to inflate prices, refuse to bargain, and sell "new antiques" at old antique prices. What they are doing is perfectly logical in the Indonesian sense of power. They have power and you have money. They will take as much of your money as they can get without relinquishing their power over you. As such, you will find you cannot play this game to your advantage. You would only loose your money to what is ostensibly your local merchant thief! So be wary, check goods carefully, and bargain hard.

On the other hand, you may have a wonderful time bargaining with the Batak women in Sumatra who appear to be honest, direct, and fun-loving merchants. You should thoroughly enjoy buying from them as well as many shopkeepers elsewhere.

6. **Combine your shopping with an appreciation of Indonesian art, culture, and craftsmen.**

   Since most of what you will purchase in Indonesia is closely tied to Indonesian art, culture, and society, we strongly recommend developing shopping plans which are closely tied to Indonesian culture. Shortly after you arrive in Jakarta, it is a good idea to visit several museums (National, Puppet, Old Batavia) as well as Beautiful Indonesia in Miniature. These initial stops will give you an excellent overview of what lies ahead for shopping. When in Jogjakarta, attend a wayang puppet show and a gamelan orchestra presentation. In Bali, the dances and village rituals are worth observing. In Toraja Land try to schedule your visit to coincide with the fascinating burial rites. And in most areas you should visit the factories, studios, and homes which produce the batik, textiles, woodcarvings, silver, sculptures, and other handicrafts. Most of these areas, including the National Museum, have shops from which you can make purchases. By combining your shopping in this manner you will find shopping in Indonesia to be more immediately fulfilling and extremely meaningful once you return home to reminisce how and where you bought particular items. Each purchase will have a special story behind it.

7. **Focus your shopping around factories, open-air stalls, small neighborhood shops and galleries, hotel shops, and department stores.**

   Indonesia has yet to develop the ubiquitous shopping malls and arcades which dominate the shopping scene for tourists in Hong Kong, Bangkok, Kuala Lumpur, and Singapore. Indonesia has shopping malls, but these are primarily oriented toward consumer goods for Indonesia's rapidly emerging middle class. Most offer little for the discriminating international shopper. The deluxe hotels in Jakarta, Bali, and Jogjakarta have the largest variety of quality shops. However, most of the good shopping will take place in small shops and galleries lining particular streets, open-air bazaar-type stalls, and the small cottage factories tucked away in various neighborhoods. One department store in Indonesia—the Sarinah chain—offers a good selection of Javanese and Balinese batiks and handicrafts. These stores usually have one floor or one section devoted entirely to batik and handicrafts. This department is a convenient starting point for many first-time visitors who wish to sample the variety of batik and handicrafts and compare Sarinah's fixed prices with those of other shopping areas and shops.

8. **Be prepared for "shopping shock."**

In many parts of Indonesia, especially Jogjakarta, Bali, and Samosir Island on Lake Toba, Sumatra, you may get weary of the over-production of what appears to be the same items. Shops on Bali often overwhelm visitors with hundreds and thousands of woodcarvings and paintings that all look the same. And to make matters worse, there seem to be too many shops and stalls selling the identical items. Indeed, many visitors are perplexed as to who buys what appears to be thousands of tacky items, and how shopkeepers can make a living by offering the same items in such large quantities. We have no answers to these questions except try to go beyond the tacky reproduction junk. You will find unique quality pieces in Indonesia, but it's like looking for a diamond in the rough. Unless you are a knick-knack collector, we strongly recommend against putting money into the tourist junk. Save your time and money for better items. When the tacky tourist shops combine with the heat and humidity begin to overwhelm you, head for a nice hotel restaurant, a designer boutique, a noted art gallery, or a famous wood carver or sculptor to begin appreciating some truly unique quality items.

9. **Don't try to shop for everything in Indonesia.**

Indonesia is a huge and diverse country. It takes a great deal of time to shop this country properly for quality items. If you only have a week for Indonesia, split your time between Jakarta and Bali, the two major shopping areas in Indonesia. With two or three weeks you can include Sumatra and Sulawesi along with Java and Bali. If you really want to shop Indonesia thoroughly and do not plan to return, set aside six weeks and shop it from northern Sumatra to the southern coast of Irian Jaya. In so doing, you will experience one of the world's great adventures, and you also will have a shipping problem with all the purchases you will accumulate along the way! Better still, leave shopping in Indonesia open for the future. Once you return home, put your purchases in their proper places, and reflect on your unique adventure, you may soon get that unexplained urge to return and tackle a whole new shopping adventure in other parts of this country. Indonesia will grow on you over time. But you must plan just enough so that serendipity can take its course and guide you through what is otherwise a helter-skelter shopping culture of elegant boutiques, factories, and street stalls beckoning you to buy their goods.

10. **The most important shopping areas are concentrated in the central business districts and a few outlying suburban areas.**

The best products in terms of quality, designs, and colors are found in shopping centers, hotel shopping arcades, department stores, and shophouses concentrated along one or two major streets in the central business districts of most major cities and towns. However, don't expect to find much shopping in rural areas other than at factory shops and cottage industry houses Bali. Knowing these shopping patterns, it's a good idea to stay at a hotel in close proximity to the main shopping streets in the center of town. Except in Bali, where you can visit factories and shops outside the central business district, expect to do 90% of your shopping along a few downtown streets.

11. **Concentrate your shopping on a few shopping areas within close proximity of each other each day.**

It's best to focus your shopping in particular shopping areas rather than continuously travel from one shop to another between areas. Compile a list of shops or areas you wish to visit, locate them on a map, and each day try to visit those close to one another.

12. **Prepare to walk a great deal within each shopping area, but use transportation to go from one shopping area to another.**

While most shops, shopping centers, and department stores are located along a few streets in the central business district, these are often very long streets requiring a considerable amount of walking. Take a good pair of walking shoes, slow your pace of walking, and take taxis whenever possible.

13. **Take your rain and sun gear whenever you go out.**

Unless you know for certain the weather forecast for the day, it's always a good idea to take an umbrella—a small collapsible one is perfect—sunglasses, and hat when you go out during the day and an umbrella at night. Indonesia's hot and humid climate can be unpredictable at times. The umbrella keeps both the rain and sun off one's head. An Indonesian version of Murphy's Law seems to operate: If you forget to take your umbrella, it invariably rains!

14. **Expect to shop in two very different shopping cultures.**

The first world is the most familiar one for visitors —shopping centers, department stores, and hotel shopping arcades. Shops in this culture tend to have window displays, well organized interiors, and fixed prices which may or may not be all that fixed, depending on your ability to get discounts. The second shopping culture consists of the traditional shophouses, markets, and hawkers which tend to be somewhat disorganized and involve price uncertainty and bargaining skills. You will most likely be able to directly transfer your shopping skills to the first culture, but you may have difficulty navigating in the second shopping culture.

15. **The day and night markets can be fun places to shop, but only if you are open to new sights, sounds, and smells not normally found in other shopping sites.**

    Many of the markets combine fresh fruits, vegetables, and meats with hawker food stalls and shop stalls selling household goods. Somewhat chaotic, these markets can be very interesting and colorful places to visit. They tend to cater to a different class of local residents—lower to lower-middle—than the department stores and shopping centers. Many locals prefer shopping in the markets, because prices appear cheap compared to other shopping alternatives. While these markets offer few items of interest to visitors, they do provide a cultural experience and are good places for exotic photo opportunities. Other markets primarily offer inexpensive clothes, household goods, electronics, handicrafts, jewelry, and antiques. These, too, are great places to experience the more traditional buying and selling culture. Depending on the market, you may or may not find good quality products in these places. In most markets the emphasis is on buying cheap goods. You may find inexpensive clothes, handicrafts, souvenirs, and fake products to make the trip to these markets worthwhile. Bargaining, with discounts ranging from 20 to 60%, is the only way to buy in these markets. You will be foolish to pay the first price.

16. **Most department stores and some shopping centers primarily cater to local residents rather than to foreign tourists.**

    Don't expect to find a great deal of quality local products in department stores and shopping centers. Most of these places orient their product lines to the local middle-class with numerous average quality consumer products and imported goods. However, you will find a few exceptional department stores in Jakarta that are primarily oriented to foreign visitors and Indonesia's upper class—Sogo and Sarinah. These are "must visit" places for most visitors.

17. **The best quality products are invariably found in the major hotel shopping arcades and a few shopping centers and department stores with reputations for quality.**

There is nothing surprising to discover that the best quality shops tend to congregate near the best quality hotels which cater to the more affluent business travelers and tourists. The shops in these places will offer a mix of expensive imported products—designer label clothes, jewelry, luggage, shoes, and accessories—as well as excellent quality local products, especially antiques, art, jewelry, clothes, textiles, and handicrafts. The prices in such shops can seem high, but they offer good quality products. The "best buys" will be on high quality local products rather than the usual mix of upscale imported goods that are available in many other cities and duty-free shops around the world.

18. **Expect to get the best prices on locally produced items that use inexpensive labor.**

Imported goods will be expensive regardless of their duty status. But any products that use inexpensive local labor, textiles, woodcarvings, woven handicrafts, handcrafted jewelry—are excellent buys because the cost of labor is increasing, and many of the handcrafting skills are quickly disappearing with the onslaught of inexpensive plastic materials and machine labor.

19. **Don't expect to get something for nothing.**

If a price seems too good to be true, it probably is. Good quality products, especially jewelry, antiques, art, batik clothes, and ikat textiles, may not seem cheap in Indonesia. But they are bargains if you compare prices to similar items found in the shops of Tokyo, Sydney, Paris, London, or New York City.

20. **Ask for assistance whenever you need it.**

At times you may feel lost and have difficulty finding particular shops or products. Whenever this happens, just ask for assistance from your hotel, shopkeepers, and people you meet on the street. While service may not be great and communications is often confusing, Indonesians are friendly and will assist you if they can.

21. **Don't be surprised if some shopkeepers take a great deal of your time in developing a personal and long-term relationship with you.**

Business in Indonesia is still a personal set of relations, regardless of all the symbols of impersonal efficiency. While some merchants may initially appear distant and suspicious, most are generally inquisitive if you will initiate a conversation that involves their family, work, or country. Many merchants in Indonesia are extremely friendly, enjoy learning more about visitors, are willing to share their knowledge about their country and products, and prefer cementing personal relationships with their customers. The lines between buyer and seller may quickly fade as you develop a friendship with the shopkeeper. You may even find some shopkeepers inviting you to lunch, dinner, or their home as well as giving you special gifts. You may even feel you are being adopted by the family! This is usually a genuine expression of interest, concern, and friendship rather than a sales tactic. Such personal encounters may well become the highlights of your shopping adventure in Indonesia and they may lead to lasting friendships with these individuals.

You will also discover other shopping rules as you proceed through the many shophouses, shopping centers, hotel shopping arcades, department stores, and markets in Indonesia. Many of these rules relate to pricing policies and bargaining practices that you can and should learn if you want to become an effective shopper in Indonesia.

PRICING PRACTICES AND BARGAINING BASICS

Bargaining still remains the way of shopping life in most parts of Indonesia. If you want to be an effective shopper in Indonesia, you need to know something about the basics of bargaining.

Most North American and European tourists come from fixed-price cultures where prices are nicely displayed on items. The only price uncertainty may be a sales tax added to the total amount at the cash register. Only on very large-ticket items, such as automobiles, boats, houses, furniture, carpets, and jewelry, can you expect to negotiate the price. If you want to get the best deal, you must do comparative shopping as well as wait for special discounts and sales. Bargain shopping in such a culture centers on comparative pricing of items. Shopping becomes a relatively passive activity involving the examination of advertisements in newspapers and catalogs.

Expert shoppers in fixed-price cultures tend to be those skilled in carefully observing and comparing prices in the print advertising media. They clip coupons and know when the best sales are being held for particular items on certain days. They need not be concerned with cultivating personal relationships with merchants or salespeople in order to get good buys.

Like a fish out of water, expert shoppers from fixed-price cultures may feel lost when shopping in Indonesia. Few of their fixed-price shopping skills are directly transferable to Indonesia's shopping environments. Except for department stores and some ads in the monthly tourist literature as well as local newspapers announcing special sales, few shops advertise in the print media or on TV and radio.

COPING WITH PRICE UNCERTAINTY

Goods in Indonesia fall into three pricing categories: **fixed**, **negotiable**, or **discounted**. The general trend in Jakarta and Bali is toward fixed prices on more and more goods. In the meantime, **price uncertainty**, negotiable or discounted prices —is the standard way to sell most goods and services in Indonesia. The general pricing guideline is this: Unless you see a sign stating otherwise, you can expect prices of most goods in small shops to be negotiable. You can safely assume that all stated prices are the starting point from which you should receive anything from a 10 to 60% discount, depending upon your haggling skills and level of commitment to obtain reduced prices.

Discount percentages in Indonesia will vary for different items and from one shop to another. In general, however, expect to receive at least a 10 to 20% discount on most items in shops willing to discount. Many will discount as much as 50 or 60%.

The structure of prices on certain goods and services varies.

The prices on items in department stores are fixed. Prices for tailors, hairdressers, airport taxis, and medical personnel are fixed. Hotel prices are subject to a variety of discounts for different categories of travelers—business, government, weekend, and tourist.

When in doubt if a price is fixed, negotiable, or subject to discounts, always ask for a special discount. After the salesperson indicates the price, ask one of two questions:

"What kind of discount can you give me on this item?"

"What is your best price?"

If the person indicates a discount, you can either accept it or attempt to negotiate the price through a bargaining process.

While skilled shoppers in fixed-price cultures primarily compare prices by reading ads and listening to special announcements, skilled shoppers in bargaining cultures primarily engage in face-to-face encounters with sellers. To be successful, the shopper must use various interpersonal skills. Once you know these and practice bargaining, you should become a very effective shopper in Indonesia—as well as elsewhere in Asia.

ESTABLISH VALUE AND PRICE

Not knowing the price of an item, many shoppers from fixed-price cultures face a problem. *"What is the actual value of the item? How much should I pay? At what point do I know I'm getting a fair price?"* These questions can be answered in several ways. First, you should have some idea of the **value** of the item, because you already did comparative shopping at home by examining catalogs and visiting discount houses, department stores, and specialty shops. If you are interested in an opal ring, for example, you should know what comparable quality jewelry sells for back home.

Second, you have done comparative shopping among the various shops you've encountered in Indonesia in order to **establish a price range** for positioning yourself in the bargaining process. You've visited a department store in Jakarta to research how much a similar item is selling for at a fixed price. You've checked with a shop in your hotel and compared prices there. In your hotel you might ask *"How much is this item?"* and then act a little surprised that it appears so expensive. Tell them that you are a hotel guest and thus you want their *"very best price."* At this point the price usually decreases by 10 to 20% as you are told this is *"our very special price," "our first-customer-of-the-day price,"* or *"our special hotel guest price."*

Once you initially receive a special price from your first price inquiry, expect to get another 10 to 20% through further negotiation. But at this point do not negotiate any more. Take the shop's business card and record on the back the item, the original price, and the first discount price; thank the shopkeeper, and tell him or her that you may return. Repeat this same scenario in a few other shops. After doing three or four comparisons, you will **establish a price range** for particular items. This range will give you a fairly accurate idea of the going discount price. At this point you should be prepared to do some serious haggling, playing one shop off against another.

Effective shoppers in Indonesia quickly learn how to comparative shop and negotiate the best deal. In learning to be effective, you don't need to be timid, aggressive, or obnoxious—extreme behaviors frequently exhibited by first-time practitioners of the Asian art of bargaining. Although you may feel bargaining is a defensive measure to avoid being ripped-off by unscrupulous merchants, it is an acceptable way of doing business in many Asian cultures. Merchants merely adjust their profit margins to the customer, depending on how they feel about the situation as well as their current cash flow needs. It is up to you to adapt to such a pricing culture. Some shopkeepers also adjust their prices depending on the nationality of the customer: highest prices for the Japanese because they are likely to think they are still getting a good deal compared to the high prices back home; relatively high starting prices for Italians because Italians want to bargain hard; and lower starting prices for Americans because they don't like to bargain and thus are likely to walk away after hearing the first price if it seems too high!

One problem you may soon discover is that every situation seems to differ somewhat, and differences between items and shops can be significant. You can expect to receive larger discounts on jewelry than on home furnishings. For example, discounts on jewelry may be as great as 60% whereas discounts on home furnishings may only be 10 or 20%.

Our general rule on what items to bargain for is this: **bargain on ready-made items you can carry out of the shop**. If you must have an item custom-made, be very careful how you arrive at the final price. In most cases you should not bargain other than responding to the first price by asking "Is this your best price?" Better still, drop a few names, agree on a mutually satisfactory price, and then insist that you want top quality for that price.

Except for custom-made items, department stores, and shops displaying a "fixed prices" sign, **never accept the first price offered**. Rather, spend some time going through our bargaining scenario. And in some cases so-called "fixed price" shops will offer a discount if you make an expensive purchase or buy several items—at least ask!

Once you have accepted a price and purchased the item, be sure to **get a receipt** as well as **observe the packing process**. While few merchants will try to cheat you, some tourists have had unpleasant experiences which could have been avoided by following some simple rules of shopping in unfamiliar places.

DEALING IN DIFFERENT AND DIFFICULT SITUATIONS

You will deal with many types of business people in Indonesia, from seasoned Chinese, Javanese, Padang, and Batak merchants to inexperienced and unpredictable shopkeepers, clerks, and peddlers. If you deal with a Chinese merchant, chances are you will be dealing with a relatively seasoned business person; he or she is a family entrepreneur who thrives on status and personal relationships, is knowledgeable about the products, and can quickly make pricing and shipping decisions. Other merchants may appear less rational in their approach to buying and selling.

As soon as you walk through the door of most shops, one expects to encounter a merchant who is eager to sell items then and there. This may or may not be true in most shopping situations you encounter in Indonesia. Customer service is not a particular strength of many shops in Indonesia. You will often have difficulty finding someone to help you. Indeed, you may enter a shop and find that no one is there! And when you do get help, the assistance can be less then informative.

On the other hand, both Padang and Batak merchants tend to be very aggressive in approaching potential customers, and they are very willing to haggle over prices and extend the largest discounts. At times Padang merchants may make you feel uncomfortable as they pester you to buy their goods. Female Batak merchants tend to be the friendliest and most fun to haggle with. But merchants in some areas, especially in Kalimantan and Sulawesi, are disappointing and may make you feel both unwelcome and uncomfortable: provide little assistance, ask high prices, refuse to bargain, and seem to indicate they would rather not be bothered with your business! Many shops will be staffed by young female clerks who know little about the products as well as lack authority to extend discounts. Shopping in these situations can be difficult since few rules seem to apply to the varied individual situations.

GETTING THE BEST DEAL

The best deal you will get is when you have a personal relationship with the merchant. Contrary to what others may tell you about bargains for tourists, you often can get as good a deal—sometimes even better—than someone from the local community. It is simply a myth that tourists can't do as well on prices as the locals. Indeed, we often do better than the locals because we have done our comparative shopping and we know well the art of bargaining—something locals are often lax in doing. In addition, some merchants may give you a better price than the locals because you are "here today and gone tomorrow"; you won't be around to tell their regular customers about your very special price.

More often than not, the Indonesian pricing system operates like this: **If the shopkeeper likes you, or you are a friend of a friend or relative, you can expect to get a good price**. Whenever possible, drop names of individuals who referred you to the shop; the shopkeeper may think you are a friend and thus you are entitled to a special discount. But if you do not have such a relationship and you present yourself as a typical tourist who is here today and gone tomorrow, you need to bargain hard.

PRACTICE THE 12 RULES OF BARGAINING

The art of bargaining in Indonesia can take on several different forms. In general, you want to achieve two goals in this haggling process: **establish the value of an item** and **get the best possible price**. The following bargaining rules work well in many shopping situations in Indonesia where the seller is also the shop owner who has the power to make pricing decisions. They work best with Chinese, Javanese, Padang, and Batak merchants. They are less effective amongst other types of shopkeepers found on Kalimantan and Sulawesi.

1. **Do your research before initiating the process.**

    Compare the prices among various shops, starting with the fixed-price items in department stores.

Spot-check price ranges among shops in and around your hotel. Also, refer to your research done with catalogs and discount houses back home to determine if the discount is sufficient to warrant purchasing the item abroad rather than at home.

2. **Determine the exact item you want.**

    Select the particular item you want and then focus your bargaining around that one item without expressing excessive interest and commitment. Even though you may be excited by the item and want it very badly, once the merchant knows you are committed to buying this one item, you weaken your bargaining position. Express a passing interest; indicate through eye contact with other items in the shop that you are not necessarily committed to the one item. As you ask about the other items, you should get some sense concerning the willingness of the merchant to discount prices.

3. **Set a ceiling price you are willing to pay, and buy now!**

    Before engaging in serious negotiations, set in your mind the maximum amount you are willing to pay, which may be 20% more than you figured the item should sell for based on your research. However, if you find something you love that is really unique, be prepared to pay whatever you must. In many situations you will find unique items not available anywhere else. Consider buying **now** since the item may be gone when you return. Bargain as hard as you can and then pay what you have to—even though it may seem painful—for the privilege of owning a unique item. Remember, it's only money and it only hurts once. You can always make more money, and after returning home you will most likely enjoy your wonderful purchase and forget how painful it seemed at the time to buy it at less than your expected discount. Above all, do not pass up an item you really love just because the bargaining process does not fall in your favor. It is very easy to be "penny wise but pound foolish" in Indonesia simply because the bargaining process is such an ego-involved activity. You may return home forever regretting that you didn't buy a lovely item just because you were too cheap to "give" on the last US$5 of haggling. In the end, put your ego aside, give in, and buy what you really want. Only you and the merchant will know who really won, and once you return home the US$5 will seem to be such an insignificant amount. Chances are you still got a good bargain compared to what you would pay elsewhere if, indeed, you could even find a similar item!

4. **Play an entrepreneurial role**.

Shopping in Indonesia involves playing the roles of buyer and seller. While Indonesians do prize individualism in certain areas of their life, they are also terrific role players, moreso than Westerners. In contrast to many Western societies, where being a unique individual is emphasized, not as high a value is placed on individualism here. Indonesians learn specific sets of behaviors appropriate for the role of father, son, daughter, husband, wife, blood friend, classmate, superior, subordinate, buyer, seller. They easily shift from one role to another, undergoing major personality and behavioral changes without experiencing mental conflicts. When you encounter an Indonesian businessperson, you are often meeting a very refined and sophisticated role player. Therefore, it is to your advantage to play complementary roles by carefully structuring your personality and behavior to play the role of buyer. If you approach sellers by just "being yourself"—open, honest, somewhat naive, and with your own unique personality—you may be quickly walked over by a seasoned seller. Once you enter a shop, think of yourself as an actor walking on stage to play the role of a shrewd buyer, bargainer, and trader. But at the same time, you may encounter a very individualistic shopkeeper who unpredictably decides to give you a special gift or invite you home for dinner just because he or she likes you.

5. **Establish good will and a personal relationship**.

A shrewd buyer also is charming, polite, personable, and friendly. You should have a sense of humor, smile, and be light-hearted during the bargaining process. But be careful about eye contact which can be threatening to Indonesians. Keep it to a mini-mum. Indonesian sellers prefer to establish a personal relationship so that the bargaining process can take place on a friendly, face-saving basis. In the end, both the buyer and seller should come out as winners. This can not be done if you approach the buyer in very serious and harsh terms. You should start by exchanging pleasantries concerning the weather, your trip, the city, or the nice items in the shop. After exchanging business cards or determining your status, the shopkeeper will know what roles should be played in the coming transaction.

6. **Let the seller make the first offer.**

If the merchant starts by asking you *"How much do you want to pay?"*, avoid answering; immediately turn the question around: *"How much are you asking?"* Remember, many merchants try to get you to pay as much as you are willing and able to pay—not what the value of the item is or what he or she is willing to take. You should never reveal your ability or willingness to pay a certain price. Keep the seller guessing, thinking that you may lose interest or not buy the item because it appears too expensive. Always get the merchant to initiate the bargaining process. In so doing, the merchant must take the defensive as you shift to the offensive.

7. **Take your time, being deliberately slow in order to get the merchant to invest his or her time in you.**

The more you indicate that you are impatient and in a hurry, the more you are likely to pay. When negotiating a price, **time** is usually in your favor. Many shopkeepers also see time as a positive force in the bargaining process. Some try to keep you in their shop by serving you tea, coffee, soft drinks, or liquor while negotiating the price. Be careful; this nice little ritual may soften you somewhat on the bargaining process as you begin establishing a more personal relationship with the merchant. The longer you stay in control prolonging the negotiation, the better the price should be. Although some merchants may deserve it, **never** insult them. Merchants need to "keep face" as much as you do in the process of giving and getting the best price.

8. **Use odd numbers in offering the merchant at least 40% less than what he initially offers.**

Avoid stating round numbers such as Rp. 50,000, 100,000, or 200,000. Instead, offer Rp. 47,000, 93,500, or 171,500. Such numbers impress upon others that you may be a seasoned haggler who knows value and expects to do well in this negotiation. Your offer will probably be 15% less than the value you determined for the item. For example, if the merchant asks Rp. 150,000, offer Rp. 90,000, knowing the final price should probably be Rp. 110,000. The merchant will probably counter with only a 10% discount—Rp. 135,000. At this point you will need to go back and forth with another two or three offers and counter-offers.

9. **Appear a little disappointed and take your time.**

Never appear upset or angry with the seller. Keep your cool at all times by slowly sitting down and carefully examining the item. Shake your head a little and say, *"Gee, that's too bad. That's much more than I had planned to spend. I like it, but I really can't go that high."* Appear to be a sympathetic listener as the seller attempts to explain why he or she cannot budge more on the price. Make sure you do not accuse the merchant of being a thief! Use a little charm, if you can, for the way you conduct the bargaining process will affect the final price. This should be a civil negotiation in which you nicely bring the price down, the seller "saves face," and everyone goes away feeling good about the deal.

10. **Counter with a new offer at a 35% discount.**

Punch several keys on your calculator, which indicates that you are doing some serious thinking. Then say something like *"This is really the best I can do. It's a lovely item, but Rp. 90,000 is really all I can pay."* At this point the merchant will probably counter with a 20% discount—Rp. 130,000.

11. **Be patient, persistent, and take your time again by carefully examining the item.**

Respond by saying *"That's a little better, but it's still too much. I want to look around a little more."* Then start to get up and look toward the door. At this point the merchant has invested some time in this exchange, and he or she is getting close to a possible sale. The merchant will either let you walk out the door or try to stop you with another counteroffer. If you walk out the door, you can always return to get the Rp. 130,000 price. But most likely the merchant will try to stop you, especially if there is still some bargaining room. The merchant is likely to say: *"You don't want to waste your time looking elsewhere here. I'll give you the best price anywhere—just for you. Okay, Rp. 120,000. That's my final price."*

12. **Be creative for the final negotiation.**

You could try for Rp. 100,000, but chances are Rp. 120,000 will be the final price with this merchant. Yet, there may still be some room for negotiating "extras." At this point get up and walk around the shop and examine other items; try to appear as if you are losing interest in the item you were bargaining for. While walking around, identify a Rp. 10,000 item you like which might make a nice gift for a friend or relative, which you could possibly include in the final deal. Wander back to the Rp. 10,000 item and look as if your interest is waning and perhaps you need to leave. Then start to probe the possibility of including extras while agreeing on the Rp. 120,000: *"Okay, I might go Rp. 120,000, but only if you include this with it."* The "this" is the Rp. 10,000 item you eyed. You also might negotiate with your credit card. Chances are the merchant is expecting cash on the Rp. 120,000 discounted price and will add a 2 to 5% "commission" if you want to use your credit card. In this case, you might respond to the Rp. 120,000 by saying, *"Okay, I'll go with the Rp. 120,000, but only if I can use my credit card."* You may get your way, your bank will float you a loan in the meantime, and your credit card company may be of assistance in case you later learn there is a problem with your purchase, such as misrepresentation. Finally, you may want to negotiate packing and delivery processes. If it is a fragile item, insist that it be packed well so you can take it with you on the airplane or have it shipped. If your purchase is large, insist that the shop deliver it to your hotel or to your shipper. If the shop is shipping it by air or sea, try to get them to agree to absorb some of the freight and insurance costs.

This slow, civil, methodical, and sometimes charming approach to bargaining works well in many cases, especially when dealing with merchants who are eager to make a sale. However, Indonesia merchants do differ in how they respond to situations, and many of them are unpredictable, depending on whether or not they like you. Some are not very entre-preneurial and thus really are not interested in making a sale! In some cases, your timing may be right: the merchant is in need of cash flow that day and thus he or she is willing to give you the price you want, with little or no bargaining. Others will not give more than a 10 to 20% discount unless you are a friend of a friend who is then eligible for the special "family discount." And others are not good business people, are unpredictable, lack motivation, or are just moody; they refuse to budge on their prices, even though your offer is fair compared to the going prices in other shops. In these situations it is best to leave the shop and find one which is more receptive to the traditional haggling process—unless it is a unique item you cannot live without!

BARGAIN FOR NEEDS, NOT GREED

One word of caution for those who are just starting to learn the fine art of Indonesian bargaining. **Be sure you really want an item before you initiate the bargaining process.** Many tourists learn to bargain effectively, and then get carried away with their new-found skill. Rather than use this skill to get what they want, they enjoy the process of bargaining so much that they buy many unnecessary items. After all, they got such "a good deal" and thus could not resist buying the item. You do not need to fill your suitcases with junk in demonstrating this ego-gratifying skill. If used properly, your new bargaining skills will lead to some excellent buys on items you really want.

EXAMINE YOUR GOODS CAREFULLY

Before you commence the bargaining process, carefully examine the item. Be sure you understand the quality of the item you are negotiating. Then, after you settle on a final price, make sure you are getting the goods you agreed upon. You should carefully observe the handling of items, including the actual packing process. If at all possible, take the items with you when you leave the shop. If you later discover you were victimized by a switch or misrepresentation, contact the local authorities as well as your credit card company if you charged your purchase. You should be able to resolve the problem through these channels. However, the responsibility is on you, the buyer, to know what you are buying.

BEWARE OF SCAMS

Although one hopes this will never happen, you may be unfortunate in encountering unscrupulous merchants who take advantage of you. This is more likely to happen if you wander away from recommended shops in discovering your own "very special" bargains or enter the *"Hey, you mister"* shops. While we have never had these problems happen to us, we do know others who have had such misfortunes. The most frequent scams to watch out for include:

- **Switching the goods.**

  You negotiate for a particular item, such as a piece of jewelry, but in the process of packing it, the merchant substitutes an inferior product.

- **Misrepresenting quality goods.**

  Be especially cautious in jewelry, leather, and antique shops. Sometimes so-called expensive antiques are excellent imitations. Precious stones, such as opals or diamonds, may not be as precious as they appear. Some substitutes are so good that experts even have difficulty identifying the difference. The antique business is relatively unregulated. Some merchants try to sell "new antiques" at "old antique" prices. Many of the fakes even fool the experts.

- **Goods not shipped.**

  The shop may agree to ship your goods home, but once you leave, they conveniently forget to do so. You wait and wait, write letters of inquiry, and receive no replies. Unless you insured the item and have all proper receipts, you may not receive the goods you paid for.

Your best line of defense against these and other possible scams is to be very careful wherever you go and whatever you do in relation to handling money. A few simple precautions will help avoid these problems:

- **Do not trust anyone with your money** unless you have proper assurances they are giving you exactly what you agreed upon. Be especially careful with your credit cards. Keep them within your sight during the transaction process.

- **Do your homework** so you can determine quality and value as well as anticipate certain types of scams.

- **Examine the goods carefully,** assuming something may be or will go wrong.

- **Watch very carefully how the merchant handles items** from the moment they leave your hands until they get wrapped and into a bag.

- **Request receipts** that list specific items and the prices you paid. Although most shops are willing to "give you a receipt" specifying whatever price you want them to write for purposes of deceiving Customs, avoid such pettiness because Customs know better, and you may need a receipt with the real price to claim your goods or a refund. However, some small vendors may not give receipts. In these cases, keep a record of how much you paid. If the shop is to ship, be sure you have a shipping receipt which also includes insurance against both loss and damage.

- **Protect yourself against scams by using credit cards** for payment, especially for big ticket items which could present problems, even though using them may cost you a little more.

If you are victimized, all is not necessarily lost. You should report the problem immediately to the local authorities, your credit card company, or insurance company. While inconvenient and time consuming, nonetheless, in many cases you will eventually get satisfactory results.

6

What to Buy

W hat types of quality products will I most likely to find in
Indonesia? Is it worth making a special trip there just
for shopping? Let's answer these questions by first
looking at Indonesia's major shopping strengths.

Indonesia is not a noted shopper's paradise simply because
it has yet to be discovered. Since few tourists visit this country,
you will encounter numerous shopping opportunities for items
that are not yet in great demand by large numbers of visitors.
However, many of Indonesia's products are in great demand by
collectors and dealers who buy for specialty shops in Europe
and North America. Like many dealers, you will be able to
purchase quality arts, antiques, textiles, and home decorative
items for a fraction of what they might cost outside Indonesia.

A UNIQUELY TALENTED AND
ARTISTICALLY PRODUCTIVE PEOPLE

Indonesia will not disappoint you if you know the "what's,"
"where's," and "how's" of shopping this country properly.
Indonesians are a particularly artistic, sensitive, gracious,

friendly, and graceful people. Moreso than other Asian countries, Indonesians express their art in daily living. They produce art for tourists, as utilitarian and aesthetic items, and as a part of religious rituals. Much of the beautiful ritual art, for example, is only produced for a few days and then destroyed as part of ceremonies. Especially in Bali, you'll discover whole villages producing woodcarvings, sculptures, and paintings.

Indonesia is a virtual living museum of artists and craftsmen producing some of the most unique arts and crafts you will encounter anywhere. If you like art, you will be fascinated with Indonesia. In Indonesia, life tends to imitate art. Indeed, it's expressed in several mediums from clever Javanese wayang puppet figures, and the power of the dalang who manipulates the puppet show, to the ritual art of Hindu and animistic Bali.

Indonesia's cultural and ethnic diversity is well expressed in its wealth of arts and crafts. Uniquely Indonesian, few of these arts and crafts are found outside the Indonesian islands. Some shops in Singapore carry Indonesia products, but the selections are limited and the prices are high. You'll also find shops in Europe and North America specializing in Indonesian products, but these are few and far between and quality items are very expensive. For the most part, you must go to Indonesia if you want to shop for quality, variety, and prices.

Indonesians are skilled carvers, weavers, painters, sculptors, musicians, dancers, and jewelers. They produce a tremendous range and variety of items, from primitive tribal masks to colorful contemporary art and exquisite textile designs.

Indonesia's major shopping strengths lie in the areas of the arts and crafts, many of which make lovely home decorative items. Your shopping choices will include:

- batik (cloth, ready-made clothes, paintings, etc.)
- wood and stonecarvings
- textiles
- oil paintings, watercolors, posters, and graphics
- lacquer boxes and chests
- arts
- wall hangings
- musical instruments
- silver decorative items, especially delicate filigree pieces
- brassware (lanterns, posts)
- gold and silver jewelry
- semi-precious stones and diamonds
- masks and costumes
- fashion clothes

- leather goods
- antiques (Dutch, Chinese, Javanese, Balinese)
- puppets (wood and leather)
- tribal artifacts (war shields, spears, masks, ancestral figures, drums, containers, decorative items)
- carved panels and house gables
- rattan items
- baskets
- pottery
- ceramics
- daggers (kris)
- furniture
- handicrafts
- cassette tapes

Shopping for such treasures in Indonesia is a very special experience, highly personal, educational, and entertaining. You'll descend into an ancient and mystical world of living art, where sights, sounds, and smells indicate you are definitely in a different time and place. You may never be the same after this shopping adventure!

While most Indonesian products are unique, reflecting the cultures of its many peoples, many of the products have international appeal and make ideal home decorative items and furnishings. In contrast to many other Asian countries, for example, Indonesia has a large, creative, and internationally famous art community producing excellent quality contemporary oils, watercolors, and batik paintings.

Indonesia's major shopping weaknesses are similar to its major tourism weaknesses—marketing and convenience. Indonesia produces wonderful arts and crafts, but they are not well marketed either inside or outside the country. While this situation has markedly improved during the past 10 years, you still must take the initiative to find what you want. This means traveling from one shop to another, digging through everything as well as visiting the various islands to discover different shopping paradises within Indonesia. Given the limited tourist facilities generally existing outside Jakarta and Bali, you will have to work at getting where you want to go. At times this means scheduling delays, bumpy and muddy roads, heat and humidity, and worn hotels and restaurants. Because of Indonesia's far flung archipelago, there is a well developed domestic air

❏ Indonesia is a virtual living museum of artists and craftsmen. It's major shopping strengths are in the areas of arts and crafts.

❏ In Indonesia, life tends to imitate art, and the *wayang* (puppets) is the purist form of life imitating art.

❏ Shopping in Indonesia is a highly personal, educational, and entertaining experience.

❏ The major batik producing centers are in and around the Javanese cities of Jogjakarta, Solo, Cirebon, and Pekalongan.

❏ If you want to buy good quality batik clothes, you need to patronize the top designer shops in Jakarta and Jogjakarta.

transportation system. Except for the most remote areas, one can get nearly everywhere by plane. But what an exciting shopping adventure awaits you!

BATIK

Indonesia is world famous for its batik. Originating in Indonesia around the 12th century, batik is produced in several large factories as well as in homes as a cottage industry. It is mainly produced on the islands of Java, Bali, Madura, as well as in Jambi on Sumatra.

True batik is a reverse dye process involving the application of various motifs and colors to cotton materials. It comes in three qualities involving different printing techniques: hand, stamped, and printed. **Handmade batik**, also known as "tulis," is produced by using a waxing instrument called a "canting." This is a small pen-like bamboo instrument with a reservoir for holding molten wax. Motifs are hand-drawn on material and then certain sections of the motif are covered with hot wax. The material is then dipped in one color. Next, wax is removed from another section of the motif, additional wax is applied to the newly dyed area, and the material is dyed in another color. The process of waxing and dying is repeated until all the desired colors in the motif appear. This is a very time consuming, labor-intensive process in which the colorization of material is a true art form.

Today, much of the batik in Indonesia is **stamped batik** produced with metal stamps called "cap." The motifs represented in the stamps are repeated throughout the material. Some batik also combines the use of the canting and cap.

Printed batik is the cheapest form of batik. In this case, batik motifs are printed on one side of cotton material. Being basically imitation batik, no waxing process is involved in making this material.

Batik is made into all kinds of apparel and decorative items. Shirts, dresses, blouses, skirts, scarves, hats, bags, napkins, placemats, coasters, slippers, purses, and pillow covers are most widely found in the shops of Jakarta, Jogjakarta, Bali, and Solo. Batik paintings and wall hangings are also widely available in a variety of traditional and contemporary designs, from abstract and surrealistic scenes to landscapes and portraits.

You will probably purchase some batik while in Indonesia. The cotton shirts, dresses, and blouses are wonderful to wear in Indonesia's hot and humid climate. Many of the batik items also make nice trip gifts and home decorative items.

But for many shoppers, Indonesian batik has its limitations given current styles, colors, quality, and sizes of finished garments. In fact, you may be more interested in observing the batik process and the infinite variety of batik motifs and colors as an art form than making it one of your major shopping goals. In the case of batik clothes, most of the designs are traditional regional designs, the colors are often muted, and the patterns are usually very busy. You will find some beautiful designer-batik in Bali, Jogjakarta, and Jakarta, but much of the batik is best left in Indonesia. Similar to the silk materials and clothes found in Thailand, most Indonesian batik has not been designed well for the Western market. With very few exceptions, Indonesia lacks designers who are sensitive to designs and colors appropriate for Western tastes. In addition, the Indonesian batik industry has fallen on hard times. Many batik clothes have been overproduced in the same patterns with poor quality materials. While batik shirts are inexpensive, some wrinkle terribly, fade quickly, and tend to fall apart.

If you want to buy good quality batik clothes, you need to patronize some of the top designer shops. Prices at these places can be expensive, but you do buy quality, and colors and designs may be more appealing to you than the mass produced "local" variety.

You will find many ready-made batik clothes in the department stores, especially the **Sarinah** chain, and in many factories and small shops on Java and Bali. However, if you are a male taller than 6 feet and weight more than 175 pounds, you may have difficulty finding ready-made clothes in your size. The largest variety of colors and patterns in batik shirts, for example, seem to be in small and medium. The selections in the large and extra-large sizes are very limited, perhaps because other tourists have already purchased them! It's virtually impossible to find large and extra large sizes in the shops of Solo (Surakarta), one of Indonesia's major batik production centers.

Much of the batik is sold in meter lengths. You may wish to purchase material and have it made into shirts, blouses, or dresses. If you have your tailoring done in Indonesia, be sure you have pictures or a model of what you want made. Indonesians are good at copying from pictures and models. You also may want to buy good quality batik for making pillow covers and wall hangings. **Sarinah** and **Keris Gallery** both carry various upholstery weight fabrics. Many of the batik motifs make very attractive accent pieces in family rooms.

Shopping for batik primarily centers on particular cities on Java. Most batik found in Jakarta comes from cities in central and northern Java. The major batik producing centers are in and around the cities of Jogjakarta, Solo, Cirebon, and Pekalongan. Each of these centers produces its own unique motifs and uses different colors. For example, batik from Solo has a creamy background whereas batik from Jogjakarta is designed with bright and clear white backgrounds. Batiks from Cirebon use a cloud and rock motif which are Chinese in origin. The batik from Jambi in southern Sumatra typically uses Arabic calligraphy and Middle Eastern geometric designs. Batik from the island of Madura is much bolder and striking in color.

Given the regional varieties of batik, the heritage underlying the production of batiks, and the fascinating and varied production techniques, you could easily spend all your time in Indonesia shopping for batik. A "batik shopping trip" would require visiting the various batik production centers on the islands of Java, Bali, Sumatra, and Madura. In each location you would go directly to the factories to view the production of batik and then make your purchases at the factory shops. You might even take a mini-course in how to do your own handmade batik clothes and paintings through one of the factories or studios. Most of these factories sell batik by the meter as well as offer a range of ready-made batik clothes and numerous decorative items. Since small shops in these cities are buying their batik directly from the factories, it is best to confine your shopping to these factories. While many places appear to have fixed prices, except for department stores, you should bargain everywhere for batik with the expectation of receiving a 10 to 50% discount on your purchases.

For excellent quality batik and for designs appropriate to Western fashion tastes, you should visit the shops of Indonesia's top international batik designers. One of Indonesia's most well noted is **Iwan Tirta**. His shops, which come under the name **P.T. Ramacraft**, are found at the Borobudur Inter-Continental Hotel shopping arcade and on Jl. Panarukan 25 (Tel. 333122) in Jakarta. We highly recommend visiting his main shop on Jl. Panarukan 25, which is located along a quiet residential street within 15-minute walking distance of the Grand Hyatt and Mandarin Oriental hotels. A "must see" stop in Jogjakarta is the famous **Sapto Hudoyo Art Batik Gallery** on Jl. Solo, near the airport (also has a small branch shop in the airport departure lounge) as well as **PT. Ardiyanto Wijayakusuma Batik** which is located at Jl. Magelang Km 5.8 (Tel. 62777). The lovely **Sapto Hudoyo Art Batik Gallery** may well become your favorite shop in all of Indonesia. A decorator's delight, this expansive shop offers a unique mix of fine batik and ikat materials and ready-made clothes along with a fine collection of jewelry, furniture, kris, masks, wayang puppets, modern and primitive art, and antiques along with excellent service. It's a virtual museum that also functions as a well appointed shop.

Numerous batik art galleries are also found in Jogjakarta, especially Jogjakarta's founding batik artist **Kuswadji K.** (located next to the Sultan's palace), **Amri Gallery**, the world famous **Affandi** (Affandi Gallery, near the Ambarrukmo Palace Hotel, next to the river off of Jl. Solo—excellent oils with some batiks), **Ardiyanto Gallery** (Jl. Magelang), **Astuti** (near Water Castle on Jl. Nagasem), and **Trimurti** (Jl. Panjutan 24). For a wide range of relatively inexpensive batik paintings (inexpensive if you bargain real hard and don't go with a guide or driver who will receive a commission), visit **Seno Batik Painting** and the many adjacent shops along Jl. Tirtodipuran. While some of these shops may seem expensive, they offer good buys considering the artistic quality and labor content of their works. You won't be disappointed with your purchases.

The quality and designs of these recommended batik shops and galleries are far superior to most other batik you will find anywhere in the world. Indulge yourself by buying some beautiful clothes, purchasing some designer batik for upholstery or home decorative items, and acquiring a beautiful traditional or modern batik painting.

If you just want to buy some inexpensive ready-made batik clothes or material, we recommend the **Sarinah** department store chain. Each branch has a handicraft section which includes one of the largest selections of batik clothes and material found anywhere in Indonesia. The quality is good to excellent and the prices are fixed. Other large shops specializing in batik clothes include **Batik Keris**, **Batik Semar**, and **Batik Danar Hadi**. These shops have factories based in Solo and branch shops in Solo, Jogjakarta, and Jakarta. However, you may have difficulty finding large and extra large sizes in these stores.

TEXTILES

While batik is Indonesia's most famous textile, other less known textiles are excellent shopping finds. In fact, Indonesia offers one of the world's most fantastic collections of traditional textiles. Many visitors immediately fall in love with the unique textile patterns, designs, and colors representing the various ethnic groups throughout the Indonesian archipelago. As with batik, you could easily spend two months shopping only for textiles on each of the major Indonesian islands, and without even looking at the more popular batik.

Textiles in Indonesia are unique. They include everything from "primitive" textiles found in Kalimantan, Sulawesi, and Irian Jaya, which use barkcloths made from fermented inner barks of trees, to weaving techniques which do not use the loom. Many textiles are extremely artistic, include primitive and geometric designs, employ unique weft and warp design techniques, and use a variety of natural dyes and colors.

Indonesians produce two major types of textiles of interest to international collectors. **Ikat textiles** are produced by weaving dyed threads into various patterns. Unique designs are created by tieing off the weft or warp threads to retain designs while the remainder of the material is dyed. The ikat comes in many different forms, motifs, and colors, all of which are extremely labor intensive to produce. Many of the smaller islands in Eastern Indonesia, such as Sumba, Flores, Timor, Tanimbar, Roti, Sawu, and Riau, are famous for producing different types of lovely ikat textiles.

The **songket textiles** are primarily produced in central and southern Sumatra. These textiles are distinguished by the use of gold threads and tinsel (silver in the case of the Minangkabau in west Sumatra) which appear to float on the top of the silk or cotton material.

Most of these traditional decorative textiles are made as clothing items, such as sarongs, head bands, and scarves or have religious and mystical significance. Historically, they have functioned as major items for trade. For most visitors, Indonesian textiles are unique works of art rather than materials to be made into clothes. Both antique and new textiles make beautiful wall hangings and upholstery material. If framed properly, they are truly works of art worthy of display in many Western homes. Many, especially the songket textiles from western Sumatra, may be too traditional to fit into your home decor.

But be prepared to pay a great deal for these textiles. Once you observe their production, you will quickly understand why many seem expensive. These are not simple weaves. They take months to produce. Once you learn the price reflects the labor content, most are a real bargain. Many are good investments since their value will continue to increase in the years ahead as fewer and fewer people practice the traditional textile crafts. Our recommendation: if you like these textiles, buy now before the good quality textiles disappear or become too expensive.

Most visitors to Indonesia know little about Indonesian textiles. In fact, many discover this unique and exciting shopping adventure during their visit to Indonesia and are disappointed they did not focus more time on examining the textile culture throughout the islands. Some would even prefer a trip just focusing on shopping for these textiles. Such a trip could take them to many of the smaller and less known islands, such as Sumba and Timor. Specialty tour groups such as Select Tours International (901 N. Pacific Coast Hwy., Suite 212B, Redondo Beach, CA 90278, Tel. 213/379-8999 or 800/356-6680) occasionally sponsor tours to Indonesia's major textile centers: Jakarta, Jogjakarta, Solo, Sulawesi, Flores, Timor, Sumba, and Bali.

To better prepare yourself for Indonesian textiles, you should read Mattiebelle Gittenger's *Splendid Symbols: Textiles and Tradition in Indonesia*. Published in 1979 by the Textile Museum in Washington, DC, this book has been largely responsible for the recent resurgence in interest for Indonesian textiles. No longer available through the Textile Museum for purchase, you may be able to examine a copy at a major library or purchase it in Singapore where it has been reprinted. An abbreviated version of this book is presented by the author in her article in the special *Arts of Asia* edition on "Primitive Arts in Indonesia" (Sept.-Oct. 1980, pp. 108-123). You can write for information or purchase this wonderful back issue: Arts of Asia Publications, 1309 Kowloon Centre, 29-39 Ashley Road, Kowloon, Hong Kong, Tel. 23762228.

You should also be aware of fake textiles. In many places individuals claim they only sell "antique" textiles—*"it's very old!"* "Antique" can mean anything from two weeks to two centuries old. While most such claims must be taken lightly as efforts to please you, beware of being charged "antique prices" for relatively new pieces. The best thing to do is to know your textiles, buy what you like without regard to age, and stay close to reputable individuals who know local textiles. Unless you are truly interested in older pieces, tell merchants and hawkers you are really not interested in antique textiles—just the newer ones.

In Jakarta the best and most reputable source for antique textiles is **Djody** at 22 Jl. Kebon Sirih Timur Dalam (Tel. 327730 or 335388). Be sure to visit the second floor of this expansive antique shop where Mrs. Djody displays her huge textile collection from numerous islands throughout the Indonesia archipelago. Another reliable source for quality textiles in Jakarta is **Caecil Papadimitriou**. She and her husband, Alex, operate one of Indonesia's finest antique shops from their home on Jl. Pasuruan 3, Jakarta Pusat (Tel. 3158748 or 3147928), just around the corner from the popular Jl. Surabaya antique row. Located unobtrusively in a residential neighborhood, Caecil and Alex know textiles and antiques. Indeed, their home should be one of your very first stops in Jakarta. Just walk through their front gate and wander around the rooms. Caecil takes care of the textile section. She has numerous antique textiles on display as well as a library of books on Indonesian textiles. A few minutes with Caecil or Alex will get you oriented to what lies ahead for you in shopping for Indonesian textiles. Prices at their shop are not cheap, but the Papadimitrious are extremely reputable and only carry good quality textiles, art, antiques, and furniture. Several antique and curio shops along Jl. Kebon Sirih Timur Dalam, such as **Shinta Art**, **Amadeus**, and **Guci Art and Curio**, carry a limited range of old and new textiles. **Hadiprana Galleries** (Jl. Palatehan 38) also has a nice selection of batik and ikat textiles, but be sure to go all the way to the third floor to find them!

If you are interested in working with textiles for either clothing or home decorative purposes, we highly recommend contacting Josephine Komara at **Bin House** (Jl. Teluk Betung 10, Tel. 335941). A talented designer, she provides custom services to many VIPs and others who have very special needs and tastes in clothing, upholstery, and window treatments as well as a whole range of other home decorative needs from furniture to antiques. She is the only designer we know of who really knows how to work with Indonesian textiles in a manner appropriate for Westerners. **Iwan Tirta** (Jl. Panarukan 25 (Tel. 333122) also has his own designer-line of textiles which are appropriate as upholstry and drapery materials.

In Bali you will find several shops in Kuta Beach and Denpasar selling textiles. Our favorite shop is **Arts of Asia** (Denpasar, Jl. Thamrin 27-37 Blok C5, Tel. 23350). The shop's reputable owner, Verra Darwiko, travels to numerous islands to collect excellent quality ikat textiles as well as numerous arts, crafts, and antiques. **Jani's Place** in the charming town of Ubud has a very large collection of quality textiles. Nicely designed clothes using ikat materials are found at **"Nogo" Bali Ikat Center** on Legian Road in Kuta Beach (Tel. 54335). One of the two **Ikat Art** shops on Jl. Bukungsari in Kuta Beach (across the street from each other) has a large selection of textiles. Several shops along the three kilometer stretch of Legian Road in Kuta Beach—especially the ethnographic shops such as **Bahao Primitive Art Shop, Manik Art Shop, Leo Shop, Thamrin Art, Afitra Shop, Kombu Art Shop, Indonesia Art Shop**, and **Dee Dee**—also offer selections of old and new ikat textiles as well as garments fashioned from these textiles.

FASHION CLOTHES

While Indonesia is not a noted fashion center, it does have numerous designers who create very fashionable garments from both batik and ikat fabrics. Fabric designs and styles range from traditional to modern. One of Indonesia's premier designers is **Iwan Tirta** who has two shops in Jakarta (see section on batik). While he mainly works in batik, creating many innovative designs, he also has an ikat line of fabrics and clothes.

Bali is fast becoming the fashion center for Indonesia. It's major strengths are fashionable ikat garments and inexpensive sportswear rather than batik. Numerous designers, both Indonesian and foreigners, have factories and shops here. You will find their shops in the major hotels as well as in Kuta Beach, Sanur Beach, and Ubud. The largest concentration of shops is found along Legian Road in Kuta Beach. We especially like the designs and styles produced at **"Nogo" Bali Ikat Center** (they have one shop along Legian Road in Kuta Beach and a garment factory and shop in Sanur Beach). Shops such as **Tropical Climax**, **Ikar**, **Andree Collection**, **Tao Galleries**, and **Biak Biak** along Legian Road offer numerous fashionable garments and sportswear. However, many of the designs respond to the type of clientele that frequent the Kuta Beach area—the young and budget crowd. Some of the best quality shops will be found in the shopping arcades of the major hotels, especially the Bali Hyatt Hotel (**Taman Boutique**, **Sari Bali Boutique**, and **Lila Shop**). Along the main street in Ubud you will find numerous clothing shops selling inexpensive garments. One of the best shops in Ubud is **Kunang Kunang**, located at the end of the main street next to Murni's Restaurant (serves the best chocolate milk shakes in Indonesia!), **Janie's Place**, and the **Lotus Boutique**.

In Jogjakarta, the main emphasis is on batik fashions rather than ikat garments. Be sure to visit **Sapto Hudoyo Art Batik Gallery** on Jl. Solo, near the airport. The shop produces some of the most fashionable batik garments in Indonesia. The owner's wife also operates the boutique in the departure lounge of the airport. Be sure to arrive at least 45 minutes early so you can browse through this excellent shop as well as see the fashion show which is performed prior to many departing flights—one of the nicest touches to any airport departure lounge in Asia! Other shops, such as **Amri Gallery** and **Ardiyanto Gallery**, also produce distinctive and fashionable batik garments. Several shops in the shopping arcade of the Ambarrukmo Hotel also offer numerous fashionable clothes.

PRIMITIVE DECORATIVE ARTS

Indonesia's various ethnic groups outside the islands of Java and Bali continue to produce some of the world's most fabulous primitive or ethnographic arts and crafts. Many of the masks, war shields, spears, staffs, storage containers, baby carriers, posts, house gables, window shutters, ancestral figures, and carvings made from wood, bone, and stone and decorated with beads and feathers make wonderful wall and end table pieces for Western homes.

The primitive or ethnographic art world of Indonesia is based to a large extent on the ancient Dong-Son culture dating from 350 B.C. and originating in south China and Vietnam. It contrasts sharply with the more refined and sophisticated art forms found on the islands of Java and Bali and developed in relation to the "high" culture of the historic Hindu Javanese and Balinese courts. In Java and Bali the original indigenous culture of animism and spiritualism was adapted to the court-induced Hindu culture. But in the Indonesian primitive art world—both visual and performing—you confront a whole new dimension of Indonesian society and culture, a world of rituals, mysticism, animism, spiritualism, ancestral worship, superstition, and once fierce warriors and cannibals. The life-death cycle of the prolific Asmat woodcarvers in Irian Jaya, for example, centers around the belief that individuals originate from woodcarvings and return to these figures at death. Such a belief provides a major impetus for the continuing production of unique Asmat ancestral figures.

In the primitive Indonesian art world you enter the world of priests and commoners who continue to produce art forms which are also utilitarian items for daily living. The cultures and lifestyles of these peoples range from primitive Stone Age and aboriginal tribes in Irian Jaya to relatively sophisticated and modern people in the cases of the Toraja in central Sulawesi and the Toba Batak in northern Sumatra. All, however, remain under the influence of the ancient Dong-Son culture which sharply contrasts from the Hindu culture of Java and Bali. Put in the simplest form, go to Java and Bali for Hindu culture and arts, but go to the other islands for Dong-Son culture and arts. However, keep in mind that today Java is primarily animistic and Muslim while Bali retains its animistic and Hindu traditions. The remaining Hindu traditions in Java are most evident in several monuments, such as the famous Prambanam complex near Jogjakarta, and in the many Javanese visual and performing arts.

The major groups producing the most interesting primitive arts are found on the islands of Sumatra, Nias, Kalimantan, Sulawesi, Timor, Leti, and Irian Jaya. The groups and their corresponding primitive arts are outlined on page 134. Other primitive arts are found on the islands of Alor in the Lesser Sundas (Moko bronze drums) and Leti in the Lesser Moluccas (wood effigy figures).

Many of these primitive motifs also are expressed in the textiles of these tribal people. Motifs showing ancestral figures, animals, and boats frequently appear in the ikat textiles of the Batak and Dayak.

Shopping for primitive arts in Indonesia can be one of the most exciting shopping adventures anywhere. It requires doing basic background reading on the various primitive art forms in Indonesia (*Arts of Asia*, Sept.-Oct., 1980 issue), and visits to the **National Museum** and **Beautiful Indonesia in Miniature** in Jakarta. The museum has a good representative collection of arts and crafts from all of the major ethnic groups. Beautiful Indonesia in Miniature has excellent displays of the architecture, arts, and crafts of each major ethnic group in Indonesia's 27 provinces. The display of Asmat art from Irian Jaya is breath-taking; it alone is well worth a visit to this interesting outdoor park, a unique museum of similar quality to Thailand's Ancient City.

Several shops in Jakarta offer primitive arts from the various islands. The stalls in the antique bazaar along **Jl. Surabaya** always yield a few new and old primitive art pieces but primarily from the Batak area in Sumatra. Like most such shops, you will have to walk into the cluttered stalls and dig around for a few minutes before you "discover" the primitive pieces. A few of the antique and curio stops along **Jl. Kebon Sirih Timur Dalam** specialize in primitive art pieces while others stock a few pieces among their Javanese and Balinese arts and antiques. Some of our favorites here include **Shinta Art**, **Djody**, **Budaya**, and **Amadeus**. Also, look for several ethnographic and antique shops along Jl. Kemang Bangka which are found near the famous Duta Art Gallery. One of our favorite shops for small and unique ethnographic pieces, especially jewelry and beads, is **Tribal** (Tel. 380-5555, ext. 76023) in the Borobudur Hotel (Jl. Lapangan Banteng Selatan). This shop is part of the art, antique, and jewelry conglomerate which currently goes under the name "The Kesenian Group." Its main shop, **Gallery 50-B**, is located at Jl. Ciputat Raya 50-B (Tel. 749-2850), which is also known as Old Bogor Road, and includes a large collection of ethnographic pieces.

Islands	Ethnic Groups	Primitive Arts	Motifs	Mediums
Sumatra	Batik (Karo and Toba)	House gables, containers, bowls, chests, masks, calendars, staffs, figures, magic horns	Lion, human figures	Wood and stone
Nias Island (Sumatra)	Nias	Figures, containers, war shields, masks	Human figures animals	Wood and stone
Kalimantan	Dayak	Masks, baby carriers, war shields, containers, figures, bead work, baskets	Human figures demons, boats	Wood, beads
Sulawesi	Toraja	House gables, panels, figures, posts	Buffalo heads, houses, graneries	Wood
Irian Jaya	Asmat	War shields, spears, blow guns, containers, canoe paddles, panels, baskets	Geometric design human figures	Wood
Irian Jaya	Dani	Axes, necklaces, penis gourds, containers	Geometric design	Wood

While the majority of primitive arts found in the shops of Jakarta are from the Batak area in northern Sumatra, you will occasionally find some Nias, Dayak, and Asmat pieces. A few shops at the **Ancol Art Market** in the Jaya Ancol Dreamland complex (Taman Impian Jaya Ancol) also carry primitive pieces. A few shops along Old Bogor Road (Jl. Ciputat Raya in the Pondok Labu area), such as **Gallery 50-B, Anang's Art Shop**, and **Indonesia Putra Art and Curio**, also have some nice ethnographic pieces.

Within the past five years numerous ethnographic shops have opened in Bali. They primarily offer ethnographic pieces from eastern Indonesia as well as from Kalimantan and Sulawesi. Our favorite shop, which also is reputed to be Bali's best antique and textile dealer, is **Arts of Asia** in Denpasar (Jl. Thamrin 27-37 Block C.S. (Tel. 23350). The selections, quality, and prices here are excellent. A well established and reputable shop, the owners are long time collectors. Another outstanding and reputable antique dealer is **Polos** which has a gallery along Jl. Legian in Kuta (Tel. 51316). It also has large warehouse/ gallery in Celuk where dealers tend to go. **"Nogo" Bali Ikat Centre** along Jl. Legian (Tel. 54335) has one of the best collections of Asmat art in Indonesia. The owner, Iwan Sumichan, imports artifacts directly from the famous artist village of Agats along the southeastern coast of Irian Jaya. This is one of our favorite shops for primitive carved shields and poles.

Most of the newer ethnographic shops in Bali are concentrated along Legian Street in Kuta Beach. Look for such shops as **Timor Arts, Rofelan Art Shop, Yanwar Antique Shop, Wijaya Antiques, Kalimantan Art Shop, H.S. Jamsuddin, AM Art Shop, Mahakam, Asmat, Thamrin Art, Kiki Antiques, Deang Antiques, Ryo Antiques**, and **Dewiyus Antiques** along Legian Road. **Anang's Place** has a very nice collection of ethnographic pieces, but be forewarned that everything in this shop is overpriced compared to similar quality products found elsewhere in Indonesia.

Two shops in particular are worth visiting in Jogjakarta: **Yamin** and **Sapto Hudoyo Art Batik Gallery**. **Yamin** (Jl. Kerto No. 9, Muja-Muju, Tel. 55165—by appointment) has one of the best selections of arts, antiques, and furniture in central Java. Since the two shop/houses may be difficult to find, you may want to contact Mrs. Yamin first at her leather shop (**Mahakam**) in the Ambarrukmo Palace Hotel to make an appointment (Tel. 88488, ext. 737). A few small shops across the street from the Ambarrukmo Palace Hotel also have some antiques and ethnographic pieces. **Sapto Hudoyo Art Batik Gallery** primarily sells batik, but the shop also has one of the best collections of ethnographic pieces we have seen anywhere in Indonesia.

Outside Jakarta, Bali, and Jogjakarta you will find many shops with primitive arts. However, there is little logic to where you should best go. Antique shops everywhere seem to yield a few pieces of primitive art. Little antique shops in Surabaya, for example, will have some wonderful primitive arts amongst their brass lamps, Chinese ceramics, furniture, and wayang puppets. Even some airport gift shops offer nice primitive art pieces. You must go from one shop to another. Since most shops poorly display items, in each shop spend some time looking under tables and chairs, surveying the walls and ceiling, and poking through cluttered piles of arts and antiques. These shops are visually disorienting, but they may yield a few gems in the midst of all the junky mess.

If you are interested in Batak and Nias art, the best places to buy these items outside Jakarta are in the city of **Medan**, at the town of **Parapat**, and in a few villages on **Samosir Island** at Lake Toba. Several antique shops in downtown Medan, along Jl Jend A Yani, stock both Batak and Nias pieces (try **Rufino** for some of the best selections and quality). At Lake Toba several shops in Parapat (on the streets adjacent to the Hotel Parapat) have limited collections of Batak arts and crafts, especially house gables, staffs, and boxes. The quality here has slipped during the past four years as fewer and fewer "original" antiques remain in this area. Most of what you find are likely to be "antiques" that were made last week. However, what old pieces you do find here are extremely reasonable compared to similar ones found in Jakarta and Singapore. On Samosir Island you will find numerous open-air stalls selling all types of Batak arts and crafts. Operating primarily for tourists, these stalls mainly sell "new" antiques which have either been buried in the ground for a few days to look old or have received a recent application of black or brown Kiwi shoe polish to look antique. Shops in other towns on Sumatra, especially in Padang and Bukittinggi, also offer a few primitive art pieces—although not enough to justify making a trip to these cities just for shopping. In all cases you should visit the local antique shops to find these arts and crafts. But do not pay "antique" prices unless you know primitive art well or are willing to risk overpaying.

A similar shopping pattern is found on the other islands, but the variety of ethnographic arts and crafts are nowhere as plentiful as those found in Sumatra from the Batak. On Kalimantan, for example, Dayak arts and crafts can be found in East Kalimantan in the towns of Balikpapan and Samarinda.

The selections are limited and the prices are often higher than in Jakarta. We recommend Kalimantan for shopping purposes, but with some reservations. You will likely be disappointed with what you find as well as the outrageous prices you must pay.

A trip to Sulawesi is necessary if you wish to acquire arts and crafts from Toraja Land (Tana Toraja). Few shops outside Sulawesi carry Toraja arts and crafts. And even there, antique items are scarce. Of particular interest are the doors, windows, and panels with carved buffalo heads taken from old homes and granaries as well as the large effigy figures. These items are even hard to find in the main cities of Ujung Padang and Manado. You must travel into Toraja Land in the central highlands of Sulawesi to find these items, and even there you will have to search hard. There you can poke around in a few shops along the main street in Rantepao, the major town in Toraja Land. In addition to finding some wonderful textiles, a few shops carry carved doors, windows, and panels with the ubiquitous buffalo motif. Near many of the burial caves and sites, you will find a few stalls selling carved panels and a variety of knickknacks made especially for tourists. If you are lucky, you may also find someone locally who will sell antique carved doors, windows, and panels from their home.

The major art center in Irian Jaya is the town of Agats along the southern coast. Extensively promoted by the Indonesian government, the Asmat in this area are producing a large variety of arts and crafts—primarily wood carved ancestral figures—for the warehouses and shops in Jayapura, Bali, and Jakarta. But it is difficult and expensive to visit this area. You must get permission from local authorities to visit this "protected" area, and permission will most likely be denied because of the lack of facilities for visitors. If you do get permission, you must first fly into the island of Biak off the northwestern coast of Irian Jaya and then proceed to the capital city, Jayapura, on the northern coast near the border with Papua New Guinea. From there you must wait until you can get a connecting flight to the southern coast.

The best places to shop for arts and crafts from Irian Jaya is in Jayapura and Biak. Both of these towns have central markets where several shops sell a large variety of newly made war shields, carvings, bags, and penis gourds. The central market in Jayapura has the largest number of shops selling Asmat artifacts —mostly handicraft items—and the prices here are excellent compared to what you must pay for the same items in Sulawesi, Bali, and Jakarta.

If Irian Jaya is not on your travel itinerary, you may want to shop for Asmat arts and crafts in Jakarta as well as in the antique shops of Jogjakarta, Surabaya, and Bali. If you are in Ujung Padang on Sulawesi, make sure you visit the airport gift shops. You will discover a nice selection of Asmat war shields and drums in this rather unexpected location.

Trips into the other islands for primitive arts and crafts will be more difficult. Before departing on such adventures, check the antique shops in Jakarta and Kuta Beach in Bali for arts and crafts from the outer islands. Shops in these cities offer the best quality antiques, arts, and crafts from these islands. You may be more successful in these shops than making a trip to Kalimantan, Timor, Sumba, Leti, or Nias.

When shopping for primitive art, be careful with claims that items are "antiques" or "old." Most primitive art pieces available in these shops are relatively new—one week to 15 years old. Nonetheless, many shopkeepers claim these items are 50 to 300 years old. In most cases they are not, and the shopkeepers simply don't know the age of the items. They say "old" because they feel that is what you want to hear!

FINE ART

Indonesia has a well developed and famous art community that produces a large quantity of fine oil and batik paintings as well as watercolors, prints, and posters. The family of Indonesia's most famous painter, **Affandi**, maintains a studio and gallery in Jogjakarta. Other famous Indonesian and expatriate painters have studios and galleries in Jakarta and Jogjakarta as well as in Bali.

Indonesia abounds with fine art galleries that offer everything from traditional and modern batik and oil paintings to sculpture. Especially in Jogjakarta and Bali, you will shop for art in the studios and shops of the artists. In many cases you will have an opportunity to meet the artists from whom you will make your purchase.

When you purchase Indonesian paintings, you may want to purchase them without frames for ease of transporting them home. In addition, framing in Indonesia, although inexpensive, leaves much to be desired in terms of designs, colors, and workmanship. We've seen few frames that go well with the art. Batik paintings are the easiest to carry since they can be folded and placed in a suitcase or carry-on bag along with your clothes. Once home, you can hand wash and iron them before having them professionally framed.

While Jogjakarta remains the center for the arts, galleries in Jakarta offer some of the best quality paintings you will find anywhere in Indonesia. While artists in Bali are prolific in producing distinctive Balinese style paintings, you may quickly become overwhelmed by the "sameness" of these paintings.

In Bali the center for artists and paintings is Ubud. You will find several galleries along the main street selling the works of famous local and European artists such as Arie Smit, Hans Snel, Wayan Rendi, Antonio Blanco, Raner Anderie, and I Gusti Nyoman Lempad. Other villages such as Mas, Batuan, Sangginyan, Pengosekan, Penestanan, and Peliatan also have several galleries. However, like the woodcarvings on Bali, many of the paintings here tend to have a monotonous "sameness" to them. The same village scenes seem to be repeated from one painting to another, with the only difference being the colors and frame. Nonetheless, you can and will find some wonderful paintings if you dig around from one studio to another.

Since Jogjakarta is the center for Indonesian art and it is here where the art of batik paintings began, you find numerous art galleries offering a wide range of batik and some oil paintings. One of Indonesia's most famous and expensive painters is Affandi, whose oil paintings are available at the **Affandi Gallery** (Jl. Solo, adjacent to the river and just west of the Ambarrukmo Palace Hotel). Some of the most famous batik painters also have studios and shops: **Kuswadji K.** (near Sultan's Palace), **Amri Gallery**, and **Ardiyanto Batik**. We especially like **Ardiyanto Batik** (Jl. Magelang Km. 5.8, Tel. 62777) which also functions as a combination art gallery and studio, batik processing center, and antique shop. Ardiyanto represents 50 young and upcoming Indonesian artists who primarily work in oils. Tourists as well as dealers especially like to shop for batik paintings amongst the many shops that line both sides of Jl. Tirtodipuran. Two of their favorite, and Jogjakarta's largest batik painting, shops are **Seno Batik Painting** and **Wiji Hartonto/Kabul Art Gallery**.

Art galleries in Jakarta offer some of the finest quality oils in all of Indonesia. The country's premier art gallery is the **Duta Fine Arts Gallery** on Jl. Kamang Raya. A beautiful gallery housed in a series of white stucco, red tiled buildings, this gallery only represents the very best in oils and sculpture produced in Indonesia. This is the gallery for serious art buyers. Nearby is the reputable **Ikawati Gallery** at Jl. Kemang Raya 50 (formerly Oet's on Jl. Palatehan). Other major galleries are concentrated along Jl. Palatehan in the Kebayoran Baru section of Jakarta. Look for **Hadiprana Galleries** (#38) for some the best quality and selections of paintings. Other good art shops in this area are **Amrus' Original**, **Fine Arts Gallery**, and **Djelita Fine Art**. Along Jl. Gajah Mada (#3-5) look for **Santi**

Fine Arts Gallery (Duta Merlin Building, #012, ground floor). Several shops at the **Ancol Art Market** and the **Indonesian Bazaar** at the Hilton Hotel.

 ## ANTIQUES AND CURIOS

If you love antiques and curios, you'll have fun in Indonesia. Numerous shops throughout Indonesia offer a large variety of Dutch, Chinese, and local antiques. In addition to primitive artifacts, these shops include Chinese porcelain, Dutch and Chinese furniture, jewelry, textiles, pewterware, brass oil lamps, puppets, containers, gables, doors, and Balinese woodcarvings and masks. In most cities and towns these shops are located next to each other along one or two streets or found in the shopping arcades of major hotels. Most of the shops are jammed with antiques. Crowded and dusty, many of these shops poorly display their goods. Consequently, you must walk into the shop and get your hands dirty by poking through everything as if you were on a treasure hunt. You will often be pleasantly surprised by what you find. Do not judge shops by their outward appearance. You must go in and investigate the details.

Shops in Jakarta offer some of the best quality antiques and curios in Indonesia. Some of the best places to shop are along Jl. Kebon Sirih Timur Dalam, Jl. Surabaya, Jl. Majapahit, Jl. Kemang Bangka (Kemang), Jl. Palatehan (Kebayoran Baru), and Old Bogor Road (Jl. Ciputat Raya, Pondok Labu).

In Jogjakarta you will find numerous shops along Jl. Malioboro as well as across from the Ambarrukmo Palace Hotel. The best antique dealer here is **Yamin** which is located on J. Wonosari, Ketandan, Banguntapan Bantul. It's best to arrange to see this warehouse/shop through the **Mahakam** shop at the Ambarrukmo Palace Hotel (Tel. 66488, ext. 7160) which is owned by Mrs. Yamin.

If you visit Solo, be sure to visit the **Antique Market** (Pasar Antik or Triwindu Market). This is one of the largest antique markets in Indonesia. Its antique stalls are crammed with lamps, beads, batik, coins, brassware, scales, irons, tools, clocks, tables, knives, porcelain, walking canes, wayang puppets, masks, and even old meat grinders! While it's fun to poke around the many stalls, you may find they are more filled with tourist kitsch than with genuine antiques—similar to the antique market along Jl. Surabaya in Jakarta.

In Bali most of the antique and curio shops are found along Legian Road in Kuta Beach as well as in several shops along the main roads that link the major arts and crafts villages in Bali. One of our favorite shops for quality antiques is **Arts of Asia** in downtown Denpasar.

WOODCARVINGS, MASKS, PUPPETS

In addition to the primitive woodcarvings and masks, many of the shops in the major cities on Java and Bali offer a large variety of woodcarvings, masks, and puppets representing traditional and contemporary Javanese and Balinese cultures. Most of the woodcarvings and masks come from Bali. These range in motif and quality from the basic human figures and mythical birds brightly colored or covered with black or brown shoe polish to intricately carved scenes of birds and trees made from hibiscus and finished with good quality oils. The former carvings are mass produced for tourists, often look tacky, and are relatively inexpensive; they are purchased by individuals who have more money than taste. The latter woodcarvings are relatively unique works of art which can be very expensive; they are class acts which make lovely home decorative pieces.

Puppets, made from leather (wayang kulit) or wood (wayang golek) are found in many shops throughout Java and Bali. The trend is to mass produce these puppets for the tourist market. Representing different characters in the popular wayang puppet shows, many of these puppets make nice home decorative pieces if displayed properly. They represent a very rich and continuing cultural tradition in Indonesia. You may wish to attend a wayang performance prior to purchasing these puppets. Many of the major hotels in Bali and Jogjakarta as well as the Puppet Museum (Museum Wayang) in Jakarta put on regular performances of the wayang puppet show.

Woodcarvings, masks, and puppets are found in many of the antique shops throughout Indonesia. In Jakarta they are also found in the handicraft sections of the **Sarinah** department stores and in several art shops along **Jl. Kebon Sirih Timur Dalam** and **Jl. Palatehan**, as well as in the **Ancol Art Market**, **Beautiful Indonesia in Miniature** complex, and the major **hotel shopping arcades**.

The woodcarving center on Java is **Jepara**, located on the northern coast of Central Java. Here you will find floral patterns, similar to batik motifs, used for furniture and panels. Other Javanese woodcarving centers are found in and around **Bandung**, **Cirebon**, and **Madura**.

But **Bali** is where you will be assaulted by a tremendous variety of these items. Most, however, are mass produced for tourists, and they have a monotonous "sameness" and tacky look to them. The antiques in **Denpasar** and the tourist stalls along the main roads of **Kuta Beach** and **Sanur Beach** and adjacent to the temple sites are filled with these items. One of the largest concentrations of such items is found in the **Sukawati Art Market** (Pasar Seni Sukawati) in Sukawati. For more unique items of excellent quality, stop at several studios and galleries in and around the village of **Mas**, the woodcarving center on Bali. Bali's top carver remains Ida Bagus Tilem who has an exquisite gallery in Mas—**Najana Tilem Gallery**—as well as branch shops in the Bali Hyatt Hotel and Hotel Bali Beach. He also has another branch shop in the Mandarin Hotel in Jakarta.

FURNITURE

If you collect unique pieces of furniture, you'll love Indonesia. This may well become the shopping highlight of your Indonesian adventure. Several shops in Jakarta, Bali, and Jogjakarta specialize in antique as well as new furniture from Java, Madura, and China. You'll discover everything from tables and bed to Madura wedding chests. Much of this furniture makes wonderful accent pieces in Western homes.

The single largest concentration of furniture shops in Indonesia is found along **Old Bogor Road** (Jl. Ciputat Raya in Pondok Labu) on the south side of Jakarta. Unknown to most tourists—indeed no tours and few guides ever visit this area—this is a popular area for expatriates who regularly shop this area and discover its many wonderful treasures. Numerous furniture shops line both sides of a 2 kilometer stretch of the road. Some shops specialize in antique furniture while others produce new furniture. Many shops also include other types of antiques, curios, and tribal artifacts. You can easily spend a whole day browsing through these shops. The best shop here is the first one you come to—**Gallery 50-B** at Jl. Ciputat Raya No. 22 (Tel. 749-2572). Other interesting shops along this road include **Maulana Art Shop, Yus Madura Art Shop, Madura Art Shop, Lampung Art Shop, Indonesia Putra Art and Curio**, and **Gondola**. Several shops along Jl. Kebon Sirih Timur Dalam, such as **Djody** and **Budaya Antique Art Shop** and a few along Jl. Palatehan, such as **Pigura**, also sell furniture.

Three of our favorite shops in Jakarta that offer top quality furniture—and also are frequented by many VIPs—are **Nilam Gallery** (Jl. Panarukan 16 pav., Tel. 3900270), **Bin House** (Jl.

Teluk Betung 10, Tel. 335941), and **Alex & Caecil Papadi-mitriou** (Jl. Pasuruan 3, Tel. 3158748 or 3147928). While Bin House primarily finds unique pieces of furniture for clients who have specific decorating or collecting needs, the other two shops also function as workshops for refurbishing antique furniture. Depending on your needs and budget, you may want to first consult with Bin House (Tel. 335941 or 3808402—talk to Josephine Komara) before running around Jakarta in an attempt to "discover" a particular piece of furniture.

Several shops in Denpasar, Kuta Beach, Sanur Beach, and the villages in Bali offer a wide range of furniture. Most of it comes from Bali or the nearby island of Madura. The best furniture shop in Bali is **Tulus Jaya** (Jl. Pantai Br. Pekandelan, Sanur, Tel. 88027). Located on a corner near the Bali Beach Hotel, this large workshop and store specializes in furniture from Madura. The quality and prices here are excellent, and many foreign dealers acquire their furniture from this place. They can conveniently arrange all shipping details for you. Another excellent antique furniture shop is **Putra Sukana** in Batubulan.

If you visit Jogjakarta, be sure to contact Mrs. Yamin Makawaru. Her two shops—**Yamin**—carry the best selections of antique furniture in Jogjakarta. You can contact her through her leather shop—**Mahakam**—in the Ambarrukmo Palace Hotel (Tel. 88488, ext. 737). As you drive from Jogjakarta to Solo, you will see numerous furniture shops along both sides of the road. These factory-shops make new furniture as well as decorative wood doors. While you may want to stop and visit a few of these factories, chances are this furniture may not meet your needs nor satisfy your tastes and quality standards.

STONECARVINGS

Except for some primitive stone work, most stonecarvings come from **Bali** and **Jogjakarta**. The Javanese use lava rock for their stone sculptures whereas the Balinese use a smoother stone. When in Bali stop in the art town of **Ubud** as well as along both sides of the road in **Batubulan** for such carvings.

JEWELRY

Indonesia is not well noted for its jewelry. Nonetheless, it does produce semi-precious stones and diamonds, especially from **southern Kalimantan** near the city of **Banjarmasin**. Several shops in the major cities offer unique pieces of gold and silver jewelry, using local and imported stones, especially diamonds, purple amethyst, black opals, and pearls. The unique Indonesian black opal is of particular interest to many visitors who discover this lovely stone while in Indonesia. More and more antique jewelry is appearing in the jewelry and antique shops. However, much of the antique jewelry is a touchy subject with the government which may soon prohibit the use of antiquity pieces by commercial jewelers.

Jakarta, Jogjakarta, and Bali are the best places to shop for Indonesian jewelry. In fact, you may want to confine your jewelry purchases to a few noted shops in Jakarta, which offer the best quality and designs for Westerners. The Spiro family, for example, has several shops in Jakarta—each under a different Spiro name—which offer many lovely designer pieces. Each shop is run independently and has different designs, but the quality is excellent in all of the Spiro shops: **Linda Spiro** (Borobudur Inter-Continental Hotel); **Joyce Spiro** (Sari Pacific Hotel and **Jay's Jewelry** in the Mandarin Hotel); and **F. Spiro Jewellers** (Hilton Hotel and Hyatt Aryaduta Hotel). Our favorite is F. Spiro Jewellers at the Hilton Hotel which has some of the most unique jewelry designs in Indonesia. Other fine jewelry shops are located in these same hotel complexes as well as at the Mandarin Oriental Hotel (**Jay's Jewelry**, which is actually a Joyce Spiro shop under a different name), and Hotel Indonesia (**Sandono**).

If you are looking for local designed gold and silver jewelry, the many jewelry shops in **Gadja Mada Plaza** are filled with numerous selections. However, with the exception of some lovely designs at **Crown Jewellery** (first floor), these shops mostly appeal to the local Jakartians.

SILVER

Silver work is well developed on Java, Bali, West Sumatra (**Kota Gedang**), and Southeast Sulawesi (**Kendari**). The silver work is produced as jewelry, bowls, flatware, and small figures, such as models of horse carts, ships, and musical instruments (gamelan orchestras). The Indonesians are particularly talented in making very delicate and artistic silver filigree figures. You can observe craftsmen working the silver in many factories in Jogjakarta and Bali. **Kotagede** near Jogjakarta is the silver center on Java. Here, you'll find the largest factory/shops **Tom's Silver** and **Yogya Silver**—two highly competitive shops that seem at war competing for customers! **Celuk** and **Mas** are the silver and gold centers on Bali. However, many tourists prefer the silver designs and prices at two large shops along Legian Street in Kuta Beach—**CV. Yusuf's Silver** and **Jonathan Silver**. Both shops are good supply sources for foreign dealers and wholesalers.

Unfortunately, tour guides in collusion with silver factory/shop owners are taking advantage of many tourists. Prices tend to be highly inflated because of the expensive commission game being played with tourists and their silver purchases. For example, many of the silver shops in the silver village of Celuk pay guides and drivers 30 to 35% commissions on all purchases made by the tourists they bring to their shops. The silver shops in Kotogede (Jogjakarta) routinely pay 15% commissions. Therefore, you can expect to pay premium prices in most of these factory shops if you go there accompanied by a driver or guide. On the other hand, expect to receive a large discount if you go to these places by yourself.

LEATHER GOODS

Indonesia produces various qualities of leather. One of its most popular leathers is a crude grade of buff-colored buffalo hide leather which is made into sandals, luggage, brief cases, belts, and purses. You may or may not be interested in these leather goods since the workmanship is crude, the styles tend to be old-fashioned, and the leather has an unpleasant odor. The handicraft sections in the **Sarinah** and **Sogo** department stores carry a good selection of these leather goods. You also will find leather shops in **Jogjakarta**, the center for producing such leather.

Some of the most interesting designer leather products are available at a shop called **Mahakam** in the Ambarrukmo Palace Hotel in Jogjakarta. This shop offers several varieties of bags which combine leather and woven materials from Kalimantan. Many foreign wholesalers purchase their stock from this shop.

The leather selections at **C. V. Usaha Jaya** (Jl. Inspectsi Raya, #46A, Tel. 583254) in Jakarta are also exceptional. This shop offers excellent quality crocodile and snake skin bags and shoes.

In Bali you will find many shops selling leather products along Legian Street in Kuta Beach. For some reason these shops are especially popular with Australian tourists. Shops such as **Andree Collection** and **Sari Bali Boutique** have a nice selection of leather bags.

HANDICRAFTS, POTTERY, DAGGERS, MUSICAL INSTRUMENTS

Indonesia produces a large variety of handicrafts. Most can be seen by visiting the handicraft section in the **Sogo** and **Sarinah** department stores in Jakarta. Among the many items you will find are a large variety of daggers, baskets, hats, placemats, cups, bowls, and toys, such as bamboo tops. Unique pottery and glazed ceramics are made on Java and Bali. The village of **Kasongan** near Jogjakarta is known for its unique earthenware. The son of one of Indonesia's most famous wayang puppet and mask makers—**Warnowaskito**—is found at his workshop/ home in the village of **Krantil** near Jogjakarta. On Bali visit the village of **Pejaten** (Tabanan area) and **Batu Jimbar** at Sanur.

One of the most popular items many visitors to Indonesia acquire is the "*kris*," the mystical, bejeweled dagger worn by Javanese and Balinese on special occasions as well as in Madura and other areas of Indonesia. The *kris* has a long and fascinating history and the workmanship is very interesting. Many visitors become collectors of the *kris*, which can become a very expensive hobby. You can buy anything from the antique *kris*, which may cost over $10,000 to inexpensive imitation *kris* for $10. Like batik and textiles in Indonesia, you could well organize a shopping trip just for buying the *kris*. Such a trip would take you to the numerous cities, towns, and villages throughout Java and Bali.

Musical instruments are found in many shops throughout Indonesia. Of particular interest are Batak string instruments, the bamboo angklung, various pieces from the Javanese gamelan orchestra, and Asmat drums. These are unique instruments which make fascinating additions to musical collections.

PLANTS AND ANIMALS

Indonesia's plant and animal life are unmatched anywhere in the world. Its rich flora and fauna make it an excellent source for buying exotic plants and animals. The variety of tropical birds, especially from Irian Jaya, is fascinating. The Perkutut song bird, for example, is an extremely prized bird among the Javanese. The Island of Biak, off the northern coast of Irian Jaya, remains the world's richest source for both legally and illegally imported birds.

If you are interested in purchasing plants or animals from Indonesia, be sure to check with the U.S. Department of

Agriculture before departing for Indonesia. You will need information on quarantines and other import restrictions. You will also have to clear the export through proper Indonesian channels.

Some good places to view the exciting variety of Indonesian flora and fauna are the **Ragunum Zoo** (10 miles south of Jakarta), the **Bird Market** (Pasar Burung at Jl. Pramuka), the Bird Park at **Beautiful Indonesia in Miniature**, the **Orchard Gardens**, and the lovely **Botanical Gardens** at Bogor (50 miles south of Jakarta). Ask the people in these locations how you can best purchase and export your favorite plants and animals. There are many experienced animal breeders and horticulturalists who regularly sell to visitors and who can help in making the necessary export and shipping arrangements for you.

THE MORE YOU LOOK

Shopping in Indonesia opens a whole new world of learning and travel. The numerous arts and crafts make lovely decorative items for Western homes. They integrate nicely in many contemporary style homes. The batik can be fashioned into clothes or used as upholstery and wall hangings. The textiles make unique wall hangings when framed properly. Most of these items are works of art as well as have utilitarian value and religious significance.

But there is a theme that runs through many Indonesian arts and crafts. To a very large extent this is a copy-cat arts and crafts culture where individual artists and craftsmen learn to copy from models. Except in many contemporary Indonesia paintings, creativity is not particularly evident nor valued. When you shop for batik, textiles, and woodcarvings, what initially appears unique may later appear boring, because you see so many similar items that look alike. Artists and craftsmen mass produce the same item over and over and over. The Balinese woodcarvings in particular become overwhelming, because they all look like the same tourist kitsch.

In many respects what you will be buying in Indonesia are various representations of Indonesian society and culture. The primitive arts, for example, are models of themes found in the ancestral worship and mysticism of the various ethnic and tribal groups. Individual wayang puppets represent very specific characters found both in the wayang puppet plays and in the personalities and roles of the Javanese. Indeed, the wayang is the purist example of life imitating art in Indonesia. When you purchase such items, you purchase examples of Indonesia's complex society.

Shopping in Indonesia is like going on a treasure hunt. You must not pre-judge shops, because many yield wonderful surprises. Most antique shops approximate Western junk, auction, or pawn shops. You must go in and dig around until you find things you are looking for or which strike your fancy.

While you may at times get bored with seeing so many of the same items, you will not be disappointed once you return home. Indonesia offers lovely decorative arts and crafts. If you know how to buy quality, these arts and crafts are best appreciated after you return home and display them in your home.

PART III

Island to Island Shopping

7

Shopping Areas and Sources

If you seek unique items and quality products, you must go beyond the typical tourist paths to find the shops that deliver uniqueness and quality. This means taking a great deal of initiative on your part to locate the many shopping areas and shops we identify in this book as some of the best places to shop. Above all, you must avoid the many "good deal" guides and merchants who want your money.

TAKE INITIATIVE FOR QUALITY SHOPPING

Knowing where to best shop is often made more difficult by tour guides and drivers who recommend specific shops. In fact, guides and drivers love to take tourists shopping. And they are prepared to make "special" recommendations on where to best shop. As you will quickly discover, such recommendations will seldom take you to quality shops. Instead, they take you to places that are a good deal for them rather than for you.

Few guides and drivers will take you to the best places to shop. More often than not, they go to places that offer mediocre quality as well as give them commissions on everything you purchase. They have special arrangements with particular shops that will give them 10 to 30% commissions. When advising you on where to shop, their judgment is clouded by their main goal—the commission. Consequently, they avoid the quality shops, because most reputable shops do not pay large commissions. Some guides and drivers will even go so far as to bad mouth the quality shops as being "no good"—poor quality and expensive. Don't believe a word they say. Insist that you be taken where you want to go.

You can and should do better than the recommendations of your local guide or driver if you understand the structure of shopping in Indonesia and take initiative to find the best shops. You must avoid the middlemen and go directly to those places that offer unique quality products. The reputable and quality places seldom play the commission game.

AREAS AND OPTIONS

When you shop in Indonesia, you visit numerous cities, towns, and villages. In these areas you will encounter hotel shopping arcades, shopping centers, department stores, retail shops, factories, markets, vendor stalls, homes, and itinerant peddlers.

Cities such as Jakarta are more or less divided into residential and commercial districts. Districts and neighborhoods tend to have reputations for offering certain types of goods. Jakarta, for example, has its Chinatown (**Glodok**) and old Dutch section (**Batavia**) as well as a modern residential and commercial area called **Kebayoran Baru**. It is in Jakarta where you will find the best quality products as well as the most well developed shopping facilities consisting of hotel shopping arcades, shopping centers, department stores, and retail shops. Yet, Jakarta also has its share of homes, markets, vendor stalls, and itinerant peddlers. Other cities primarily have small shopping areas consisting of retail shops in one or two sections along major streets as well as markets, vendor stalls, and peddlers.

Each of these shopping areas yields different types of shops and products as well as becomes a different type of shopping experience. When we examine specific cities, towns, and villages, we will identify the hotel shopping arcades, shopping centers, department stores, retail shops, homes, markets, and vendor stalls appropriate for each area.

HOTEL SHOPPING ARCADES

Hotel shopping arcades in Indonesia are by no means as well developed as those in Hong Kong, Bangkok, or Singapore. Most deluxe hotels will have a few jewelry, clothing, arts, and crafts shops offering a variety of goods for upscale international shoppers. The **Spiro family**, for example, has most of its jewelry shops located in Jakarta's deluxe hotels. **Iwan Tirta**, Indonesia's famous batik designer, maintains a small shop in Jakarta's **Borobudur Hotel** as do two of Indonesia's top antique dealers—**Djody** and **Tribal**. Shops in these hotels are normally branches of a main shop or factory located in the owner's home or in another commercial area. Jakarta's **Plaza Indonesia** on Jl. MH. Thamrin boasts Southeast Asia's largest hotel (Grand Hyatt) shopping arcade with 490 shops.

❑ Guides and drivers love to take tourists shopping, but they avoid quality shops, because the best shops will not pay them commissions.

❑ Most Indonesian shopping centers have little to offer international shoppers.

❑ Indonesia has one chain of department stores worth visiting—the Sarinah Department Store.

❑ Most major antique and curio shops tend to be located next to each other or at least within a short walk.

❑ Street or roadside vendors are prevalent in many parts of Indonesia. Be sure to visit the antiques vendors along Jl. Surabaya in Jakarta at least once during your visit. If you're lucky, you may find a "diamond in the rough."

❑ Much of the quality shopping in Indonesia is found in the homes of Indonesian entrepreneurs who maintain home-based studios, galleries, and shops.

SHOPPING CENTERS

Multi-level shopping centers are beginning to emerge in Jakarta. However, most of these are oriented toward consumer goods for local residents. They are heavily patronized by Jakarta's growing middle class, especially young people who roam the levels window-shopping and listening to the latest tunes over the loud speaker system. These centers have little to offer international travelers except for jewelry stores. **Gajah Mada Plaza** in Jakarta, for example, has more than 20 jewelry stores offering locally produced gold and silver jewelry as well as necklaces, earrings, and bracelets made with semi-precious stones, pearls, and diamonds. These centers are good places to purchase CDs.

DEPARTMENT STORES

While Indonesia has few department stores, more are opening each year as Indonesia follows the shopping trends of other developing countries. Several of the department stores are excellent sources for purchasing Indonesian handicrafts.

Indonesia has one chain of department stores which is well worth visiting. The **Sarinah Department Store** has several branches throughout Jakarta as well as in other cities on Java and the outer islands. These stores have a good selection of Indonesian batik, cottons, and handicrafts. Each store has either one floor or a section devoted to Indonesian handicrafts and ready-made batik clothes. We highly recommend visiting this department store early in your visit in order to get an overview of the type and quality of tourist handicrafts you can expect to encounter elsewhere as well as survey prices. Department store prices are fixed, and they appear to be reasonable compared to prices elsewhere. The **Sarinah Department Stores** carry several relatively nice and inexpensive lines of batik shirts with a good selection of large and extra large sizes. The main store at Jl. HM. Thamrin 11 has the largest selections of Indonesian products.

The **Pasa Raya** department store in Blok M (Kebayoran Baru, Jl. Iskandarsyah II/2), formerly known as Sarinah Raya Department Store, is an upscale department store offering similar products as the main Sarinah Department Store. It has an excellent arts and crafts section.

The **Keris Gallery** department store has an "Indonesian Handicraft Centre" on the second floor where Batik Keris brand batik garments and accessories are sold.

The popular and upscale **Sogo Department Store** is found at the Indonesia Plaza shopping center which is attached to the Grand Hyatt Hotel at Menteng Circle in Jakarta.

RETAIL SHOPS

Retail shops tend to be scattered throughout each city. Many are clustered along certain sections of the downtown area or in particular neighborhoods. Each city and town will have a particular area which has a reputation for retail shops selling a variety of items of interest to international travelers. Most of the major antique and curio shops tend to be located next to each other or at least within a short walking distance. In **Jakarta**, for example, the major such areas for arts, antiques, furniture, and ethnographic artifacts are Jl. Kebon Sirih Timur Dalam, Jl. Surabaya, Jl. Palatehan, Jl. Kamang Raya, and Old Bogor Road (Jl. Ciputat Raya). In **Medan** it's Jl. Jend A Yani. In **Ujung Pandang**, it's Jl. Somba Upu. In **Surabaya**, it's Jl. Basuki Rachmat (shops adjacent to the Hyatt Bumi Surabaya). In **Jogjakarta**, it's Jl. Malioboro, Tirtodipuran, Solo, and

Taman Garuda. And in **Bali**, it's Jl. Gajah Mada (Denpasar) and Legian Street (Kuta Beach).

If you head for a particular retail shop, chances are you will find several other shops selling similar items in the immediate vicinity. As soon as you arrive in such areas, it is a good idea to survey the shops around the one you plan to visit. This quick survey will give you some idea of the range of goods and prices.

FACTORIES

Many cities, towns, and villages have small to large factories producing a variety of Indonesian handicrafts. Large batik factories are found in Jogjakarta, Solo, Cirebon, and Pekalongan. There you can observe the batik process, from the initial waxing to dying, and purchase batik in meter lengths, as ready-made garments, or as small gift items from their factory shops. Silver, woodcarving, and leather factories abound in Central Java and on Bali. These are well worth visiting.

Two words of caution about these factories. First, do not expect to find top quality goods at these factories. Second, expect your guide or driver to receive anywhere from a 10 to 35% commission on everything you buy at the factory shop.

Most factories produce handicrafts for the mass market. They supply the department stores and retail shops in Jakarta and elsewhere. After a while these factories begin to look the same; they may well become a boring aspect of your shopping adventure. Do visit a few to see how the batik and handicrafts are made, but don't treat them like factory outlets in other countries such as Hong Kong or Australia. These are cottage industries run by families; they produce goods for the mass market of tourists and exporters.

Your best approach to finding these factories is to ask at your hotel what factories are found in the area and how and when to visit them. Most factories are open to tourists. But it is wise to plan your factory visits ahead of time. Especially in Jogjakarta and Solo, you may want to hire a car and driver for a full day just to tour and shop at these factories.

MARKETS

Each city and town has open-air and enclosed markets which sell fresh fruit, vegetables, and meats as well as ready-made clothes, meter lengths of cotton and batik, numerous household goods, and some handicrafts. Items found in these areas are usually less expensive than in the retail shops, but in general the quality is not as good as elsewhere.

The market experience in Indonesia is similar to market experiences in other Third World countries. The food sections of markets tend to be very crowded, dirty, and smelly. They are indeed a cultural experience, one which you may wish to forego, especially if you have visited similar markets in other Third World countries. Do not expect to do quality shopping in these areas. If you do shop in the markets, be sure to bargain hard. You should be able to get 20 to 50% discounts off the asking price. Also, watch your head and feet. It is easy to bump your head on hanging baskets and garments as well as step into puddles of dirty water and trip on trash. The smells and sights of food may get to you if you linger.

The **antique markets** in Jakarta (Jl. Surabaya) and Solo (Pasar Triwindu, off Jl. Diponegoro) are well worth visiting. You may find a few treasures amongst the tourist kitsch. Be sure to bargain hard in these areas, expecting anywhere from a 30 to 70% discount off the initial asking price. The **handicraft market** at Sukawati in Bali (Sukawati Art Market) is also well worth visiting for bargain hunters. In Jayapura (Irian Jaya), the major shopping area for acquiring Asmat artifacts are at several tribal artifact stalls that front on the market at Hamadi Beach.

VENDOR STALLS

Many cities, towns, and sights frequented by tourists will have various sections lined with vendors who sell goods from mobile, temporary, or permanent stalls. One of the most famous areas is the **Jl. Surabaya** antique row in Jakarta. This is a "must" area to visit at least once, even if you don't buy anything. In Bali you will encounter roadside vendors displaying all types of goods, from puppets to paintings. Similar to the market areas, you must bargain hard with these vendors. Most, however, offer a great deal of tourist junk. On the other hand, you may find a "diamond in the rough" if you stop and explore enough stalls.

HOMES

Much of the quality shopping in Indonesia is found in the homes of Indonesian entrepreneurs. Moreso than in other Asian countries, families in Indonesia tend to operate their businesses from their homes. You must ask around to find who has a reputation for producing and selling certain types of items. In many cases the answer will take you to someone's home which also doubles as a cottage production center. This pattern is particularly evident and most developed on Bali where hundreds of homes have been transformed into studios, galleries, and shops.

The home pattern of shopping is the most unfamiliar for visitors to Indonesia. International shoppers are used to visiting shopping centers and retail shops where items are on display. In the home pattern of shopping, you will meet someone who has a reputation for specializing in particular goods, such as antiques, paintings, and woodcarvings. The family may or may not have items on display. In the Batak area of Sumatra, or in Ujung Pandang on Sulawesi, you may visit someone's home. Upon arriving, the owner will go to a back room to show you his collection which is for sale if the price is right. Other homes display their items nicely in particular rooms, because they have a steady flow of visitors. In many cases you will arrive in the middle of a residential area and knock at a door or gate. Once you enter you will be escorted to the display area.

We highly recommend the home shopping pattern since many of these homes have excellent quality goods and are run by specialists who know quality. These places take you off the beaten tourist path. But you will most likely need a car with a driver who has instructions on where to take you. A good example of such shopping is **Alex and Caecil Papadimitriou's** excellent textile, furniture, and antique selections which are only available by visiting their home at Jl. Pasuruan 3, Jakarta (Tel. 315-8748 or 314-7928). Just knock at the gate and you will be escorted through the display rooms of their home. In one neighborhood in Jakarta—Jl. Panarukan—you will find two of Indonesia's top clothing, furniture, and home decorative shops that are operated from homes: **Iwan Tirta** and **Nilam Gallery**. In another neighborhood, you'll discover one of Indonesia's top textile designers and producers—Josephine Komara at **Bin House** (Jl. Teluk Betung 10, Tel. 335941).

PEDDLERS

The pattern of buying from peddlers is particularly unique in Indonesia. It is a major source of wonderful antiques and textiles for local residents. Unfortunately, few short-term visitors ever come into contact with these suppliers.

If you lived in an Indonesian city, your residential area would be frequented by peddlers who sell a variety of goods they collect. If, for example, you were interested in antiques and let the peddler know this, you might be visited once a week by the peddler who has "found" something for you. Indeed, many expatriates in Jakarta have put together some nice antique collections because of these door-to-door peddlers.

As a short-time visitor, your chances of finding such peddlers are not good. At best, you should find an expatriate who might know where to locate a particular peddler or what day of the week he is most likely to return with another load of goods. This "home shopping" pattern takes you off the beaten tourist path and may well become one of the highlights of your shopping adventure. The prices of peddlers are relatively inexpensive, but be sure to bargain.

BROADCAST SHOPPING

A final shopping pattern is ideal for the short-term visitor to Indonesia. This involves broadcasting the fact that you are interested in examining particular items.

Given the difficulty in finding good detailed city maps, limited self-directed shopping information, and the helter-skelter locational patterns of shops, factories, homes, and street vendors, one of the easiest ways to cut through this confusing and disorganized maze is to "put out the word" that you are interested in making certain purchases. The informal communication networks will work for you.

Start at your hotel by asking the concierge for recommendations on the what, where, and who of local shopping. Let him know what you want. He or someone else close to the hotel will begin strategizing where to send you. In some cases, you may be visited by someone who heard you are interested in making purchases. Repeat this informational approach at other hotels, restaurants, and museums. After a while you will begin discovering places both on and off the beaten tourist paths, many of which are in the homes of Indonesians who specialize in certain types of goods.

However, be careful about broadcasting your desires too fervently while in a shop. The price will quickly double or triple, and you run the risk of goods being misrepresented. On our first visit to Jl. Surabaya, for example, we casually mentioned we were looking for primitive artifacts from Irian Jaya. In each stall we visited thereafter, vendors pointed out that several of their pieces were from Irian Jaya. However, most were Batak pieces from Sumatra—an area located more than 3,000 miles west of Irian Jaya! These entrepreneurs merely told us what they thought we wanted to hear, however inaccurate, in order to make a sale.

8

Jakarta

Jakarta is Southeast Asia's largest city. A melting pot of over 9 million people drawn from throughout the archipelago, it's a bustling, cosmopolitan city offering wonderful shopping opportunities for those who have the time and persistence to seek its many treasures.

Jakarta has undergone major transformations since the bleak '60s and '70s when the city seemed to be one vast slum. Today, it impresses visitors with its fine hotels, restaurants, commercial buildings, and shops as well as numerous attractions for international travelers and tourists.

A CITY ON THE GO

Like many other Asian and Third World cities, Jakarta is a big sprawling tropical city punctuated with numerous pockets of poverty and wealth. Lacking a well-defined city center, it consists of several major sections which have their own unique commercial and residential character. Currently one of Southeast Asia's most rapidly developing and economically booming cities, Jakarta also tends to be choked with traffic throughout the day. It's a crowded and bustling city that offers everything from traditional noodle stands to a Planet Hollywood!

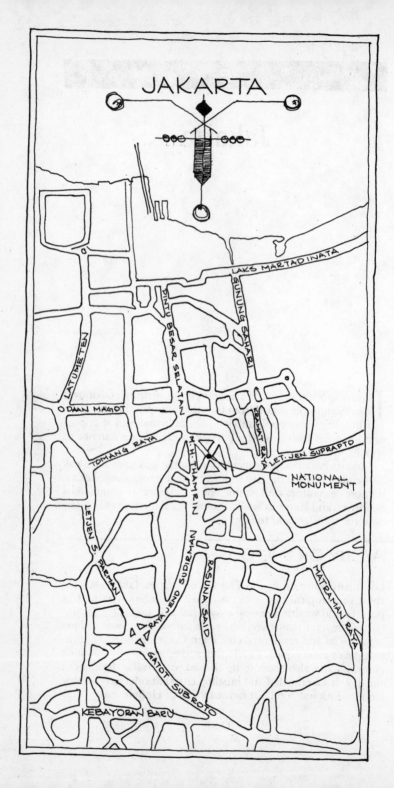

While Jakarta may initially appear disorienting and unattractive, after awhile its peoples and places grow on you. Over the years we have come to enjoy this city more and more. Each visit brings new surprises and even better shopping. While Bali may offer more numerous shopping opportunities, Jakarta remains our number one Indonesian shopping destination for quality products and one of our "must" stops on any trip to Southeast Asia.

GETTING TO KNOW YOU

If you travel to Indonesia without visiting Jakarta, you'll miss some of Indonesia's best shopping, dining, sightseeing, and accommodations. Yet, Jakarta is not on every traveler's Indonesian itinerary. For many people, it has a negative reputation. This is in part due to the fact that 25 to 30 years ago Jakarta was indeed an unattractive city with little to do; it has yet to completely shed its *Year of Living Dangerously* image. It is also due in part to the fact that Jakarta has not been promoted like Bali as a major international tourist destination.

Above all, Jakarta is a working city that is far more likely to attract international businesspeople than the average tourist. Indeed, many travelers go directly to Bali to experience all of their Indonesian adventure. Even many dealers avoid Jakarta, because they believe most shopping is found in Bali. This is unfortunate because Jakarta has a great deal to offer visitors, from Southeast Asia's oldest museum to one of the world's most interesting traditional working harbors. For shoppers, it can be a better buy than Bali, and the quality of products in Jakarta is generally superior to what you will find in Bali or elsewhere in Indonesia.

❑ While Bali may offer more numerous shopping opportunities, Jakarta remains our number one Indonesian shopping destination for quality products.

❑ Jakarta is a working city that is far more likely to attract international businesspeople than the average tourist. However, it has a great deal to offer visitors.

❑ Shopping in Jakarta is work. Be sure to plan ahead before you take to the streets in search of this city's treasures.

❑ Don't plan to do much walking in Jakarta. Distances between shopping areas are great enough to require taking taxis or hiring a car with driver. Forget the buses!

❑ We strongly recommend starting your Jakarta adventure by visiting the National Museum and Beautiful Indonesia in Miniature.

With one of Asia's fastest growing economies and a booming tourist industry, Indonesia is well on its way to becoming Asia's next great economic success story. And it is Jakarta that first benefits from the new-found wealth as it responds with new hotels, restaurants, shopping centers, more automobiles, expanded roads, and improved urban infrastructure. Jakarta is fast becoming a sophisticated international city which has much to offer travelers. It is quickly being discovered by travelers who once thought Indonesia was equivalent to Bali. Unfortunately— but perhaps fortunate for us—most tour groups still by-pass Jakarta in favor of shopping for tourist kitsch in Bali and Jogjakarta. Consequently, much of the "good stuff" remains in Jakarta!

OPPORTUNITIES AND STRATEGIES

While Jakarta is not known as a shopper's paradise, it does offer some unique shopping opportunities. The city is well worth a three-day visit during which time you should combine sightseeing with visits to the major shopping areas.

Jakarta is a "must" shopping stop, because it serves as the central crossroads and market for goods from all over Indonesia. If you are a dedicated shopper with limited time in Indonesia, you are well advised to spend some of it in Jakarta. Other areas, such as Jogjakarta and Bali, do offer wonderful shopping opportunities, but they do not have the same quality shopping as found in Jakarta.

Your Jakarta shopping experience will take you to hotel shops, department stores, shopping centers, galleries, open-air stalls, and small shops and homes along main streets and down dusty roads and lanes. Shopping here is a wonderful adventure in discovering antiques, textiles, fashion batik, clothes, brassware, Chinese ceramics, furniture, jewelry, woodcarvings, and paintings. Like shopping in many other Third World cities, shopping in Jakarta is work. Unlike Hong Kong and Singapore, the quality shops are not just there for you to stumble on by chance. You must plan ahead and then take to the streets in search of Jakarta's many unique shopping treasures.

GETTING ORGANIZED

While Jakarta is a very large and sprawling city, it's a relatively easy place to get around in if you organize yourself properly. The main streets are wide, most attractions are within a short driving distance, transportation is convenient, and shopping areas are well defined.

Orientation to the city is easy if you focus on a few key streets, landmarks, hotels, and areas. With a map in hand, it's best to first look at Jakarta horizontally. Most major roads and areas run from north to south. The northern section of the city is bounded by the ocean, harbor, and Ancol Dreamland Complex. The southern edge of the city continues on to the city of Bogor. Between these north and south points is one road that links most hotels and shopping areas together—Jl. MH. Thamrin which also becomes Jl. Jend Sudirman as you travel south. At the center is the Menteng traffic circle where several major hotels are located.

Try orienting yourself to Jakarta's shopping by considering Menteng traffic circle (Jl. MH. Thamrin) as the center of the city. All major streets, areas, hotels, shopping centers, department stores, and attractions seem to radiate from this central reference point. Menteng traffic circle is easy to find since it is surrounded by three of Jakarta's major hotels—Mandarin Oriental, Grand Hyatt, and Hotel Indonesia—and has the dramatic Welcome Statue towering at the center of the circle. All other major areas relevant for shopping and sightseeing can be easily located in reference to Menteng traffic circle:

North: Sarinah Department Store, Sari Pacific Hotel, Jl. Kebon Sirih Timur Dalam, Merdeka Square, National Museum, National Monument, Old Batavia (Fatahilah Square), Chinatown (Glodok Plaza), Old Harbor, and Ancol Dreamland Complex.

Northeast: Borobudur Inter-Continental Hotel and the Hyatt Aryaduta Hotel.

East: Jl. Surabaya and Jl. Pasuruan.

West: Jl. Panarukan and Jl. Pekalongan.

South: Sahid Jaya Hotel, Jakarta Hilton Hotel, Shangri-La Hotel, Regent Hotel, Kebayoran Baru, Blok M, Pasa Raya Department Store, Jl. Palatehan, and Jl. Kemang Bangka.

Southeast: Old Bogor Road (Jl. Ciputat Raya) and Indonesia in Miniature.

Don't plan to do much walking in Jakarta other than within specific areas. Shopping areas are well defined, but you will need transportation to get to each area. The best way to get around this city is to take air-conditioned taxis or hire a car and driver for a half or full-day. We do not recommend taking buses or other forms of public transportation, such as bajajs. Although cheap, they are inconvenient, hot, and crowded—not our idea of how one should best spend precious travel time. However, if you want to meet many local people, sweat a lot, and do Jakarta on the cheap, buses and bajajs will do the trick!

Most of the major hotels, such as the Grand Hyatt, Borobudur Inter-Continental, Mandarin Oriental, Hilton, Shangri-La, Regent, Hyatt Aryaduta, Sahid Jaya, and Sari Pacific, are conveniently located in relation to most shopping areas and attractions. If there were one best location to start a Jakarta shopping adventure, we would begin with the hotels and department stores around the Menteng traffic circle, especially the huge shopping complex attached to the new Grand Hyatt Hotel. In addition to the Mandarin Oriental, Hotel Indonesia, President, and Sari Pacific hotels, you are only a short distance from the Sarinah Department Store, Hilton Hotel shopping complex (Indonesian Bazaar), Jl. Surabaya ("antique" stalls), Jl. Pasuruan (Papadimitriou) Jl. Panarukan and Jl. Pekalongan (Iwan Tirta, Nilam Gallery), Jl. Teluk Betung (Bin House), Jl. Kebon Sirih Timur Dalam (ethnographic, furniture, textile, antique, arts, and crafts shops), the Borobudur Inter-Continental Hotel (shopping arcade)—as well as such major attractions as the National Museum, National Monument, and National Mosque. From here you can travel directly south to three of Jakarta's other major shopping areas—Keboyaran Baru/Blok M, Jl. Kemang Bangka, and Old Bogor Road (Jl. Ciputat Raya)—as well as the Indonesia in Miniature Park (regional theme park) or north to Chinatown, Old Batavia, the Old Harbor, and the Ancol Art Center (located within the Ancol Dreamland Complex).

We strongly recommend that you start your Jakarta shopping adventure by visiting the **National Museum** (Museum Nasional) and **Beautiful Indonesia in Miniature Park** (Taman Mini Indonesia Indah). Several tour companies provide half-day or full-day tours of Jakarta that include these two major attractions. If you spend a half day surveying these two orientation points, you will have an excellent overview of Indonesian society, culture, arts, and crafts. In addition, the National Museum has a small shop which offers some nice artifacts. At the front entrance to the park you will find a two-story shopping center with numerous shops selling handicrafts from the 27 provinces of Indonesia.

If you do take a city tour, don't expect to see many shopping areas along the way. At best, most tours only stop at the antique stalls along Jl. Surabaya (called a "Flea Market" in some brochures) and at the Indonesia Bazaar in the Jakarta Hilton Hotel compound. While these are two interesting shopping areas, they are not the most important ones for quality shopping. If you want to do some serious shopping, you'll have to organize your own shopping tour by taking taxis or hiring a car and driver to take you to the shopping areas we recommend.

WHERE TO SHOP

Most shopping in Jakarta is found in hotel shopping arcades, department stores, shopping centers, and shops that line key streets in various sections of the city. If you want to thoroughly shop this city for unique and quality products, plan to spend at least three days just for shopping. If you have limited time for shopping, we recommend concentrating your shopping on a few key hotel shopping arcades, department stores, and streets with shops that specialize in products that most interest you.

HOTEL SHOPPING ARCADES

Most of Jakarta's major deluxe hotels have small shopping arcades worth visiting. Many of them house some of Indonesia's finest shops for jewelry, fashion clothes, arts, crafts, and antiques.

Jakarta's major hotel shopping complex is the **Plaza Indonesia** which is attached to the Grand Hyatt Hotel on Jl. MH. Thamrin, adjacent to three other major hotels—Mandarin Oriental, Hotel Indonesia, and the Hotel President. Opened in 1990, this is Southeast Asia's largest hotel shopping arcade with 490 shops. This also is Jakarta's first large upscale air-conditioned shopping center. Similar to the River City Shopping Complex in Bangkok or the Marina Square Shopping Arcade in Singapore, this arcade has literally put Jakarta on the shopping map for Southeast Asia. It includes numerous name-brand clothing, jewelry, music, sporting goods, and electronic stores along with art galleries and handicraft shops. Prices on many name-brand imported goods are excellent here. We were pleasantly surprised to finally purchase a Gucci watch here for US$217 (Centre Watches, 3rd floor) that we had priced in several other countries, some of which had claimed duty-free prices (U.S. $269; Cancun, $249; Florence, $480; Singapore, $279; Hong Kong, $289). Be sure to visit several shops on the first floor: **Batik Keris** and **Batik Samar** for batik clothes; **Silver Threads** for unique filigree silver produced in Ugung Padang (Sulawesi); **P.T. Pelangi** and the **Jakarta Pearl Center** (same owners related to the Kesenian Group) for jewelry. Be sure to visit the third floor of the **Sogo Department Store** which has a large antique (run by the Kesenian Group) and handicraft section. For a sampling of Balinese handicrafts, visit **Garuda Bali** on the third food where you will also find a large food court with numerous fast-food restaurants. This shopping arcade also boasts a Baskin-Robbins and a Swenson's for ice cream—a nice treat after spending a hot and humid day pounding the pave-ment in search of Jakarta's treasures!

The shopping arcade occupying the second and third floors of the **Borobudur Inter-Continental Hotel** (Jl. Lapangan Banteng Selatan) remains one of our favorite places to shop for top quality products in Jakarta. Here, you will find a few excellent quality shops:

- **Iwan Tirta**: Also known as P.T. Ramacraft, this fashion boutique offers excellent quality batik and ikat clothes. If you don't have a chance to visit his main shop on Jl. Panarukan 25, be sure to visit this small shop. Located on the second floor.

- **Tribal**: Tel. 3805555, ext. 76023, 9am to 10:30pm. Also located on the second floor, this small but unique shop offers one of Indonesia's nicest collections of eth-nographic pieces. Owned by the Kesenian Group (pre-viously known as P. D. Pelangi Indonesia Opal and Jewelry Center), Tribal has a fine collection of primi-tive carvings, antiques, textiles, jewelry, beads, and other ethnographic pieces from Sumatra, Kalimantan, and other islands throughout the Indonesian archipel-ago. If you collect such items, you'll love this shop and its truly unique collection of items not found else-where in Indonesia. This is one of several shops operated by the Kesenian Group. The personnel working here will probably urge you to visit their main shop, **Gallery 50-B**, at Jl. Ciputat Raya 50-B (Tel. 7492850). However, it takes over one hour to get there. We still prefer this shop to the larger one.

- **Djody**: Also located on the second floor, this is a branch shop of one of Indonesia's best antique stores —Djody at 22 Jl. Kebon Sirih Timur (Tel. 327730). Unfortunately, this small shop does not do justice to the much larger and well defined collection found at the main shop. Nonetheless, you may find some nice one-of-a-kind items here. This shop also operates the art gallery on the third floor. Be sure to visit the main shop which has an extensive collection of Javanese antiques, primitive art, and textiles.

- **Linda Spiro:** Also located on second floor, this is one of Jakarta's best jewelry shops. Offers some lovely rings, bracelets, and necklaces uniquely designed with diamonds, pearls, opals, and other precious stones; they offer some of the largest pieces of jewelry in Indonesia.

The **Jakarta Hilton Hotel** actually has two shopping complexes—a few small shops inside the hotel and the **Indonesian Bazaar**, an international shopping bazaar located on the beautiful hotel grounds. Inside the hotel look for **F. Spiro Jewelry**, a small but wonderful shop offering old designs in new forms. Here you will discover pins, earrings, rings, and necklaces designed around ethnographic figures and themes representing the cultures of Central Java, Sumatra, Kalimantan, Sumba, Flores, Timor, Southern Moluccas, and the Asmat of Irian Jaya. If you are looking for some truly unique jewelry representative of Indonesia, be sure to visit this shop.

The **Indonesian Bazaar** has been an ambitious attempt to bring together numerous shops within a lovely outdoor water and garden setting reminiscent of Balinese and Sumatran architecture. Each shop occupies a separate building. While this is an interesting place to visit, and you will find several good shops offering arts, crafts, and jewelry, it's a rather quiet shopping area that has not become as successful as the creators had envisioned. Only about 50% of the shops are occupied. The problem is two-fold: few tours include this shopping area because of competing tour activities, and shops do not pay tour guides commissions to steer tourists here to shop. Nonetheless, the Indonesian Bazaar is worth visiting. You'll enjoy the ambience of this outdoor shopping setting which also offers dining opportunities. Especially interesting is **Sanggar Pratita Indone sia**, a cooperative art shop representing 15 artists who create unique paintings from chicken and bird feathers. **F. Spiro Jewelry** also has a small shop here as does **P.D. Pelangi Indonesia Opal and Jewelry Center**. You'll find some nice arts, crafts, and souvenir shops here.

The **Mandarin Oriental Hotel** has a very small shopping arcade. It only has three shops of special interest. **Jay's Jewelry**, which is actually a Joyce Spiro shop, offers nice jewelry, especially neckpieces, using Indonesia ethnic designs in silver as well as some items using pearls. You'll see similar items in the Joyce Spiro shop at the Sari Pacific Hotel. **Ida Bagus Tilem**

Gallery represents the works of Bali's most famous carver—Ida Bagus Tilem. Each carving is a one-of-a-kind piece. Expensive, but you buy top quality at this shop. If you've visited the main gallery in Bali (Mas), this shop will seem very small. **Le Drugstore** sells some fashionable neckpieces under the "Devi Tana" label as well as porcelain.

The shopping arcade at the **Sari Pacific Hotel**, located near the Mandarin Oriental Hotel on Jl. MH. Thamrin, has a few shops worth visiting. The **Joyce Spiro** shop offers nice contemporary jewelry designs using gold and silver. We especially like their ethnographic motifs used in silver rings, earrings, and necklaces. **Seni Indonesia** offers numerous handicrafts from Java and Bali. The **Sari Gift Shop** has a nice collection of imported porcelain and glass.

The **Hyatt Aryaduta Hotel** has three shops of interest to visitors. The **F. Spiro Jewelry** shop on second floor carries the same line of ethnographic jewelry found in the F. Spiro Jewelry shops at the Jakarta Hilton Hotel. **Pusaka Art-Drugstore** carries batik shirts and blouses, textiles, puppets, Asmat artifacts, and woodcarvings from Bali. Although a very small shop, the **Newsstand** has an excellent selection of books on Indonesia.

Several other hotels will have a shop or two of interest to visitors. The **Sahid Jaya Hotel**, for example, has a few clothing, handicraft, and gift shops. The new **Shangri-La Hotel** (Jl. Jend Sudirman Kav. 1) and **The Regent Hotel** (Kl. Karang Asem Raya 35) also have a few shops.

MAJOR SHOPPING STREETS

Some of the best shopping in Indonesia is found in shops along several major shopping streets in Jakarta. Nine streets in particular are well worth visiting. In some cases, such as Jl. Kebon Sirih Timur Dalam, Old Bogor Road, and Jl. Palatehan and Blok M, you can easily spend a half day or more visiting the many intriguing shops that line each street.

With the exception of Jl. Surabaya, few tour groups ever visit these shopping streets. As a result, most first-time visitors to Jakarta do not have a chance to experience the best of Jakarta's shopping. But to visit Jakarta without exploring at least four of these streets is to truly neglect some of Jakarta's major attractions!

JL. MH. THAMRIN AND JL. JEND SUDIRMAN

Jl. MH. Thamrin is the main thoroughfare that connects north and south Jakarta. It is also the street on which you will find the major hotels, high rise commercial buildings, and shopping complexes. Like many Indonesia street names, Jl. MH. Thamrin changes its name to become Jl. Merkeda Barat as you travel north; it becomes Jl. Jend Sudirman as you travel south toward the Kebayoran Baru area. The major landmark is the huge and somewhat monolithic Welcome Statue—a man and women with arms outstretched—that is elevated at the center of the Menteng traffic circle.

The best place to begin shopping in this area is at the Menteng traffic circle. This circle is surrounded by several luxury hotels which offer excellent shopping opportunities. Here you will find the **Plaza Indonesia** attached to the Grand Hyatt Hotel with nearly 500 shops, the **Mandarin Oriental**, **Hotel Indonesia**, and the **President Hotel**. Just to the north of the circle is the **Sari Pacific Hotel**, Jakarta's major department store, the **Sarinah**, and the famous **Jl. Kebon Sirih Timur Dalam** antique and ethnographic shopping area. Be sure to visit the third and fourth floors of the Sarinah department store since it has one of the largest collections of batik clothes, arts, and crafts found anywhere in Indonesia.

Immediately to the west of the Menteng traffic circle are two quiet neighborhood streets adjacent to each other—Jl. Panarukan and Jl. Pekalongan. Here you will discover two exquisite home shops for clothes, antiques, and home decorative items, **Iwan Tirta** and **Nilam Gallery**.

To the east of Menteng traffic circle are the famous antique and curio stalls lining Jl. Surabaya as well as adjacent Jl. Pasuruan which is home to one of Indonesia's best antique shophouses—**Alex & Caecil Papadimitriou**. Further to the northeast is the **Hyatt Aryaduta Hotel** and the **Borobudur Inter-Continental Hotel** with its quality shopping arcade.

Further to the south of Menteng traffic circle, where Jl. MH. Thamrin becomes Jl. Jend Sudirman, look for the **Hotel Kartika Plaza** (includes a shopping center popular with locals), **Sahid Jaya Hotel**, and the **Jakarta Hilton Hotel** with its adjacent Indonesian Bazaar shopping complex.

You can easily walk from Menteng circle to the Sarinah Department Store, Sari Pacific Hotel, and Jl. Panarukan/Pekalongan. However, since the distances from Menteng circle to the other locations to the north, northeast, east, and south are far on foot, we recommend that you take a taxi to get to these places. Most places are a short Rp. 5,000 (US$2.30) taxi ride from Menteng traffic circle—no more than five or 10 minutes. You could well spend a very hot and sweaty half hour to an hour or more walking to these places. You may want to stop at the Jakarta Hilton Hotel on your way south to the Kebayoran Baru and Blok M areas.

JL. KEBON SIRIH TIMUR DALAM

Jl. Kebon Sirih Timur Dalam is a "must visit" shopping street for anyone interested in Indonesian antiques, textiles, ethnographic pieces, arts, and crafts. You will find more than 30 shops selling a large variety of items, including Chinese ceramics, porcelain, lacquerware, war shields from Nias and Irian Jaya, Balinese woodcarvings, Javanese and Chinese furniture, Dayak masks and baby carriers, Batak staffs and gables, baskets, antique jewelry, kris, instruments, door panels, chests, wayang puppets, beads, Madura and Minangkabau chests, vases, drums, spears, and even Thai Buddhas and Korean chests! This is a treasure hunter's paradise. Shopping here is both fun and rewarding for those who have the time and patience to browse through each shop. Within an hour or two, you will learn a great deal about Indonesian antiques, arts, crafts, and textiles by visiting these shops.

A narrow and crowded one-way street, with car repair and upholstery shops interspersed amongst the other shops, few if any tour groups ever visit Jl. Kebon Sirih Timur Dalam. This is a shame because some of the best shopping in Indonesia is found along this street. But the street is simply too narrow and parking places are nonexistent for tour buses. Therefore, you will have to visit this area on your own. We recommend taking a taxi to the beginning of the street and then walking its length, visiting shops on both sides of the street. If you go by way of a car and driver, instruct your driver to meet you at the other end of the street. He may, however, be able to squeeze out a parking place along this congested street. Please be very careful as you walk down this narrow and congested street. Watch out for the speeding traffic as you crisscross the street several times. It's very easy to get hit by a car.

During the past five years several changes have taken place along this street: more and more antique shops have opened as well as closed; many shops have gone upscale with nice displays and air-conditioning; textiles, puppets, porcelain, and furniture have increasingly become popular shop items; and shops are generally cleaner and less cluttered. While the shops along this street used to primarily specialize in ethnographic pieces from Sumatra and Kalimantan as well as Javanese and Chinese furniture, more and more shops now offer antiques, textiles, arts, and crafts from all over Indonesia. Unfortunately, this area has been targeted for "urban renewal." If and when this area will be razed, and where the shops are likely to relocate, remains uncertain.

You can easily spend two hours browsing through these shops. Many are cluttered and dusty, the perfect places to discover a wonderful treasure from Sumatra, Nias, Kalimantan, Madura, Irian Jaya, Sulawesi, Lombok, Sumba, or Java.

The quality of products in these shops are some of the best you will find anywhere in Indonesia—much better than similar shops found in Bali. As with any antique shop you encounter, be careful about buying "new" antiques which are supposed to be "old." Some shops sell fakes. For example, Chinese ceramics and porcelain purchased in Indonesia—but made locally or imported from Hong Kong and Taiwan—have been known to fool even the experts. Indeed, they have been the subject of one of the most interesting antique scandals in recent years.

If you like shopping for the types of products represented in these shops, Jl. Kebon Sirih Timur Dalam may well become your favorite shopping area in all of Indonesia. Our experience has been very positive here. We've traveled to Sumatra, Kalimantan, Sulawesi, Bali, and Irian Jaya, but we always find the best quality and selections from these areas in the shops along this street. Just when we think the quality and selections are declining here, we always discover another unique treasure that confirms the wisdom of always visiting this street when we return to Jakarta.

Some of our favorite shops along Jl. Kebon Sirih Timur Dalam include:

- **Djody:** Jl. Kebon Sirih Timur Dalam 22, Tel. 327730. A large shop with two floors filled with all types of antiques, arts, crafts, textiles, and curios. This is one of those "must visit" shops. It is reputed to be Jakarta's, if not Indonesia's, best antique shop. It also has one of the most extensive textile collections found anywhere in Indonesia. The shop also has branch shops in the major hotels in Bali (Nusa Dua and Bali Hyatt) and at the Borobudur Hotel in Jakarta. While this shop appears small from the outside, and the window displays may not be attractive, be sure to go all the way into this shop and then keep walking to your right. This is an L-shaped shop where many of the most interesting items are found in the back as well as upstairs. In fact, the upstairs has two major sections—one for textiles and the other for primitive art.

- **Budaya Antique Art Shop:** Jl. Kebon Sirih Timur Dalam 21, Tel. 740-4441. Offers a very good collection of carvings, vases, furniture, pottery, doors, jewelry, textiles, masks, Batak staffs and house gables, Nias shields, and wayang puppets. The second floor is devoted to textiles. If you are looking for a good quality Madura chest, this shop may still have a few in stock.

- **Shinta Art:** Jl. Kibon Sirih Timur Dalam 5E, Tel. 320258. Always has some unique ethnographic pieces, from baskets, stools, knives, masks, antique wayang puppets to textiles, stonecarvings, and tribal head racks. This used to be the best shop on the street until newer shops opened and now offer larger selections and better prices.

Other interesting shops to look for along Jl. Kebon Sirih Timur Dalam include **Terracotta Art and Antique, Amadeus, Bahni Art Shop, Makassar Art Shop, Soni Art Antique, Kapuas Art, Dewata Art and Curio, Nasrun, Guci Art Shop, Dornis,** and **Krisna Art and Curio.**

JL. SURABAYA AND JL. PASURUAN

Since Jl. Surabaya and Jl. Pasuruan are nearly adjacent to each other and each offers a different shopping experience, it's best to visit both streets on a single trip to the Menteng section of Jakarta. Jl. Surabaya, or **Pasar Barang Antik**, is to some people a "flea market" and to others an "antique market." Call it what you want, but it's still fun to shop here amongst the many dilapidated, worn, and cluttered stalls filled with everything from tourist kitsch to an occasional real antique. Many tour buses stop here for 30 minutes or more, just enough time to take pictures and discover a treasure at a 40 to 60% discount. For some tourists, this is the highlight of their guided Jakarta tour. Here, they finally have a chance to try out their bargaining skills, as outlined in Chapter 5. And everyone seems to have a great time trying to beat up the vendors on price, or getting beat up by the vendors instead!

Consisting of numerous stalls packed with woodcarvings, sculptures, masks, brass and silverware, porcelain, puppets, and furniture, Jl. Surabaya is a fun place to shop. Many of the antiques are "new." In fact, if you arrive early in the morning, around 8am, you can see many of the so-called "antiques" receiving a fresh coat of brown Kiwi polish. This is also the best time to strike good bargains. The vendors are very aggressive, pester you to no end, and initially quote you ridiculously high prices. The best way to shop this area is to start at one end and proceed to explore several of the stalls along the way. The gems are often tucked away under piles of junk. Whenever you seem to show an interest in an item, you will probably draw a crowd of other vendors who have similar items and want to sell you their's at a *"very cheap price."* Keep moving on to other stalls and pretend you are not too interested. Only after surveying all shops and getting a sense of prices should you begin making your selections and bargaining hard. In the meantime, say over and over to the hawkers *"Just looking right now"* or in Indonesian say *"jalan jalan,"* which roughly translates as *"just walking."* This Indonesian phrase has a magical quality about it—most hawkers indeed leave you alone when you say *"jalan jalan"*!

Our general rule of thumb for pricing goods along Jl. Surabaya is that you should get at least a 50% discount. You may end up with a 60 to 70% discount, depending on the time of day and your bargaining skills. If you pay more than 50% you are probably getting "taken."

You may want to visit Jl. Surabaya several times during your stay. The goods filling these stalls are always changing. Each visit will result in a new shopping experience. In fact, one of our major reasons for visiting Jakarta is to try our luck on Jl. Surabaya, and we do so at least twice during our visit.

Jl. Pusaruan is located just around the corner from Jl. Surabaya. If you are interested in high quality antiques, furniture, textiles, and art, you should visit one shophouse on this street—**Alex & Caecil Papadimitriou** (Jl. Pasuruan 3, Tel. 315-8748 or 314-7928). This unassuming shophouse may be difficult to find at first, because it blends into this residential street like all the other houses. You will have to go up to the rusting metal gate and knock until someone comes out to let you in. Once in, walk through the front entrance of the house which is located on your right. Once inside, you will discover a wonderful collection of antique furniture, textiles, and local oil paintings. The furniture refinishing workshop is located on the left. Caecil is the expert on textiles and furniture. Alex specializes in paintings and other collectibles.

Like the outside, the inside of this shophouse is cluttered. You may have to look two or three times through the clutter in order to discover items that appeal to you.

Long acknowledged as Indonesia's leading antique and

textile collectors, Alex and Caecil Papadimitrious' shop is for serious collectors who are looking for some unique and high quality pieces. Here you'll discover some lovely Madura wedding chests, small chests, instruments, masks, carvings, doors, wayang puppets, Dayak pig sticks, and a large assortment of Javanese, Chinese, and Madura furniture, including Minangkabau chests. Serious textile collectors consider Caecil to be one of Indonesia's leading experts on textiles. If you are looking for something special, talk to Caecil. The inside room with the textiles and oil paintings is also filled with books on Indonesia textiles. You can always learn something new about Indonesian textiles by visiting with Caecil or her assistant. If you collect fine art, Alex has an excellent collection of original oils done by Indonesia's leading artists, including Affandi.

Please keep in mind that Alex and Caecil Papadimitriou have a reputation for top quality and reliability. While they once traveled widely throughout the archipelago to collect antiques and textiles, today most of the quality pieces literally come knocking on their door because of their reputation. Indeed, during your visit, you may see some Indonesians selling their antiques here. As a result, the Papadimitrious only stock the best of the best. Therefore, don't expect to find cheap prices here nor practice your bargaining skills with expected results. In the trade, Alex and Caecil are considered collectors' collectors. They represent the best of the best. Given their reputations and business success, they really don't need new business.

JL. PANARUKAN AND JL. PEKALONGAN

Jl. Panarukan and Jl. Pekalongan are located just west of the Menteng traffic circle and adjacent to one another. A quiet and unassuming residential area, these are two of our favorite shopping streets because of two high quality shophouses located near each other.

- **Iwan Tirta:** Jl. Panarukan 25, Tel. 333122. This is the premier batik fashion boutique in Indonesia. It is to Indonesia what Jim Thompson Silk is to Thailand. This lovely shop offers fashionable women's and men's clothes designed by the creative Iwan Tirta. The shop also sells some ikat materials and garments as well as a few textiles. If you only visit one batik shop in Indonesia, make sure you visit this one. The designs are beautiful, although a bit ethnic for some foreign tastes, and the quality of the materials and clothing are excellent. While the clothes here are more expensive than in most other shops, you will be buying top quality here. The shop also has a small gallery selling batik paintings and silver. Don't leave Indonesia without at least looking at Iwan Tirta's shop. He also has a small shop in the Borobudur Hotel as well as the Grand Hotel Preanger in Bandung and the Nusa Indah Hotel and Convention Centre in Nusa Dua, Bali.

- **Nilam Gallery:** Jl. Pekalongan 16 pav., Tel. 390-0270. Another fine quality shop specializing in antique furniture (Dutch, Javanese, Chinese), old prints and maps, textiles, baskets, jewelry, ethnographic pieces, lamps, collectibles, and home decorative items. Its major strength is refinished antique furniture. If you are not an antique furniture collector, the outstanding selections here may quickly turn you into a convert. This is the type of shop Bin House would recommend for solving an antique furniture problem. If you are looking for some of the best quality antique furniture in Indonesia, Nilam Gallery may have what you're look for. The owner, Wieneke Degroot, also designs her own line of clothes using hand woven fabrics from Eastern Java which she designs. She also designs small silver gift items. While prices here may seem high compared to other shops, they are actually reasonable given the quality of their products and compared to prices abroad. Like Bin House, Nilam Gallery is for serious shoppers. And like Caecil and Alex Papadimitriou, this residential shop is very unassuming; you may think you are at the wrong address because it looks like a private residence. Don't worry; you're at the right place. Just knock on the gate or ring the bell until someone comes to let you into the shophouse which is filled with wonderful treasures.

Also nearby these two quality shops is the **Jakarta Handicraft Centre** (Jl. Pekalongan No. 12a, Tel. 338157). Several tour buses and guides stop here since it is a one-stop shopping center for handicrafts. This shop stocks a large number of woodcarvings from Bali—including large and colorful flowers, fruits, banana trees, palm trees, and cactus. You'll also find batik and ikat textiles, shirts, leather bags, purses, baskets, paintings, wayang puppets, and jewelry here. Everything here is nicely displayed and the selections are generally good but by no means in the class of the other three shops on Jl. Panarukan and Jl. Pekalongan. Indeed, you may think you're "slumming" if you visit this shop after stopping at Iwan Tirta and Nilam Gallery! Given the tour guide and tour bus orientation of this shop, you may want to first examine the fixed prices on similar items found in the handicraft sections of the Sogo Department Store (Hyatt Plaza), Sarinah Department Store (Jl. MH. Thamrin), and Pasa Raya (Blok M) before coming here. However, this shop offers many items not found at the Sarinah Department Store and Pasa Raya Department Store.

JL. TELUK BETUNG

There's really only one shop here—**Bin House**—and it's difficult to find because taxi drivers don't seem to know how to find the street. You may want to call ahead to get directions. Previously located on Jl. Panarukan, Bin House moved to this location two years ago: Jl. Teluk Betung 10, Tel. 335941 or 334948. This is a very special shop and shopping experience for individuals who are looking for top quality textiles, antiques, furniture, upholstery, fashion clothes, art, and interior decorating services. It's much more than an interior design or fabric shop. If you decide to visit this shop, you should have very specific shopping questions in mind as well as shopping problems you need solved. Bin House's real strength is its capability to find quality items and provide shopping services that you can't find elsewhere in Indonesia. The shop does not keep much inventory on hand since it is more of a consulting and customized shopping service than a shop selling products off the shelf. Interior decorators, collectors, and individuals with very special shopping needs for quality textiles, antiques, and custom-made furniture will love Bin House. If, for example, you are interested in an ikat fabric for draperies or upholstery, Bin House can design something special for you and have it woven in its factories in Solo. Indeed, one of Bin House's specialties is silk and cotton *ikat*; they also work with wool ikat. Best of all, they are one of the few places that knows how to work with Indonesian textiles. If you are interested in a special piece of furniture—either antique or new—Bin House can find it for you or have it made. If you want to have a particular garment made using batik or ikat—an evening dress for example—Bin House will arrange to have it made using the best fabrics and tailors in town. If you are interested in contemporary Indonesian artists, Bin House also manages two young artists—Teguh and Arifiem. Depending on your shopping needs, Bin House could well become your most exciting shopping discovery in Indonesia. But you will first need to know how to use this shop. It's not for the typical walk-in customer who expects to see items displayed. If you need help with an eye toward top quality, Bin House is the place for you. The person to see at Bin House is Josephine Komara.

JL. MAJAPAHIT

Jl. Majapahit is a very crowded and congested street and of limited interest to most shoppers. However, it does have three good antique and handicraft shops that may be well worth making a special trip to this area.

If you take a taxi to Jl. Majapahit, ask to be dropped at **Lee Cheong** (Jl. Majapahit No. 32, Tel. 348570). A long established and reputable shop, this is one of Jakarta's finest antique shops for Chinese ceramics, jade, and collectibles. You'll find some exquisite pieces here. The nearby **Arjuna Craft Shop** (Jl. Majapahit 16A) and **Garuda** (Jl. Majapahit 12) both have good collections of Indonesian handicrafts.

JL. PALATEHAN AND BLOK M

The Jl. Palatehan and Blok M area is located a few kilometers south of Menteng traffic circle, along Jl. Jend Sudirman, in an upscale suburban area adjacent to the Kebayoran Baru district. Here you will find three styles of shopping—department stores, shopping centers, and small shops. Like many other large shopping areas in Jakarta, this one is very crowded and congested. You can easily spend three to four hours browsing through the main department store and the many shops that line Jl. Palatehan.

We recommend starting your shopping adventure in this area at the **Pasa Raya Department Store**. Formerly known as the Sarinah Raya, this is the largest and most upscale department store in the Kebayoran Baru and Blok M areas. It's open from 9am to 7pm. Similar to the Sarinah Department Store on Jl. MH. Thamrin, it's filled with consumer goods as well as offers extensive local fashion and handicraft sections for tourists. The third floor has a good selection of batik garments and numerous Indonesian handicrafts. This is a good place to shop for some inexpensive "trip gifts."

Next to the Pasa Raya Department Store are two shopping centers—**Melawai Plaza** and **Aldiron Plaza**. Extremely crowded, noisy, and offering numerous imported and local products for middle-class shoppers, these unattractive shopping centers are of little interest to tourists. You may find the vendors along the sidewalk of greater interest. They sell everything from live rabbits to oranges and offer numerous photo opportunities!

The best shopping in this area is just around the corner from the department and shopping centers—Jl. Palatehan. While this area has declined in recent years, especially since Oet's Fine Art Gallery moved to Jl. Kemang Raya, this short one block street has soom excellent shops on both sides of the street. Here you will discover a few art galleries and handicraft shops. **Hadiprana Galleries** (Jl. Palatehan I/38, Blok K-5, Tel. 722-1023) is an excellent art gallery (first and second floors) that includes much more than just paintings. You will find both oil and batik paintings, including those by Ardiyanto, one of Jogjakarta's famous batik artists. Be sure to explore all floors of this shop. You'll find some excellent quality Balinese carvings (ducks and birds), batik clothing, greeting cards, stuffed toys, children's clothes, and jewelry here. Don't forget to walk up to the third floor for a real shopping treat. This level has a wonderful selection of ikat and batik fabrics which are organized by colors. It includes antique textiles from Sumba, Flores, Sulawesi, and Bali. Unfortunately, most of the ready-made clothes are for small sizes; custom-made garments will take about one week for completion—which may be longer than you can wait.

You will also find two other small art galleries along this street: **Fine Arts Gallery** and **Amrus' Original**. The **Fine Arts Gallery** (Jl. Palatehan I/32-33) has changing exhibits of Indonesian and European artists.

Pigura (Jl. Palatehan I/41) is a real discovery if you are looking for furniture, textiles, and ethnographic pieces. This large shop has an extensive collection of furniture on the second floor, including Madura, Batak, and Minangkabau chests. The downstairs area is filled with Balinese carvings, silver, bags, ivory, masks, baskets, bells, antique textiles, kris, Javanese lacquer. At the very back of the shop you will find one room devoted to ethnographic pieces, including many nice carvings.

Most of the remaining shops along Jl. Palatehan specialize in handicrafts, textiles, and antiques. **Gramedia Art Gallery** has a good selection of paintings, Balinese carvings, and ethnographic pieces from the Batak and Asmat. **Pura Art Shop** also has Balinese carvings along with silver, lacquerware, wayang puppets, lamps, and kites. **Mini Antiques** specializes in new furniture and antique clocks.

KEMANG TIMUR (FORMERLY JL. KEMANG BANGKA)

Three adjacent streets in the Kebayoran Baru area, Jl. Bangka, Jl. Kemang Raya, and Jl. Timur, have become one of the newest and most interesting shopping areas in Jakarta. However, this area may be somewhat confusing because of street name changes. Drivers seem to get lost here. Kemang Bangka, for example, is now known as Kemang Timur. Since 1986 this area has seen the opening of Indonesia's premier art gallery—**Duta Fine Arts Gallery**—and the opening of several small arts, antiques, and handicrafts shops. We recommend starting your shopping adventure in this area at the art gallery.

This area is well worth visiting just to see the outstanding **Duta Fine Arts Gallery** (Jl. Kemang Utara 55A, Tel. 799-0226). Opened in October 1986, this spacious gallery is housed in a series of beautiful white stucco, red tiled Spanish-style buildings. Representing nearly 100 artists, the gallery also has special monthly exhibits. You will find a wonderful selection of both traditional and modern oil paintings as well as sculptures on display here. The gallery represents only the best of Indonesian artists. Of all the art galleries we have visited in Southeast Asia, this one remains our favorite for both ambience and quality art.

Just down the street is one of Jakarta's best art galleries. **Ikawati Gallery** (Jl. Kemang Raya 5), formerly known as Oet's Fine Arts Gallery on Jl. Palatehan, is a large gallery representing many of Indonesia's top artists. You'll find an excellent selection of oil paintings, water colors, and sculptures here.

Just down the street and around the corner is the **Rattan House** (Jl. Bangka Raya), a large and interesting shop selling rattan furniture. This is a popular place with expatriates.

Nearby Jl. Kemang Timur (Kemang Bangka) has nearly 40 art, antique, ethnographic, and handicraft shops worth visiting. We especially like **Sulewesi Arts and Antiques**, **Morrys' Art**, and **Gusnel Art Shop** (Jl. Kemang Timur I/17), three shops adjacent to each other that offer good selections of ethnographic arts and antiques such as Asmat war shields, antique beads, textiles, Dayak masks, silver, and bows and arrows. These shops also carry Madura chests, kris, pots, baskets, wayang puppets, and porcelain. Also look for **Empress, Prabanam, Denas Art and Curio,** and **Kodannes**. Further down this street around Jl. Kemang Timur I/51 you will find seven shops offering a wide selection of arts and crafts. **Burung Burung Terbang**, for example, is a nice shop offering a unique selection of stuffed toys and Christmas decorations. **Kodena Art Shop** specializes in furniture and masks. If your travel plans do not include visiting Bali, stop at **Cer Aki** which has a large selection of Balinese woodcarvings. **Fifty One Art Shop** offers furniture (chests), lamps, instruments, carvings, and ethnographic pieces. **Bangka Art Shop** also offers similar items.

OLD BOGOR ROAD (JL. CIPUTAT RAYA)

Old Bogor Road, also known as Jl. Ciputat Raya in the Pondok Labu area, is a shopper's paradise for both old and new furniture as well as many ethnographic and collectible antique pieces. In fact, this area is perhaps Indonesia's best kept shopping secret. It's a popular area with expatriates who come here to furnish their homes with antique furniture. Once you discover this area, you may forgo shopping in other parts of Jakarta as well as Bali!

Located on the south side of Jakarta, along a narrow one kilometer stretch of Jl. Ciputat Raya, you'll find over 50 shops offering some of finest selections of furniture found anywhere in Indonesia. In fact, many of the shops selling furniture elsewhere in Jakarta buy wholesale from these shops. Therefore, you should be able to realize some major savings on furniture by buying directly from the shops in this area.

Few tourists ever come here because it is off the normal tour routes and beaten tourist paths. Expatriates who live nearby as well as dealers and a few independent travelers have long known about this area. Best of all, during the past five years the area has blossomed as several new shops and workshops have opened to offer even better selections.

Since few tourists ever visit this area, you can expect to get good prices here, similar to those received by expatriates and dealers. If you are really interested in furniture, you may want to plan to spend the day shopping along Old Bogor Road area or perhaps combine a visit here with shopping in the Jl. Kemang Bangka area. It may be most convenient to rent a car and driver for the day since it's difficult to get a taxi once you're here (it can take a half hour to flag down a taxi). The problem with this area is the amount of time it takes to get here as well as the traffic situation. Given the narrow two-lane road that serves this major traffic artery, traffic is bad all day long, but especially from 6-8:30am and 3-7:30pm. The road is a constant traffic jam. If you come here from one of the major hotels near Menteng traffic circle, expect to spend at least one hour before arriving at the first shop along this road, which should be **Gallery 59**, on your left, at Jl. Ciputat Raya 22.

But the traffic and time involved in getting here is justly rewarded with many excellent shops and buys you'll discover as you shop both sides of this road. Keep in mind that most of the shops in this area are also workshops. Many shops primarily sell and restore antique furniture—chests, beds, benches, tables, chairs, doors, carved window and wall panels, and even bird cages. Much of this furniture is from the island of Madura. But you will also find furniture from Java and Bali. Other shops primarily make new furniture. And some shops sell both old and new furniture. If you are interested in having furniture custom-made, Old Bogor Road is the place to visit. All you need to do is bring your plans, pictures, and ideas.

Given the large number of shops as well as the similar items offered, Old Bogor Road is a good place to do comparative shopping. You may want to initially spend two hours just browsing from one shop to another until you have a good idea of what's available and pricing practices. Then return to those shops that particularly stood out from the rest. If you want custom work done, you may need to spend more than a day shopping along Old Bogor Road.

While all the shops offer similar items, each shop tends to specialize in certain items. Most shops include "Arts" or "Curios" in their name, but they are primarily furniture shops which may include a few textiles and ethnographic pieces amongst all the furniture. Many shops are dusty and cluttered, with the definite look of a traditional antique shop. Others have gone upscale with large air-conditioned display rooms. All of the shops are experienced at packing and shipping abroad, which they do regularly for the many dealers visiting this area.

Among the many shops found in this area, nine in particular stand out as special. These are good places from which to orient yourself to many other shops along this road:

- **Gallery 59**: Jl. Ciputat Raya 22, Tel. 749-2572, Fax 749-2572. This is unquestionably the best antique and furniture shop along Old Bogor Road. It's the first shop you come to on your left. It's filled with four floors of tables, chairs, desks, chests, benches, doors, lamps, mirrors, and carvings. This is the type of shop that appeals to serious collectors and designers. Good quality and a great place to start your Old Bogor Road adventure. You can see and touch quality here.

- **Gallery 50-B**: Jl. Ciputat Raya 50-B, Tel. 749-2850 or Fax 380-9595. One of the best shops for ethnographic art in all of Indonesia. Operated by the Kesenian Group, which also runs Tribal at the Borobudur Hotel and P.T. Pelangi (jewelry), this shop includes three floors of good quality ethnographic art. The collection here represents only part of a much more extensive collection which the owner, an American expatriate, has collected during the past 25 years. The owner has been a major force in shaping, and perhaps cornering, much of the Indonesian antique market. The shop claims to have the largest collection of antiques and ethnographic art in all of Indonesia. Maybe, maybe not. We know they have lots of overhead given their far-flung antique empire! They do offer an impressive collection fit for serious collectors. Prices also are very expensive.

- **Anang's Art Shop:** Jl. Ciputat Raya 36E, Tel. 749-2776. Less oriented toward furniture, this shop has some very unique ethnographic pieces you will not find elsewhere in Jakarta or even in Indonesia. Look for jewelry, silver, carved doors, containers, and textiles here. Much less expensive and friendlier than the brother's shop (Anang's) in Kuta Beach, Bali.

- **Yus Madura Arts Shop:** Good selection of wood panels as well as Madura chests, benches, beds, doors, tables, and chairs.

- **Madura Art Shop:** A large shop offering Madura chests, beds, panels, doors, tables, chairs, wedding chests, cabinets, and bird cages.

- **Lampung Art Shop:** Includes ethnographic pieces (Batak and Nias carvings) and Lampung textiles amongst its chests, tables, chairs, beds, lamps, vases, and porcelain.

- **Nina Art and Curio:** A large shop offering stone carvings, tables, chairs, cabinets, Madura chests, carved ethnographic doors, and vases.

- **Indonesia Putra Art and Curio:** One of the few air-conditioned shops with nice displays. Look for Batak bowls and carvings, tables, chairs, cabinets, porcelain, beads, kris, textiles, Toraja Land (Sulawesi) doors, Madura furniture, carved panels, silver, jewelry, lacquerware, and even canons! Be sure to go upstairs where you will find a nice collection of Batak panels and vases.

- **Gondola:** Another air-conditioned shop with nice displays. This is one of the best shops in the area in terms of selections. Look for canons, vases, cabinets, large carved house and wall panels, benches, tables, chairs, Madura chests, and textile hangers. The work-shop produces new furniture and carved panels using old motifs.

Other good shops to look for are **Citra**, **Ujang**, and **Revin**. You'll encounter a very large range of traditional Javanese and Madurese furniture in the many shops lining this busy road. Be very careful going back and forth across this very busy road. It can be very dangerous stepping out in front of speeding cars, buses, and trucks. The problem with this area is that you never really know where to begin or end. We normally start walking down one side of the road, beginning at **Gallery 59** (Jl. Ciputat Raya 22) and go all the way to **Anang's Art Shop** (Jl. Ciputat Raya 36E), which is on the other side of the road, and then walk back to Gallery 59. We're usually exhausted by the time we get to Anang's. Indeed, this is a very long walk, about 2-3 kilometers, and takes two to four hours. You'll find a small air-conditioned shopping center on the left hand side, near **Gallery 50-B**, where you can stop for a cold drink or a bite to eat.

JL. PASAR BARU

Jl. Pasar Baru is another major shopping area in Jakarta. However, we have yet to find anything in this highly congested area to warrant a special trip here. Selections are both limited and disappointing. If you do visit here, look for the **Irian Art and Gift Shop** (Jl. Pasar Baru 16A) for handicrafts and three department stores—**Ginza**, **Matahari**, **Micky Mouse**, and **Levi's**. You will also find some outlet shops here selling sports wear manufactured in Bandung.

DEPARTMENT STORES

Jakarta has a few department stores worth visiting. The major ones of interest to international travelers are **Sarinah Depart-ment Store** (on Jl. MH. Thamrin, just north of the Menteng traffic circle and adjacent to the Sari Pacific Hotel) and **Sogo Department Store** (in the Plaza Indonesia at Menteng traffic circle). These two popular department stores cater to both locals and tourists. The first two floors of **Sarinah Department Store** are filled with popular consumer goods, including cosmetics and clothes. The third floor is devoted to handicrafts; the fourth floor is reserved for batik clothes and fabrics. Indeed, this department store offers one of the largest selections of such products conveniently displayed in different sections. You'll find Balinese woodcarvings, pottery, textiles, bags, baskets, boxes, pillow covers, *ikat*, Asmat carvings and shields, lacquerware, bronze figures, puppets, purses, furniture, paintings, instruments, mats, and bird cages here. If you are interested in such garments and handicrafts, need to quickly purchase some "trip gifts," or wish to know the going fixed prices on items for comparative shopping purposes, we recommend visiting this department store early in your visit to Jakarta. The selections and quality are good and prices are fixed. Even Iwan Tirta has a small boutique section on the fourth floor where you can purchase batik shirts. **Sogo Department Store** is more upscale than Sarinah and a more pleasant area to visit because of all the other surrounding shops and restaurants. You may be most interested in visiting the antique, art, and handicraft section on the third floor of Sogo. It has similar selections to those found at Sarinah.

The **Pasa Raya Department Store**, previously known as the Sarinah Jaya, in Blok M (Jl. Iskandarsyak II/2, next to the Melawai Plaza and Aldiron Plaza) is a relatively new department store rebuilt in a phenomenal eight months on the ashes of a previous department store. It offers similar products as the Sarinah Department Store on Jl. MH. Thamrin. For example, you'll find a wide selection of batik garments and handicrafts on the third floor. If you are in the Kebayoran Baru and Blok M areas—especially after walking nearby Jl. Palatehan and Jl. Kemang Bangka—this air-conditioned department store is a nice place to stop for shopping as well as for fast food (food court on the lower level).

The **Keris Gallery** (Jl. H.O.S. Cokroaminoto) is another department store also worth visiting for batik garments, batik and ikat materials, and handicrafts. It also has a small branch shop in the Grand Hyatt Hotel and Shopping Plaza. While the first floor is filled with imported cosmetics, the second floor, called the "Indonesian Handicraft Centre," is primarily devoted to Indonesian products. Previously the Batik Keris brand of batik garments were available in the boutique section of the Sarinah Department Store. But no longer. During the past two years Batik Keris established their own department stores offering a wide selection of batik and ikat garments, materials, and handicrafts. The Indonesian Handicraft Centre has one of the best selections of batik and ikat fabrics, available by the meter, and clothes in Jakarta. This section also has someone demonstrating the hand drawn batik (*tulis*), complete with hot wax and the drawing instrument (*canting*). However, men who take a large size will have difficulty finding shirts here that fit. The store primarily stocks Batik Keris shirts in small and medium sizes; you'll find very few in sizes 17 and 18—the local equivalent to a large. Although not as big as the other department stores, the handicraft section does have a good selection of wayang puppets, pottery, paintings, carvings, lamps, leather bags, and brass items. You will also find a few other department stores in Jakarta. One of the largest is the **Golden Truly Supermarket** (Jl. Palatehan 68, Jl. MH. Thamrin 9, Jl. Suryo Pranoto 18a, and Jl. H. Samanhudi 14-16). Others include **Ginza** (Jl. Pasar Baru 26), **Matahari** (Jl. Pasar Baru 52-56, J. H. Samanhudi 8, Jl. Melawai III/24), **Micky Mouse** (Jl. Pasar Baru 110), **Nikko** (Gaja Mada Plaza), **Renee** (Ratu Plaza), **Levi's** (Jl. Pasar Baru 15A), and **Hero**. These department stores primarily cater to Jakarta's growing middle class with a large range of consumer and imported goods. You may find few things of interest in these stores.

SHOPPING CENTERS

Jakarta has several shopping centers that are especially popular with local shoppers. We hesitate to recommend any of them since we have yet to find many shops of interest to international shoppers. They are more a cultural experience for observing middle class Jakartians, especially young people, than worthwhile shopping experiences.

The major air-conditioned shopping centers in Jakarta include **Plaza Indonesia** (see previous section on hotel shopping arcades), **Pondok Indah Mall** (in Pondok Indah town), **Ratu Plaza** (Jl. Jendral Sudirman, Senayan) and **Gajah Mada Plaza** (Jl. Gajah Mada 19-26, Kota). Ratu Plaza has the largest concentration of name brand shops. Gajah Mada Plaza has the largest concentration of jewelry shops in Indonesia, although the styles and designs are geared more toward the local market than for international tastes. Other shopping centers, such as **Aldiron Plaza** and **Melawa Plaza** in Blok M of Kebayoran Baru, and **Duta Merlin Shopping Centre** (Jl. Gajah Mada), **Glodok Plaza** (Chinatown), **Hayam Wuruk Plaza**, and **Pusat Perbelanjaan Pasar Baru** in Kota, are more appropriate for local residents in search of ready-made clothes, household goods, appliances, records, and restaurants. You may want to skip most of these shopping centers.

If you want to visit a couple of shopping centers, we only recommend **Ratu Plaza** and **Gajah Mada Plaza**. **Ratu Plaza** is Jakarta's newest and most upscale shopping center. This five-story air-conditioned shopping plaza comes complete with fountains, a movie theater, and a department store (**Matahari**

Department Store). Here you will find many name brand clothing and leather products available in such shops and boutiques as **Benetton**, **Bally**, **Lanvin**, **Etienne Aigner**, **Esprit**, **Cartier**, and **Charles Jourdan**. You'll also find jewelry stores (**Dynasty Collection**, **Monet**, **Jewel DeVille**) along with fabric, optical, and book, leather, tailor, men's fashion, children's, home furnishings, and greeting card (**Hallmark**) shops here. **Batik Keris** has a clothes and handicraft store in this plaza. International fast food restaurants are well represented: Churches' Texas Fried Chicken, Pizza Hut, Diary Queen.

Gajah Mada Plaza and the adjacent **Gajah Mada Shopping Centre** (between the Duta Merlin Shopping Centre and Gajah Mada Plaza) is another multi-level air-conditioned shopping mall especially popular with local residents. Anchored by a **Nikko Department Store**, Gajah Mada Plaza is filled with small shops selling everything from furniture, clothes, shoes, and leather bags to the latest imported electronic goods. This plaza is famous for its many jewelry stores—the largest concentration found anywhere in Jakarta. With the exception of the nice designs found at **Crown Jewellery** (2nd level), most of the jewelry stores appeal to locals.

ANCOL ART CENTER

Another place you may want to visit is the **Ancol Art Center** which is adjacent to the Jaya Ancol Dreamland recreational center in the northeast section of the city. Here you can stroll in the pleasant tropical surroundings viewing a potpourri of small shops and open-air stalls with craftsmen and artists producing and displaying their arts and crafts. While somewhat "touristy," you will find many worthwhile items you may have difficulty finding elsewhere. Several well-noted painters display their unique creations here. Many will do portraits while you wait. One shop (**Pondok Primtif**) sells a limited selection of Asmat arts and crafts, items which are often difficult to find elsewhere, along with Balinese carvings and Madura wedding chests. **Batik Samar** has a boutique and handicraft shop here. Other shops such as **Sastra Leathercraft** offer unique leather goods, and several shops produce interesting furniture, large woodcarvings, and stone sculptures.

BEAUTIFUL INDONESIA IN MINIATURE

Indonesia's cultural theme park—Beautiful Indonesia in Miniature (Taman Mini Indonesia Indah)—also offers some limited shopping opportunities. Located southeast of the city on the road toward Bogor, it takes approximately 45 minutes to get here from Menteng traffic center. Expect to spend at least a half day here. And its well worth the trip since you will learn a great deal about the cultures and lifestyles of the many peoples that define Indonesia's 27 provinces. You will also find a small two-level shopping center near the entrance to the park. It's filled with many handicraft shops offering products from the different provinces. While it's not worth making a special trip here just to shop, be sure to stop here to browse through the shops when visiting this park.

QUALITY SHOPPING

Shops in Jakarta tend to offer the best quality products in Indonesia. Some of our favorite shops for quality products include the following, most of which were identified in our earlier discussion of shopping areas.

BATIK AND IKAT CLOTHES/FABRICS

- **Bin House:** Jl. Teluk Betung 10 (Tel. 335941). An exclusive fashion and home decorative consultant specializing in silk, cotton, and wool ikat materials. Produces some of the most creative designs based upon traditional weaving techniques. Also does custom weaving to customers' color and design preferences. A one-of-a-kind place for acquiring beautifully designed fine silk materials (scarfs and clothes) and for ikat upholstery materials or having special garments designed and made. Knows how to work with Indonesian ikat textiles for other cultural settings. Excellent source for corporations, interior designers, and individuals with special needs. A top quality shop that is taking traditional Indonesian textiles into new directions. This is not a typical retail outlet. You'll need to communicate your needs to the personnel who have a limited number of examples in the shop. If she is available, see the owner, Josephine Komara, who is responsible for the exciting work going on here. An exclusive shop which appeals to the most discriminating shoppers. Popular with discriminating Japanese buyers, expatriates, and international designers. Maintains two retail outlets on the island of Bali (**Plaza Bali**, just five minutes from the airport, and the airport departure lounge).

- **Iwan Tirta:** Main shop at Jl. Panarukan 25 pav. (Tel. 333122) and a small shop in the shopping arcade of the Borobudur Inter-Continental Hotel. Also has a small boutique on the fourth floor of the Sarinah Department Store on Jl. MH. Thamin. The main shop also goes under the name of **PT Ramacraft**. Iwan Tirta used to be Indonesia's most famous batik fashion designer who hob-knobs with the rich and famous. He has trained some of Indonesia's young and creative designers who now have their own shops and are taking Indonesian textiles in new directions. Offers excellent quality batik garments in the latest traditional styles. However, his current work tends to be somewhat touristy and too ethnic for many Western shoppers. We increasingly have difficulty finding things here that integrate well with our home and warerobes. Iwan Tirta also is developing a growing line of ikat materials and garments as well as offers some antique textiles, jewelry, batik paintings, and a line of exquisitely designed silver.

- **Sarinah Department Store:** Jl. MH. Thamrin (adjacent to Sari Pacific Hotel). Fourth floor is devoted to batik garments and materials—one of the largest selections in Jakarta. Offers a good range of batik, from inexpensive to expensive. Includes a small Iwan Tirta boutique. Most garments are average quality and reasonably priced. Tourists requiring large size garments should be able to find more choices here than in most other stores. A good place to do last minute gift buying.

- **Keris Gallery:** Jl. H.O.S. Cokroaminoto. This relatively new department store is owned by one of Indonesia's largest batik manufacturers—Keris Batik—based in Solo. The second floor and its "Indonesian Handicraft Centre" is largely devoted to batik garments and materials (yardage) as well as handicrafts. Offers a limited selection of "Large" sized garments; many designs are very traditional and colors tend to be muted. Medium range quality and prices on batik garments. Also has a shop on the first floor of the Plaza Indonesia.

- **Other batik shops:** You'll discover several other shops throughout Jakarta offering batik material and ready-made garments. Among these are **Berdikari** (Jl. Mesjid Pal VII, Pal Merah Barat, Tel. 5482814); **Danar Hadi**

(Jl. Raden Saleh 1A; Jl. Melawai Raya 70; and 6 Jl. Panglima Polim III); **Yamarco** (Jl. Pasuruan 16, Tel. 3802210); **Hajadi** (Jl. Palmerah Utara 46, Tel. 5480584); **Batik Mira** (J. MPR Raya 22, Tel. 761138); **Semar** (Jl. Tomang Raya 54; Jl. Hang Lekir II 23; Plaza Indonesia, and Soekarno-Hatta International Airport); **Sidamukti** (Jl. Prof. Dr. Sahardjo 311, Tel. 8291271); **Batik Srikandi** (Jl. Melawai VI, 6A Blok M, Tel. 736604; Hias Rias Market; and Jl. Cikini Raya); and **Winotosastro** (1 Jl. Wijaya IX, Flat 4, Tel. 770370). The Batik Keris brand garments are available in several department stores and shops.

TEXTILES

- **Djody:** Jl. Kebon Sirih Timur Dalam 22 (Tel. 327730). This is one of Indonesia's oldest and most reputable antique shops. The second floor of this expansive shop is filled with new and old textiles collected by Mrs. Djody from throughout Indonesia. She is a leading expert on Indonesian textiles. You'll have a wonderful time exploring the quality traditional ikat textiles represented here. If you find something you like, buy it now because the quality found here is quickly disappearing.

- **Caecil Papadimitriou:** Located in a private residence turned shophouse on Jl. Pasuruan 3 (Tel. 315-8748 or 314-7928), just around the corner from the famous Jl. Surabaya "antique market." One of Indonesia's leading experts on traditional ikat textiles. Knows and collects only the very best quality. While this shophouse may appear to be primarily an antique and furniture shop, look carefully as you enter the main house. You'll find a few textiles on display but most are folded in a cabinet. The shophouse also has an excellent library of books on Indonesian textiles.

- **Hadiprana Galleries:** Jl. Palatehan I/38, Blok K-5, Kebayoran Baru (Tel. 722-1023). This is actually a 3 in 1 shop, and it's not the most convenient place to find. Each floor goes by a different name, but for all practical purposes, let's just call this Hadiprana Galleries. Otherwise you'll have difficulty finding the textiles which are confined to the third floor. The first two floors are called **Hadiprana Galleries** which includes a nice collection of contemporary and Balinese paintings, arts, wood carvings, and handicrafts. The second floor is shared by **Puri Mira Boutique**, which is a small boutique filled with clothes for babies, teenagers, men, and women, as well as stuffed toys and Christmas decorations. The third floor goes by the name of **Taman Batik**. Here is where you will find the textiles. This section offers an excellent collection of batik fabrics, silk batik scarfs, wall hangings, and contemporary and antique ikat materials which are nicely displayed. Excellent quality and displays of special appeal to fashion and interior designers as well as individuals looking for something special for the home or wardrobe. Only place in Indonesia where ikat textiles are organized by colors on racks! Antique textiles are from Sumba, Tana Toraja, Flores, Borneo, and Bali. Also includes a small collection of modern and antique jewelry.

- **Jl. Kebon Sirih Timur Dalam shops:** More and more shops along this street have begun offering old and new textiles—both batik and ikat. However, be sure you know your textiles before buying since some may not be as old as they are supposed to be. In addition to Djody, some of the best shops for textiles include **Shinta Art** (#5, Tel. 320358), **Budaya Antique Art Shop** (#21, Tel. 320881), **Amadeus** (#5D, Tel. 324664), **Guci Art and Curio** (#158, Tel. 320274), and **Krisna Art and Curio** (#7A).

ETHNOGRAPHIC ARTS AND CRAFTS

- **Tribal:** Located on the second floor of the Borobudur Inter-Continental Hotel shopping arcade (#6, Tel. 370108, ext. 76023). One of the most unique shops for quality ethnographic arts and crafts. This is always one of our first stops in Jakarta and we usually find some exquisite items here. Has quickly become one of our favorite shops in Indonesia. Specializes in small items, especially jewelry, beads, carvings, and textiles from the outer islands. Owned and operated by the Kesenian Group (P.D. Pelangi Indonesian Opal and Jewelry Center). Expensive but excellent quality.

- **Gallery 50-B:** Jl. Ciputat Raya 50-B, Tel. 749-2850 or Fax 62-21-380-9595. Claims to be the largest and best shop for Indonesian ethnographic art. Operated by the Kesenian Group (Tribal, P.T. Pelangi, Jakarta Pearl Center), this shop includes three floors of good quality ethnographic art displayed in a rather cluttered manner. You may find some treasures here. Ask about other items they may have on display elsewhere. During the first five years the Kesenian Group has undergone several marketing changes, opening and closing galleries, and operating shows, and displaying their collection in restaurants and office buildings. We don't know where they are headed next. In the meantime, it's probably best to keep in contact with this group through the Tribal shop at the Borobudur Hotel. Starting there will save you a great deal of time and hassle of having to fight the traffic to get to this Old Bogor Road shop. Can be very expensive.

- **Djody:** Jl. Kebon Sirih Timur Dalam #22 (Tel. 327730). One of the largest shops for ethnographic arts and crafts. If you go in the main entrance, make sure you go all the way into the shop—keep to your left and go upstairs—since it appears small from the outside. Carries everything from large pieces of furniture to Batak carved doors, Dayak medicine man boxes, and Asmat war shields, and textiles. Has other more expensive shops in the Borobudur Inter-Continental Hotel as well as the Nusa Dua Hotel and Bali Hyatt Hotel in Bali.

- **Shinta Art:** Jl. Kebon Sirih Timur Dalam #5 (Tel. 320258). Usually has excellent quality and unique carved pieces as well as textiles from all over Indonesia. Good place for collectors. While recent visits have been disappointing, this may be a temporary supply situation.

- **Budaya Antique Art Shop:** Jl. Kebon Sirih Timur Dalam #21 (Tel. 320881). Excellent quality and selections carvings, furniture, doors, jewelry, Batak textiles, Madura chests, Nias war shields, and carved Batak staffs.

- **Anang's Art Shop:** Jl. Ciputat Raya 36E (Old Bogor Road, Tel. 749-2776). Includes many unique ethnographic pieces from the eastern islands (Sumba, Flores, Timor) as well as from Sumatra, Kalimantan, and

Sulawesi. Look for carvings, jewelry, silver, doors, and textiles.

- **Indonesia Putra Art and Curio:** Jl. Ciputat Raya (Old Bogor Road) #86. Good selection of nicely displayed bowls, beads, textiles, carvings, and Tana Toraja doors. Be sure to go upstairs where you will find several Batak house panels.

- **Jl. Kebon Sirih Timur Dalam shops:** This street has Jakarta's largest concentration of ethnographic shops. In addition to several already identified as special, you'll discover many other shops along this street that will yield numerous treasures from Sumatra, Nias, Kalimantan, Sulawesi, Timor, Lombok, and Irian Jaya. Occasionally you'll come across a rare piece from Sumba or Flores. Most shops tend to be more oriented toward ethnographic pieces and antiques from Sumatra and Kalimantan than from eastern Indonesia—the area best represented in the shops of Bali.

- **Jl. Kemang Timur shops:** Three shops (**Sulewesi Arts and Antiques, Morrys' Art**, and **Gusnel Art Shop**) located at Jl. Kemang Timur I/17 offer a wide assortment of ethnographic arts and crafts from Sumatra, Kalimantan, Sulawesi, and Irian Jaya: antique beads, textiles, baskets, masks, war shields, carvings, bows and arrows, and musical instruments.

- **Jl. Palatehan shops:** Blok M/Kebayoran Baru. Several arts and crafts shops—**Gramedia Art Gallery, Pigura**, and **Urip Store**—also carry a limited range of textiles and ethnographic pieces (Asmat carvings, silver, furniture, baskets, Lombok boxes, musical instruments) from Sumatra, Lombok, and Irian Jaya.

JEWELRY

- **Linda Spiro:** Borobudur Inter-Continental Hotel shopping arcade (2nd floor). Excellent quality and uniquely designed jewelry. Specializes in large necklaces, bracelets, and rings using precious and semi-precious stones.

- **Joyce Spiro:** Sari Pacific Hotel (Tel. 323707, ext. 1911). Offers a unique collection of contemporary designs in gold and silver using many ethnographic motifs.

- **F. Spiro Jewellers:** Jakarta Hilton Hotel (Tel. 587995, ext. 9019) and the Hyatt Aryaduta Hotel (Tel. 376008, ext. 88188). Another Spiro family shop offering unique ethnographic designs in gold and silver.

- **Jay's Jewelry:** Mandarin Oriental Hotel (Tel. 321307, ext. 1383). This is actually a Joyce Spiro jewelry store under a different name. Offers similar selections as found in the Sari Pacific Hotel shop—ethnographic designs in gold and silver—as well as some lovely neckpieces using pearls.

- **Gajah Mada Plaza jewelry shops:** Jl. Gajah Mada 19-26, Kota. This shopping center houses Indonesia's largest number of jewelry shops under one roof. Most of the shops are oriented toward local consumers rather than international travelers. However, you may find a few shops offering unique designs and excellent quality, such as **Crown Jewellery** (2nd level).

ANTIQUES

- **Alex and Caecil Papadimitriou:** Jl. Pasuruan #3 (Tel. 315-8748 or 314-7928), near Jl. Surabaya. One of Indonesia's most famous and reputable antique dealers. Offers a wide range of quality antique furniture as well as textiles and paintings.

- **Lee Cheong:** Jl. Majapahit 12. Indonesia's best shop for Chinese antiques, especially jade, ceramics, jewelry, and some furniture. If you appreciate Chinese antiques, this is a "must visit" shop.

- **Nilam Gallery:** 16 pav., Jl. Pekalongan (Tel. 390-0270). A small shophouse offering some of the finest quality antique furniture in Indonesia. Specializes in antique Dutch, Javanese, Chinese, and Madura furniture. Also includes many collectibles, including textiles, jewelry, prints, maps, baskets, dishes, lamps, and ethnographic pieces. Designs own line of clothes.

- **Gallery 59:** Jl. Ciputat Raya 22 (Tel. 749-2572, Fax 62-21-749-2572). This is the best antique and furniture shop found along Old Bogor Road, a trip you will want to set aside for one day in order to visit this and several adjacent shops stretching along with 2+ kilometer section of road. It's the first shop you come to on your left. You'll find four floors of excellent quality tables, chairs, desks, chests, benches, doors, lamps, mirrors, and carvings. Good prices and very reliable. Serious collectors and designers frequent this shop.

- **Bin House:** Jl. Teluk Betung 10 (Tel. 335941). Offers custom services for those who have special needs. If, for example, you are looking for a particular piece of antique furniture, Bin House should be able to find the best of the best for you. Chances are they will find it at the Nilam Gallery or in certain shops along Old Bogor Road.

- **Stalls along Jl. Surabaya:** Menteng area. This is more of a "flea market" for antique reproductions, arts, and crafts than for real antiques. However, occasionally a real antique actually appears amongst the stalls!

FURNITURE

- **Alex and Caecil Padimitriou:** see Antiques

- **Gallery 59:** see Antiques

- **Nilam Gallery:** 16 pav., Jl. Pekalongan (Tel. 390-0270). Excellent quality antique Dutch, Javanese, Chinese, and Madura furniture.

- **Gondola:** Jl. Ciputat Raya (Old Bogor Road) #87. Offers some antique furniture. Makes new furniture and house panels using old motifs.

- **Pigura:** Jl. Palatehan I/41 (Tel. 711143). Second floor is filled with a wide range of furniture, including Minangkabau chests.

- **Old Bogor Road shops:** Jl. Ciputat Raya. You'll discover numerous shops and workshops along this road that offer antique furniture—both finished and unfinished—as well as new furniture. Much of the new furniture is made-to-order from old motifs. If you are looking for antique furniture or need custom-made furniture, the shops along Old Bogor Road are the best places to shop in Indonesia.

- **Jl. Kebon Sirih Timur Dalam shops:** Numerous shops along this street offer a wide range of furniture. Most of it is antique Javanese, Chinese, and Madura furniture. You'll even find a few antique Minangkabau chests! Some of the best shops include **Budaya Antique Art Shop** (#26) and **Djody** (#22).

FINE ART

- **Duta Fine Art Gallery:** Jl. Bangka I/55A Kemang (Tel. 799-0226). Perhaps Indonesia's top art gallery. Offers oil paintings and sculptures produced by Indonesia's top artists. Nice gallery housed in a pleasant Spanish hacienda setting.

- **Ikawati Gallery:** Jl. Kemang Raya 50. Located near Duta Fine Art Gallery. Formerly known as Oet's Fine Arts Gallery on Jl. Palatehan, this is one of Indonesia's largest and most reputable galleries. Displays the works of Indonesia's top artists. Includes prints, oils, watercolors, and sculptures, both framed and unframed.

- **Hadiprana Galleries:** Jl. Palatehan I/38, Blok K-5, Kebayoran Baru (Tel. 722-1023). An eclectic gallery displaying everything from contemporary and Balinese paintings and wall hangings by Ardiyanto and Karna to woodcarvings, jewelry, handprinted greeting cards, and lampshades. Be sure to explore the second and third floors where you will find additional paintings, batik, ikat, and even ready-made fashionwear for children.

- **Bentara Budaya:** Located on Jl. Palmerah, across from the main Kompas Foundation building. Includes nearly 400 paintings of both noted and aspiring artists.

- **Alex & Caecil Papadimitriou:** Jl. Pasuruan #3 (Tel. 315-8748 or 314-7928). Alex Papadimitriou is a major collector of works produced by Indonesia's leading artists. Many of these paintings are on display in this shop.

- **Santi Fine Arts Gallery:** Duta Merlin Building (Pusat Pertokoan Duta Merlin) #012, Jl. Gajah Mada #3-5

(Tel. 361411). Owner is one of Indonesia's expert art dealers. Offers paintings produced by Indonesia's leading artists.

- **Ancol Art Market (Pasar Seni) shops:** Located at the Ancol Dreamland Complex in northeast Jakarta. A large open-air market with numerous small shops operated by noted as well as aspiring artists selling oils and watercolors. Some artists will do portraits while you wait. A good place to discover some unique styles as well as meet the artists. Prices range from inexpensive to expensive.

ARTS AND CRAFTS

- **Sarinah Department Store:** Located along Jl. MH. Thamrin, just north of Menteng traffic circle and adjacent to the Sari Pacific Hotel. Go to the third floor where you will find a very large collection of arts and crafts from all over Indonesia.

- **Sogo Department Store:** Grand Hyatt Hotel and Shopping Plaza at Menteng traffic circle. Visit the third floor which has an extensive collection of Indonesian arts and crafts, similar to those found at the Sarinah Department Store.

- **Pasa Raya Department Store:** Jl. Iskandarsyah II/2, Blok M, Kebayoran Baru. Previously called the Sarinah Raya Department Store, sometimes referred to as the Pasaraya Sarinah, and similar to the Sarinah Department Store, the third floor has a large collection of Indonesian arts and crafts.

- **Keris Gallery:** Jl. H.O.S. Cokroaminoto. One of Jakarta's major department stores. Includes a handicraft center on the second floor selling everything from wayang puppets to leather bags.

- **Jakarta Handicraft Centre:** Jl. Pekalongan #12A (Tel. 338157). Offers a wide selection of quality arts and crafts, included Balinese carvings, jewelry, paint-ings, leather products, puppets, and new textiles.

- **Hadiprana Galleries:** Jl. Palatehan I/38, Blok M/Kebayoran Baru (Tel. 722-1023). Includes excellent quality handicrafts amongst its many works of arts. Look for Balinese carvings, especially birds and ducks, as well as stuffed toys.

- **Pigura:** Jl. Palatehan I/41, Blok M/Kebayoran Baru (Tel. 711-143). Offers a large selection of Balinese carvings, silver, bags, masks, kris, lacquerware, baskets, and musical instruments amongst its many textiles, ethnographic pieces, and furniture.

- **Urip Store:** Jl. Palatehan I/40, Blok M/Kebayoran Baru. Look for a wide selection of souvenirs, gifts, and antiques, including carvings, paintings, lac-querware, masks, puppets, baskets, and musical instruments.

- **Jl. Palatehan shops:** Blok M/Kebayoran. Several additional shops—**Djelita Art Shops**, **Gramedia Art Gallery**, and **"Pura" Art Shop**—offer a wide range of arts and crafts, including silver, Balinese carvings, lacquerware, puppets, lamps, and kites, along with some textiles, antiques, and ethnographic pieces.

- **Jl. Majapahit shops:** Somewhat off the beaten tourist path and in a heavily congested part of town, you'll find two well established shops offering a wide range of Indonesian arts and crafts—**Arjuna Craft Shop** (#16A) and **Garuda** (#12).

- **Indonesian Bazaar shops:** On the spacious grounds of the Jakarta Hilton Hotel. Numerous small shops offer a wide range of Indonesian arts and crafts. We especially like **Yakinda**, **Sanggar Pratita Indonesia**, **Rama Shinta Art Shop**, **Padi Kawi Art Shop**, **Batak Art Shop**, **Fine Arts Gallery**, and **Sari Bali**.

- **Ancol Art Center (Pasar Seni) shops:** Located in northeast Jakarta in the Ancol Dreamland Complex this is also referred to as the Ancol Art Market. You'll find a large collection of arts and crafts shops selling everything from Balinese carvings to leather goods. Some of the more unique shops include **Pondok Primtif** and **Sastra Leathercraft**.

- **Jl. Surabaya "antique" stalls:** Ostensibly termed "antiques," most items found here are best considered arts and crafts. Some fall in the category of "tacky."

- **Jl. Kemang Timur shops:** Located south of Keba-yoran Baru and Blok M, several shops offer a combination of arts, crafts, and antiques. **Burung Burung Terbang**, for example, has a unique collection of stuffed toys and Christmas decorations. **Cer Aki** (#51) specializes in Balinese woodcarvings. The three ethnographic shops at Jl. Kemang Bangka I/17—**Sulewesi Arts and Antiques, Morrys' Art**, and **Gusnel Art Shop**—offer a wide range of arts, crafts, and antiques from the outer islands.

- **Beautiful Indonesia in Miniature shops:** Located just inside the gate of this interesting outdoor museum/park complex, numerous shops are found in a two-story shopping center. The shops sell hand crafted items produced in the 27 provinces which are represented in this park.

ENJOYING YOUR STAY

You'll find plenty to do in Jakarta in addition to shopping. Indeed, you can easily spend three to five days just sightseeing in and around the city.

SEEING THE SIGHTS

Among the many attractions available in Jakarta, several tend to be special. Many, especially museums displaying Indonesian products, are also relevant to shopping:

- **National Museum:** Jl. Merdeka Barat. Also referred to as the Museum National, Central Museum, and Jakarta Museum. This is Southeast Asia's oldest and most interesting museum. If you want a quick introduction to Indonesian history, culture, and art, make the National Museum one of your first stops. Genesha Volunteers provide guided English language tours every Tuesday, Wednesday, and Thursday at 9:30am as well as the last Sunday of the month at 9:30am. Plan to visit the museum in the morning since it closes early. Hours are Tuesday to Thursday, 8:30am to 1pm; Friday, 8:30am to 11am; Saturday and Sunday, 8:30am to 2pm. Don't plan to visit on Monday since the museum is closed all day. The small museum shop sells some good quality arts and crafts.

- **Beautiful Indonesia in Miniature (Taman Mini Indonesia Indah):** Located in southeast Jakarta along the road toward Bogor, this 300 hectare complex is one of Asia's finest outdoor cultural parks. Surrounding an artificial lake with islands forming a replica of the archipelago, individual buildings and pavilions house the cultural treasures found in each of Indonesia's 27 provinces. The interesting architecture alone is worth the visit to this park. Some pavilions, such as Bali, have regular cultural performances and handicraft demonstrations. The buildings housing the arts and crafts from Irian Jaya are outstanding and awe inspiring. Near the entrance to the park you'll find a shopping complex with several shops offering arts and crafts from each of the provinces. It takes 45 minutes to an hour to get here from the major hotels near Menteng traffic circle. Plan to spend at least a half day here. Expect to do a great deal of walking, although a cable car does operate between a few sections of the park. On a hot day you may want to approach this park very leisurely rather than rush through it in the steam bath of heat and humidity awaiting the avid walker.

- **National Monument:** Located in central Jakarta at Freedom Square (Medan Merdeka). This 450 foot marble monument is the tallest structure in Jakarta. It's topped with a gold flame. This is a good place to get a panoramic view of the city from the observational tower at the base of the flame (elevator operates daily from 9am to 5pm). Be sure to visit the historical museum hall in the basement. Here you will get a quick overview of Indonesia's revolutionary history by viewing the 48 dioramas that line this marble gallery. This is also a cool place to escape into during the heat of the day!

- **Old Harbor (Sunda Kelapa port):** Located on the north shore of town, this is an interesting and picturesque harbor filled with the old wooden Buginese sailing ships that still ply the Indonesian waters, transporting lumber from Kalimantan to Jakarta. If you see someone with a small row boat, a few thousand rupiah will get you a ride to view the ships close up. A fascinating experience and a great photo opportunity.

- **Old Batavia:** This is the original Dutch settlement that established the city of Jakarta in the 1620s. The old town square, known as Taman Fatahillah (Fatahillah Square), is all that remains of the old city. History and cultural buffs will enjoy visiting the **Jakarta History Museum**, **Wayang Museum**, and the **Fine Arts Museum** adjacent to the town square. All are open Tuesday, Wednesday, Thursday, and Sunday from 9am to 12 noon; Friday from 9am to 11am; Saturday from 9am to 1pm. The museums are closed on Monday.

- **Wayang Museum:** Excellent collection of Indonesia *wayang* puppets from throughout the archipelago as well as from other Southeast Asian countries are on display in the old Dutch colonial residence on the west side of Fatahillah Square, Old Batavia. If you don't have time to sit through a shadow puppet (wayang kulit) performance, an abbreviated performance is presented here every Sunday morning.

- **Textile Museum:** Jl. Sasuit Tubun #4, central Jakarta. Represents one of Indonesia's most important living traditions—the importance of textiles in both traditional and contemporary Indonesian life. Displays nearly 600 Indonesian batik and ikat textiles—in both cotton and silk. If textiles are on your shopping agenda, or if you wish to learn more about techniques and significance of textiles in Indonesian cultural life, you should visit this museum.

- **Ancol Dreamland Complex:** Located along the north shore, this sprawling recreational complex is the ideal place for those interested in swimming, aquariums, fishing, and boating. The Fantasy World (Dunia Fantasi) includes bowling alleys and evening entertainment. The complex used to include a popular gambling casino. Local religious pressure resulted in closing the casino. The complex also includes the Ancol Art Center (Pasar Seni), often called the Ancol Art Market, where you can spend an hour or two browsing through the many arts and crafts stalls.

FOOD, RESTAURANTS, AND PUBS

If you enjoy exotic foods and good restaurants, Jakarta's offerings will not disappoint you. You'll find a full range of restaurants from street vendors and fast food (Pizza Hut, Dairy

Queen, Burger King, Big Boy, Ponderosa) to elegant international dining, including Chinese, Indian, Japanese, Korean, Thai, Vietnamese, French, Italian, and Mexican restaurants. Even a Planet Hollywood has opened in Jakarta.

One of our favorite "must visit" restaurants in all of Asia is the **Oasis** (Continental, Jl. Raden Saleh Raya #47, Tel. 326397 or 327818). This is as much a cultural experience as an evening in fine dining. You'll enjoy the ambience, service, and entertainment of this unique restaurant. Our favorite restaurant for buffet breakfasts and lunches is the **Bogor Brasserie** coffee shop at the Borobudur Inter-Continental Hotel. The **Peacock Cafe** in the Jakarta Hilton Hotel also serves excellent international buffets.

Some of the best and most elegant restaurants are found in the major hotels: **Taman Sari Grill** (Jakarta Hilton, Tel. 583051); **Toba Rotisserie** (Borobudur Inter-Continental, Tel. 370108)); **The Club Room** and **The Spice Garden** (Mandarin Oriental, Tel. 321307); **Sahid Grill** (Sahid Jaya Hotel, Tel. 587031); and **Jayakarta Grill** (Sari Pacific). Reservations are recommended for these restaurants.

Other good restaurants in Jakarta include **Black Angus** (American, Jl. Cokroaminoto #86A, Tel. 331551); **Paregu** (Vietnamese, Jl. Sunan Kalijaga 63, Blok M); **Memories** (Continental, Jl. Jend Sudirman, Tel. 5781008); **Le Bistro** (French, Jl. K.H. Wahid Hasyim 75, Tel. 364272); **Castelo do Mar** (Southern European/Portuguese, Jl. Kemang Raya); **The Pink Qasbar** (Western/Indonesian, Jl. Kemang Raya 14, Tel. 7992605); **Moon Palace** (Chinese/Hakka, Jl. Melawai VII/15A, Blok M); **Summer Palace** (Chinese/ Cantonese/Sichuan, Tedja Buana Building, Jl. Menteng Raya, Tel. 332989); **Kikugawa** (Japanese, Jl. Kebon Binatang IV); **Taichan Rarmen** (Japanese, Jl. Gondangdia Dalam); **Tora-Ya** (Japanese, Jl. Gereja Theresia 1, Tel. 310-0149); **Yamazato** (Japanese, Hotel Indonesia, Jl. MH. Thamrin, Tel. 323875); **Griya Selera** (Jl. HOS Cokroaminoto 122); **Omar Khayyam** (Indian, Jl. Antara 5-7, Tel. 356719); **Art and Curio** (Indonesia/European, Jl. Kebon Binatang III/8A); **Sari Nusantara** (Indonesian, Jl. Silang Monas Timur); **Sari Kuring** (Indonesian, Jl. Silang Monas Timur 88, Tel. 352972); and **Tan Goei** (Indonesian, Jl. Besuki 1A).

Some of the most popular pubs in Jakarta include **Jaya Pub** (Jl. MH. Thamrin); **Top Gun** (Jl. Palatehan I/32, Kebayoran Baru, Tel. 735436); **Green Pub** (Jakarta Theatre Bldg., Jl. MH. Thamrin or Jl. H.R. Rasuna Said, Setia Budi Bldg.), and **The Tavern** (Hyatt Aryaduta Hotel, Tel. 376-008).

Accommodations

Jakarta has a full range of accommodations, from deluxe hotels to inexpensive guest houses (losmen). Hotels in general tend to be expensive, moreso than in Kuala Lumpur and Manila, on the par with Bangkok and Singapore, but not as expensive as in Hong Kong or Tokyo. Expect to pay US$180 or more for first-class and deluxe hotels.

Several new hotels are under construction in Jakarta in response to the rapidly expanding international business sector and tourism. Most of the hotels are conveniently located for shopping and sightseeing. The country's largest shopping complex is attached to the Grand Hyatt Hotel.

Jakarta's best deluxe and first-class hotels include the following. The major deluxe hotels are:

- **The Regent Hotel**: Jl. Karang Asem Raya 35, Tel. 520-5577.
- **The Shangri-La Hotel**: Jl. Jend Sudirman Kav. 1 (Tel. 570-7440.
- **Grand Hyatt Hotel**: Jl. MH. Thamrin, Menteng traffic circle at Plaza Indonesia.
- **Borobudur Inter-Continental Hotel**: Jl. Lapangan Banteng Selatan, Tel. 70108.
- **Mandarin Oriental**: Jl. MH. Thamrin, Tel. 321307.
- **Jakarta Hilton International**: Jl. Jend Gatot Subroto, Tel. 583051.

Jakarta has a growing number of first-class hotels:

- **Sari Pacific**: Jl. MH. Thamrin, Tel 323707.
- **Hyatt Aryaduta**: Jl. Prapatan, Tel. 376008.
- **Sahid Jaya**: Jl. Jend Sudirman, Tel. 587031.
- **Kartika Chandra**: Jl. Jend Gatot Subroto, Tel. 511008.
- **Hotel Indonesia**: Jl. MH. Thamrin, Tel. 322008.
- **President**: Jl. MH. Thamrin, Tel. 320508.
- **Horison**: Taman Impian Jaya Ancol, Tel. 680008.

Less expensive, and frequently less convenient and comfortable, are several three and two-star hotels:

Three-Star

- **Garden**: Jl. Kemang Raya, Tel. 71808.
- **Jayakarta Tower**: Jl. Hayam Wuruk, Tel. 624408.

- **Kartika Plaza:** Jl. MH. Thamrin, Tel. 321008.
- **Kemang:** Jl. Kemang Raya, Tel.793208.
- **Sabang Metropolitan:** Jl. KH. Agus Salim, Tel. 354031.
- **Wisata International:** Jl. HM. Thamrin, Tel. 320308.

Two-Star

- **Asri:** Jl.Pintu Satu Senayan, Tel. 584071.
- **Cikini Sofyan:** Jl. Cikini Raya, Tel. 320695.
- **Grand Hotel Paripurna:** Jl. Hayam Wuruk, Tel. 376311.
- **Interhouse:** Jl. Melawai Raya, Tel. 716408.
- **Kebayoran Inn:** Jl. Senayan, Tel 716208.
- **Metropole:** Jl. Pintu Besar Selatan, Tel. 677921.
- **Natour Transaera:** Jl. Merdeka Timur, Tel. 351373.

Budget travelers are well advised to consult two travel guides that list the least expensive accommodations. Bill Dalton's *Indonesia Handbook* and Lonely Planet's *Indonesia on a Shoestring*. Be forewarned, however, that many of their recommendations may be more appropriate for backpackers and others seeking a cultural experience with the lower classes than for shoppers who focus on quality. But they do know where to find really cheap accommodations.

GOING ELSEWHERE

After finishing with Jakarta, your Indonesian shopping choices are numerous. At this point you need to decide the "where" and "what" of your trip in relation to your remaining time in Indonesia. Many visitors head immediately for **Bali** where they encounter a shopper's paradise. Others head for **Central Java**, the cultural and artistic heartland of the Javanese, and the northern coast. The **Jogjakarta-Solo (Surakarta) area** is a treasure-trove of Javanese batik, paintings, and handicrafts. **Cirebon** and **Pekalongan** on the northern coast are famous batik centers. More adventuresome travelers head for the outer islands for textiles, antiques, and primitive artifacts.

Let's next go to Bali where most tourists, world travelers, and dedicated shoppers and dealers tend to congregate. Then we'll do Jogjakarta-Solo and several other islands as we put more adventure into your search for Indonesia's many unique treasures and pleasures!

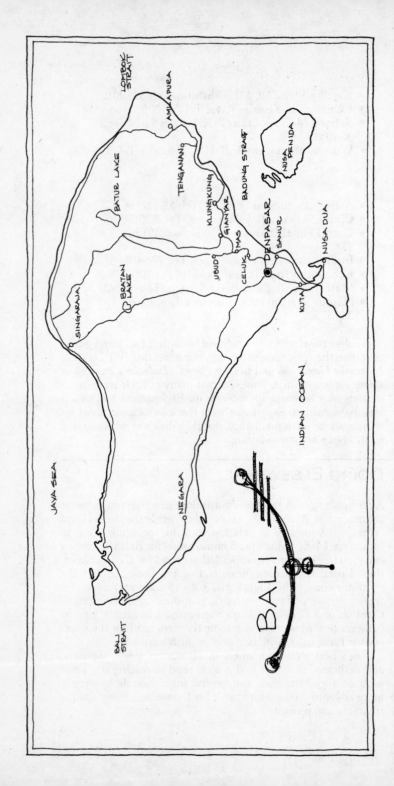

9

Bali

Here's one of the world's most unique traveling and shopping experiences. Different from the rest of Indonesia, it's unlike any other place in the world you will ever visit. For many visitors, Bali simply is the closest they will ever get to paradise. It's stunning architecture, landscapes, beaches, ceremonies, and crafts immerse you in a different world. This alluring place may captivate you as you later yearn to return to experience its many pleasures, including its excellent shopping.

Everything about this place is exotic, from sights to smells to sounds. Bali's highly religious and communal society differs greatly from all other Indonesian societies. While most Indonesians are Moslems, the Balinese continue to practice their centuries-old Hindu and animistic customs and rituals in the midst of a rapidly developing tourist industry. The lush volcanic island is beautiful and alluring; its nearly 3 million people are delightful; the performing arts are colorful; shopping is centered around workshops, studios, homes, villages, shops, stalls, and hotel shopping arcades; and everything about this place is exotic. In addition to leaving Bali with many purchases, you will have some exciting memories of this very different Asian and Indonesian experience.

THE BASICS

Located off the eastern coast of Java, Bali is a small volcanic island of only 5,561 square kilometers with a population of nearly 3 million. Approximately the size of Rhode Island in the U.S., Bali has a very large presence in the tourism industry because of its rich culture, beautiful landscapes, and expanding tourist infrastructure of hotels, restaurants shops, and inbound travel services.

It's relatively easy to get to Bali. Direct international flights to Bali originate in Europe (Garuda), the U.S. (Garuda and Continental), Australia (Qantas), and Singapore (Qantas). Other international airlines servicing Bali include Lufthansa, KLM, Singapore Airlines, Cathy Pacific, Malaysia Airlines, Korean Air, JAL, China Airlines, UTA, Air New Zeland, Thai International Airways, and Royal Brunei. Daily connections between Bali and Jakarta and Jogjakarta are frequent.

Upon arrival at the relatively new Ngurah Rai International Airport, go to the tourist information booth for literature on Bali or assistance with accommodations. During the high season (May-August), you should have hotel reservations since Bali tends to be fully booked at this time of the year. Many hotels run mini-vans between the airport and the hotel. If your hotel does not provide this service, take a taxi from the airport to your hotel. Go directly to the taxi counter where you will pay a fixed amount for a taxi. Next, take your receipt to a driver who will take care of you and your bags.

If you plan to spend a few days or a week or two in Bali, we highly recommend getting a copy of Bill Dalton's new ***Bali Handbook*** (Moon Publications). This excellent guidebook is detailed, informative, and well written. It covers everything from history, art, and culture to hotels, restaurants, sightseeing, and shopping. The sections on arts, crafts, and culture will give you a good background on many items you will likely purchase on Bali.

LIFE IMITATES ART

Bali has the best developed tourist facilities in all of Indonesia. Air connections to Bali are frequent. The island boasts many fine hotels and resort complexes. You will have plenty to do, be it lying on the beach, sailing, scuba diving, observing village ceremonies and dance performances, exploring the island, or "shopping 'til you drop!" Indeed, many visitors make Bali their only Indonesian stop. Falling in love with this island of beauty, art, and tradition, many visitors yearn to return to further experience the pleasures of a place where time appears to have stopped and life seems so unreal.

The Balinese are master craftspeople and artists. Everywhere you go on this island, you see people producing arts and crafts. Villages specialize in particular products. If, for example, you are interested in woodcarvings, then you should visit the village of Mas, which is Bali's woodcarving center. If you are interested in clothes, antiques, and textiles, Kuta Beach should be your destination. Silver production is concentrated around the village of Celuk. For paintings, you should go to Ubud.

CHOOSING THE PERFECT RESORT

The best way to organize yourself for the Bali experience is to select a hotel from which you will drive to the various villages to observe craftspeople and shop. As soon as you arrive at the international airport in Bali, you can contact several hotels through the information counter. Hotels, bungalows, and losmen range in price from $4.00 to $500 a night, depending on how you wish to experience Bali.

There are essentially six major areas where you can stay in Bali: Denpasar, Nusa Dua, Jimbaran, Kuta Beach, Sanur Beach, and Ubud. Each has its own character as well as certain advantages and disadvantages for shopping and sightseeing.

Denpasar, a bustling, crowded, and congested city of 300,000, is the major city on Bali. Similar to many other provincial cities in Indonesia, there is nothing particularly Balinese about this utilitarian city. Downtown Denpasar is not an exciting place to stay, and the shopping here is limited to a few small antique, batik, and handicraft shops along **Jl. Gadah Mada, Jl. Arjuna, Jl. Dresna, Jl. Veteran**, and **Jl. Gianyar**. Nonetheless, a shop such as **Arts of Asia Gallery** (Jl. Thamrin 27-37, Blok C.5, Tel. 23350) is one of the best "must visit" places on Bali for quality arts, antiques, and textiles. Denpasar also has a few central markets, a wholesale crafts market, and cooperative arts market that offer a wide range of inexpensive products of interest to both tourists and dealers.

Most visitors to Bali stay in one of the remaining five areas. **Sanur Beach** is located along the southeast coast. This is one of the older and quieter hotel and resort areas. Three of Bali's best hotels are found here: Bali Hyatt, Bali Beach, and Tanjung Sari. Shopping is largely confined to the shopping arcades in the Bali Hyatt and Bali Beach hotels as well as a few shops along the main road, Jl. Tanjung Sari. The beaches are not as expansive as those in the south, but Sanur Beach is a very peaceful and pleasant area to stay and stroll along the beach and roads. This also is a relatively expensive area to stay in comparison to Kuta Beach, Ubud, or Denpasar.

Kuta Beach in the south is a popular area for budget travelers and young people looking for a good time. You'll either love or hate this place, depending on your travel interests. Very noisy, chaotic, congested, and touristy, it has a free-wheeling, frontier town feel to it. Kuta Beach does have a good beach and offers inexpensive accommodations (some for US$4.00) along with a few deluxe and first-class hotels and an occasional good restaurant on an island noted for mediocre food and restaurants. One of the best located hotels in this area is the **Bali Padma Hotel** (Jl. Padma No. 1, Legian, Kuta, Tel. 52111). Its beautiful grounds and well appointed rooms provide an oasis from the maddening crowds in the nearby streets. This is our favorite hotel in the Kuta area. At the very end of the long and narrow main street—Legian Road—you will discover one of Indonesia's best hotels—the **Bali Oberoi**. This is an oasis of class and ambience at the end of what is unquestionably Indonesia's most chaotic shopping street. However, the Oberoi is not within most people's conception of "walking distance" of Kuta's shopping areas. Kuta Beach also has spectacular sunsets. Bars, restaurants, car and motorbike rental offices, and clothing and souvenir shops and stalls line the main roads in Kuta; hawkers pester tourists everywhere. It's usually "party-time" in this fun area where budget-traveling Australians have long preferred its cheap pleasures. If you are into bar hopping, people watching, crowds, surfing, and abusing another culture, this is the place to go.

But Kuta is full of contradictions. While it has lots of tourist knickknack and T-shirt shops lining both sides of Legian Road, here you also can find some excellent shops offering clothes, jewelry, textiles, antiques, and ethnographic art. Overall, however, the quality of products available here largely reflects the spending habits of Kuta's youthful traveling-on-a-shoestring clientele—mediocre to low. More than any other place, Kuta Beach symbolizes why quality shopping is largely found in Jakarta rather than in Bali. This place is not for everyone. Indeed, for many visitors Kuta Beach merely confirms the worst effects of tourism on paradise. On the other hand, many visitors love the festive atmosphere of Kuta, and they come away with some exciting shopping discoveries. See for yourself if this is your style.

Nusa Dua is Bali's newly developed resort area just southeast of Kuta Beach. Set away from the hustle and bustle of

Denpasar and Kuta Beach, the style here is strictly luxury. If your idea of traveling is "having it better than back home," and you're not particularly interested in mingling with the locals, then this area is for you. It's expensive here, but a great place to pamper yourself.

Jimbaran, located between Kuta and Nusa Dua on the northeast tip of Bukit peninsula and within 15 minutes of the airport, is Bali's newest area for upscale hotels and resorts. Here you will find the fabulous Four Seasons Resort and the Inter-Continental Hotel. We consider the **Four Seasons Resort** (Tel. 71288 or Fax 71280) to be Indonesia's best hotel/resort, and possibly the best in all of Asia. You simply can't do better than this place. It's an incredible resort with 147 private villas which include plunge pools, outdoor pavilions, and knock-your-socks-off views of Jimbaran Bay and Bali's sacred Mount Agung. The sleeping, bathing, and dressing pavilions in each of the quest quarters are spacious as is the outdoor dining and lounging paviolion. The restaurants here (The Dining Room, Pantai Jimbaran Restaurant, Pool Terrace Cafe) are outstanding. Indeed, we had two of the best meals we have ever enjoyed in Bali at the Four Seasons. The resort also provides one of the best upscale shopping boutiques with a dazzling array of quality antiques as well as good quality, but lesser priced, handicrafts. If you really want to pamper yourself and experience the best of the best in Indonesia, stay here for a few days. You won't want to leave! If you only stay at one five-star hotel in Indonesia, make sure it's the Four Seasons Resort in Jimbaran.

Ubud is fast becoming a popular place to stay. Indeed, many travelers regret not staying here or spending more time in Ubud. Located inland and north of Sanur Beach, Ubud is a center for artists and world travelers. It's a favorite destination for budget travelers who prefer a local cultural alternative to Kuta Beach. However, with the recent arrival of electricity and telephones as well as the construction of new deluxe hotels, especially the Amandari, the character of Ubud is quickly changing. Nonetheless, many travelers still prefer staying in Ubud, because it is less "touristy" and closer to the "real Bali" they remember than any of the other major areas. The best hotel/resort here is the world famous **Amandari** (P.O. Box 33, Ubud, Bali, Tel. 95333 or Fax 62-361-95335). Consisting of nearly 30 plush bungalows, the Amandari is in a class of its own. It also has an excellent gift shop offering a fine selection of Indonesian arts, crafts, and antiques. Two other Aman-resorts, the **Amankila** and **Amanusa** near Nusa Dua, as well as the Amandari, can be booked through the Hong Kong Aman-resort offices at 852-845-6711 (Tel.) or 852-845-5983 (Fax). If you really want to pamper yourself in Bali, spend a few days at the Four Seasons Resort in Jimbaran and then move to the Amandari in Ubud for a few days. While the resorts are very different, they are the best of the best in Indonesia.

Transportation in Bali is convenient. You can rent bicycles, motorbikes, and self-drive cars, or hire a car with driver. While driving yourself is relatively easy, it may not be safe given the continuing traffic congestion, especially in the southeastern section of the island. If you drive and get into an accident, your departure could be delayed. A car with driver is most convenient and relatively inexpensive. You can arrange your transportation at the airport or your hotel or visit the many rental offices dotting the main roads near the major tourist areas.

TACKLING THE ISLAND

Getting around Bali is relatively easy given the good road system and maps available for visitors. Regardless of where you stay, your shopping adventure requires traveling from one area to another. In this sense it really doesn't make much difference—perhaps 15 minutes—where you stay in relation to the shopping. We still prefer the Sanur Beach area for its quiet, ambience, and central location for shopping, restaurants, hotels, and beaches. Do not plan to walk from your hotel to most shops!

One of the first things you should do is look at a map of Bali. The island is best viewed in terms of regions: South, Central, East, North, and West. **Southern Bali**—including Denpasar, Kuta Beach, Jimbaran, Sanur Beach, and Nusa Dua—is the most urbanized and least Balinese. Most tourists stay here to enjoy the beaches and tourist facilities. Ironically, the Balinese prefer the upland areas and are not particularly keen about one of the favorite pastimes of tourists—the beaches. The upland central region, just to the north of Denpasar and Sanur Beach, is where most of the major arts and crafts villages are found. Your village-centered shopping will take place within a 10-mile radius of the noted artist village and tourist center of **Ubud**. Village after village perform dances and produce the arts and crafts Bali is so well noted for.

Eastern Bali is perhaps the most beautiful part of Bali with its picturesque volcanos, terraced rice fields, quaint villages, and interesting temples. For centuries this region has been the center for Bali's major kingdoms. You travel here to view the scenery, especially Mt. Agung, and tour various temple complexes. You also will pass through **Gianyar**, Bali's famous textile center where you can tour the factories and workshops and also shop for local jewelry; **Klungkung**, a market town noted for basketry; and **Kamasan**, a village with wayang paintings and gold and silver products.

Northern Bali is one of the most peaceful sections of the island. It's largely devoid of tourists. Since trips from the south to the northern coast take a long time, you may wish to stay overnight if you visit this area. This area is best noted for its spectacular scenery—volcanos, lakes, hot springs, and beaches —and temples. You will find several nondescript market towns, such as Singaraja and Kubutambahan, in this area. Go here for the scenery, peace and quiet, but don't expect to do any quality shopping.

Western Bali is the largest region. Several villages in this area are noted for temples, music, dancing, bull races, and textiles. This is the region of the famous seaside temple Tanah Lot, the monkey forest, and snake caves.

WHAT AND HOW TO BUY

Bali offers an incredible variety of arts, crafts, antiques, jewelry, and clothing. Of particular interest to visitors are the Balinese woodcarvings, paintings, gold, silver, and pottery as well as antiques, furniture, ethnographic pieces, and textiles from other areas in Indonesia, especially from Sulawesi, Madura, Lombok, Timor, and other eastern islands. Numerous shops also sell the latest in resortwear, leather products, fashion clothes, home decorative items as well as surfboards, backpacks, cassettes, and a wide assortment of tourist kitsch. Shopping is found in hotel shopping arcades, shopping centers, markets, roadside stalls, small shops and boutiques, home factories and galleries, and among hawkers. Less well known to visitors, but of most importance to the Balinese, are the **ritual arts**. These consist of many beautiful sculptures made as ceremonial offerings. Most last no more than two weeks and are usually destroyed as part of a ceremony—cremations being the most spectacular. These are the real Balinese arts. For the Balinese, art is used as offerings to the demons and gods—not collectibles for decorating homes. In the meantime, the Balinese produce other forms of art primarily for tourists. Like the tourist preference for the beaches, this permanent art is designed to satisfy the Western concept of arts and crafts used primarily for display.

While Bali offers a great deal in terms of shopping, it also offers some of the worst aspects of tourist shopping. Much of what you find in the small shops, roadside stalls, factories, and galleries is simply tourist junk. Most of the Balinese woodcarvings and paintings are copies of each other. You will enter galleries and literally see hundreds of "busy" Balinese oil paintings that look the same. After visiting two or three of these shops, you will probably never want to see another Balinese painting the rest of your life! Many of the woodcarvings have a similar fate—hundreds of the same figures assault your eyes. You will have to dig around in many different shops to find unique pieces which appeal to your sense of quality shopping.

Bali offers quality shopping, but you have to work to find it. The problem with quality shopping in Bali is readily apparent by observing the type of tourists who frequent this island. Bali has a reputation for attracting budget travelers and backpackers who come here for cheap accommodations, inexpensive food, and free fun. They are not big spenders with a taste for quality shopping. When they shop, they look for small inexpensive items they can either wear or fit into their backpacks. Quality shops simply cannot survive amongst many of these types of tourists. What quality shops do exist tend to be found in and around the deluxe hotels or they sell primarily to quality dealers who purchase their products for resale abroad or shops in Jakarta. Bali is especially a shopping paradise for dealers who purchase inexpensive carvings and jewelry for resale abroad.

You should also be prepared for hawkers, commissions, rip-offs, and mangy dogs on Bali. In many areas hawkers will pester you with their tacky goods. Just say *"jalan jalan"* and keep moving if you want to rid yourself of this annoyance. Since many sellers are used to dealing with rich and naive tourists, they are not above taking advantage of you. Be careful about claims of items being "old" and "antique," and bargain everywhere for your 30 to 60% discount. Indeed, some antiques dealers in Singapore have been known to unwittingly buy antique reproductions in Bali. After discovering they have been cheated, their only recourse was to send them back to Bali where they can be sold to tourists who think they are getting a real bargain! Indeed, you may discover prices for some items made in Bali to be higher than those found abroad for the same item. Be especially careful of antique shops which have recently experienced a tremendous increase in acquisition of so-called antique items.

The commission game in Bali is almost as bad as the notorious commissions that gouge tourists in Chiangmai, Thailand. Most guides and drivers steer tourists to particular shops that give them commissions on everything you purchase. Merchants, of course, pass this commission charge on to the purchaser. Most commissions range from 10 to 20%. However, commissions on silver purchases in the famous village of Celuk range as high as 30 to 35%. If you want to reduce your price as well as your driver's commission, some merchants may suggest that you lie to your driver/guide. Instead of telling the driver than you actually paid US$100 for an item, tell him you only paid US$20. Remember, top quality shops in Bali don't pay commissions, because they have a steady clientele based on their reputation. Many guides and drivers will not want to take you to such shops because there is no payoff for them in doing so. For example, the **Ida Bagus Tilem** gallery shop/workshop in Mas—Bali's top woodcarver—is not popular with tour guides and drivers. If you don't tell your guide or driver that you want to visit this place, chances are you will miss what is the most important woodcarver in Bali as well as Indonesia. In fact, some guides and drivers may bad-mouth this place as being "very expensive," which it is, and then try to take you to one of their recommended shops where in fact they get a commission. The prices will most likely to cheaper at this other shop, but you will see a definite difference in the quality of products.

The old saying that "You get what you pay for" is doubly valid in Bali where you also get to pay a hidden commission for poor and mediocre quality items. Shops that are frequented by tour buses invariably pay commissions to guides. In addition, many of the shops targeted by guides and drivers offer mediocre products. If you visit such shops on your own, when bargaining over the price, remind the salesperson that you are not with a guide or driver and thus you expect a substantial discount for your lone efforts. Consequently, you may want to direct your guide or driver to many of the quality shops recommended in this chapter. While not all of these shops are commission-free, at least you get quality for your money.

Keep clear of the mangy dogs that roam the streets through-out Bali. They are not cute, so don't pet or feed them, unless you want to risk rabies shots!

SHOPPING STRATEGIES

A good approach to shopping in Bali is to visit the Bali Museum, the Mandera Giri Art Center, and Central Market (Pasar Padung) in Denpasar to get an overview of Balinese arts and crafts. Next, survey a few antique, textile, and curio shops along Jl. Gajah Mada, Jl. Arjuna, Jl. Dresna, Jl. Veteran, and Jl. Gianyar in Denpasar. After that, survey some of the hotel shops in the major resort hotels, such as the Bali Beach, Bali Hyatt, and the Nusa Dua Beach Hotel, and stroll along the main streets in Kuta Beach (Legian Road) and Sanur Beach. Plan to return to these areas after visiting several arts and crafts villages in central Bali. If you want to see what real quality shopping is, visit Arts of Asia in Denpasar and the shops at the Four Seasons Resort in Jimbaran and the Amandari resort in Ubud.

We recommend hiring a car with driver who speaks some English to make the village shopping tour. Know though that many drivers or guides will make known to the shop owners that they brought you there (even though you may have selected the shop) in order to collect commissions on your purchases. Alternatively, armed with a good map, which may be difficult to find, you may want to rent a self-drive car. But you may get lost since roads are not well marked in Bali. While motorbikes are fun for sightseeing, they are not very safe nor convenient for shopping.

You might develop a checklist of villages for planning your shopping adventure into central Bali. Most villages tend to specialize in producing one or two particular products. If you're interested in wood carvings, for example, you go to one village. If its silver or paintings, you go to another village or villages that only specialize in these items. Indeed, some villages only specialize in producing carved doors, banana trees, and flowers. In addition to factories and shops, many villages will have dance and musical performances and ritual ceremonies going on during your visit. You will probably immerse yourself in the local culture while shopping. Within a 10-mile radius of Ubud, the most important arts and crafts villages are:

Village	Specialty
Celuk	Bali's silver and gold center. Family factories produce the unique Balinese filigree jewelry. Expect deep discounting since most shops pay high commissions (as much as 35%) to tour guides and drivers.
Batuan	Famous village for Balinese paintings and dance and musical performances. Great place to first observe the performances and then shop.
Mas	Famous village of woodcarvers with numerous galleries to explore. World famous wood carvers live and work here. The mecca for carved figures and masks.

Ubud This town is Bali's best kept shopping secret. The island's creative art center, it's linked to a cluster of artistic villages, such as Campuan, Penestanan, Juti, Pujung, Sebatu, Taro, and Pengosekan. The streets are lined with shops and stalls selling woodcarvings, masks, textiles, paintings, clothes, leather goods, and a variety of knickknacks. Many famous Indonesian and expatriate artists live in and around this town and have homes and galleries open to the public. Ubud is a great place to stroll for shopping, dining, and viewing the countryside. Fast becoming a major tourist destination in Bali for both budget and deluxe travelers and an especially pleasant alternative to Kuta Beach. If there is one place in Indonesia visitors really regret not having spent more time visiting, it definitely is Ubud. Plan to spend two or three days in this area. Trust us. You'll be glad you came and spent some time here.

Outside the central region you will find several other villages specializing in arts and crafts. Among these are:

Village	Specialty
Blayu	A textile village noted for producing good quality songket. Located northwest of Mengwi.
Gianyar	Famous for its cottage textile industry and architecture. 18 miles northeast of Denpasar.
Kamasan	Center for producing wayang style painting as well as large silver bowls and gold jewelry. Located just south of Klungkung.
Peliatan	Famous dance and gamelan orchestra village with a gallery displaying the works of artists from nearby Pengosekan, a village less than one mile from Mas.
Pengosekan	Famous village with some of Bali's finest painters. Located just south of Ubud.

Sukawati	Bali's *wayang* center. Has a popular and congested market selling colorful masks, woodcarvings, batik, and ikat. Located 8 miles northeast of Denpasar.
Tenganan	Extremely traditional and conservative walled village noted for producing *gringsing* cloth.

You will also find small shops and souvenir stalls near some of the major tourist sites, such as the Elephant Cave (Goa Gajah). Most of these places sell woodcarvings, baskets, leather goods, and a variety of knickknacks which you may or may not want to acquire.

Another way of approaching Bali is to seek out particular shops specializing in quality arts and crafts. The real shopping problem in Bali is how to go beyond much of the boring copycat tourist junk to find quality items. Thousands of artisans continue to produce arts and crafts solely for the tourist market. If you are looking for quality, explore the following locations:

Items	Location

Textiles	**Arts of Asia** in Denpasar and several shops in Kuta Beach, along Legian Road, have good selections. Kuta is also a good place to shop for batik beachwear. Try the towns of Gianyar and Ubud and the villages of Tengganan (for unique double ikat, or "gringsing," cloth), Sideman, Batuan, Blayu, Gelgel, and Mengwi. **Jani's** in Ubud is well worth visiting for his nice and reasonably priced textile selections.
Clothes	Bali is fast becoming a center for fashionable sports and casual wear using batik and ikat materials. Numerous shops along Legian Road in Kuta Beach as well as in the major hotels offer locally designed clothes. One of the best such shops is **"Nogo" Bali Ikat Centre** on Jl. Legian (Kuta Beach) and Jl. Tanjung Sari 173 (Sanur). Also look for the **Keris Gallery Department Store** (Nusa Dua) for batik clothes and fashionable shops at the two-storey **Plaza Bali** near the airport. In Ubud, **Lotus Studios,**

Mutiara Art Bali, Toko, and the **Bamboo Gallery** (see their adjacent clothing shop) offer uniquely designed clothes.

Paintings

Head for Ubud and the nearby villages of Mas, Batuan, Sangginyan, Pengosekan, Penestanan, and Peliatan. Visit the **Neka Museum**, **Gallery Munut**, and the **Pengosekan Community of Artists**. Klungkung is the center for traditional wayang style paintings. In Peliatan, visit the **Agung Rai Gallery**. Several world-renowned artists in Ubud have galleries in their homes: Arie Smit, Hans Snel, Wayan Rendi, Antonio Blanco, Rainer Anderle, and I Gusti Nyoman Lempad. In Ubud, be sure to visit the **Neka Gallery** (established artists) and the **Bamboo Gallery** (young, promising artists).

Wood-carvings

Woodcarvings, both old and new, are found in several shops in Kuta, Sanur, and Klungkung. The major woodcarving center is Mas. Be sure to stop at the Ida Bagus Tilem Gallery and the Tantra Gallery in Mas. Ubud also is a wood-carving center as are the villages of Pujung, Batuan, and Jati. They produce a large variety of woodcarvings using teak, ebony, and jackfruit woods. Each town and village tends to produce its own unique styles.

Stone-carvings

Batubulan is the center for sandstone carvings. You'll see stonecarving shops lining both sides of the road. Stop by I **Made Suasa** and **Made Kakul** for a nice range of selections. This is a great place to buy traditional Balinese figures and animals carved in sandstore for fountains and garden pieces. The shops are experienced in packing and shipping abroad.

Gold/silver

Celuk, Kamasan, and Kuta are the centers for gold and silver work. Shops in Denpasar along Jl. Sulawesi and Jl. Kartini offer a good selection of traditional Balinese jewelry. One of the best shops in Celuk is **Melati Silver**. Watch out for guides and drivers who steer you into mediocre shops which give them 20-30% commissions on everything you buy.

**Pottery &
porcelain**
Be sure to visit the village of Pejatan (12 miles west of Denpasar) for a distinctive style of contemporary Balinese terra-cotta pottery. You will find glazed ceramics in Batu Jimbar, Sanur. Visit **Djody** in Mas for porcelain.

Antiques
The best locations for antiques are the major hotel shopping arcades and shops in Kuta Beach, Sanur, Denpasar, Klungkung, Batubulan, and Singaraja. In Kuta Beach (Jl. Legian), one of Bali's best antique shops is **Polos**. Also, look for **Mahakam, Ujung Padang Art, H. Sjamsuddin Art, Ryo Antique Shop, Nogo Bali Ikat**, and **Timor Arts**. Along Jl. Tunjung Makar, look for **Thamrin Art** and **Kiki Antiques Shop**. In Batubulan and Celuk, stop at **Puri Sakana** and **Polis**. Denpasar has one of Indonesia's best antique shops—**Arts of Asia**. In Sanur a few antique shops are found along Jl. Sanur. For excellent one-of-a-kind treasures, try the gallery shops at the **Four Seasons Resort** in Jimbaran and the **Amandari** in Ubud.

Furniture
Numerous shops offer a wide assortment of furniture. Most furniture is either from the nearby island of Madura or produced locally. One of the best shops for both quality and prices is **Sekar Tanjung** in Sanur (Jl. Pantai Br. Pekandelan, Tel. 88027). Many other shops are found along the road near Celuk and Batubulan, especially **Polis** and **Puri Sakana**.

Handicrafts
You will find handicrafts everywhere, in souvenir shops, markets, and stalls. For baskets, visit Bona, Bedulu, and Goa Gajah. For bone carvings, visit Tampaksiring. For a large assortment of inexpensive woodcarvings, batik, ikat, and tourist kitsch, visit the popular handicraft market in **Sukawati**. For good quality handicrafts, visit the shops at **Plaza Bali** near the airport.

To shop Bali properly, you need at least four days, but preferably a week to absorb other aspects of this wonderful island. Bali is not a big island, but its narrow and winding roads and numerous shops along the way make going slow.

WHERE TO SHOP

Shopping in Bali seems to be everywhere, from hotel shopping arcades to village workshops. You'll encounter numerous shops along main streets as well as alongside the major roads connecting one village to another. Above all, you need a car, driver, good map, and time to explore the many shopping cities, towns, villages, and roads.

DENPASAR

Denpasar is no one's favorite city but it does have its own treasures and pleasures. Functioning as the major city on Bali, it is typical of so many Indonesia cities—large, crowded, congested, polluted, worn, and ugly. It's an administrative and commercial center rather than a major tourist destination. Most visitors pass through this city on their way to the major tourist areas—Nusa Dua, Kuta Beach, Sanur Beach, or Ubud.

Yet, you should not overlook shopping in Denpasar. The city does have some noted shopping opportunities. It has a few markets worth exploring. The three-story market along the river in downtown Denpasar, **Pasar Badung,** has everything from fish, fruit, vegetables, and hardware to clothing, textiles, and baskets. On the opposite side of the river the **Kumbasari Shopping Centre** functions as an arts, crafts, and clothing market. Here you will find a large number of small stalls on the second and third floors selling woodcarvings, textiles, bags, hats, T-shirts, masks, and batik. This is a good place to purchase inexpensive gift items. The center is open until 8pm each night. Denpasar also has a night market—**Pasar Malam**. Located just south of the Kumbasari Shopping Centre, this lively market consists of brightly-lit food stalls as well as vendors selling inexpensive clothes, shoes, batik fabric, and other items. Good buys on arts and crafts can be found at the **Pasar Satria,** Denpasar's version of an art dealer's wholesale market. Located at the corner of Jl. Nakula and Jl. Veterans (two streets north of Jl. Gajah Mada), Pasar Satria's two upper floors are devoted to wholesaling woodcarvings, paintings, and other craft items.

Denpasar also has a few good art and antique shops. One of the best antique shops in Indonesia is found in Denpasar—**Arts of Asia** (Jl. Thamrin 27-37, Blok C.5, Tel. 23350). A well established and reputable shop, Arts of Asia offers excellent quality textiles, furniture, Chinese porcelain, Dayak and Balinese masks, jewelry, wayang puppets, Batak gables, drums, and paintings. The owners—a husband and wife team—are very knowledgeable about antiques and textiles and only offer top quality. This shop also has a branch shop in Kuta Beach. You will also find several arts shops along Jl. Thamrin, Jl. Supraman, Jl. Arjuna, and Jl. Gratot Kaca. Jl. Gadjamata has a few clothing and gift shops. **"Mega" Art Shop** at Jl. Gajah Mada No. 36 has an excellent selection of woodcarvings, wayang, paintings, silver, ceramics, leather purses, kris, and textiles. Its larger shop— **"Mega" Gallery of Arts** on the outskirts of Denpasar (Jl. Gianyar, Km. 5.7, Denpasar, Tel. 28855) is a huge emporium for Indonesian arts and crafts. In fact, this was the first shop established in Bali. One section of this shop includes the owner's private collection of textiles and kris which, of course, are not for sale but well worth a visit if you're interested in these items. **Popiler** (Tel. 35162, 35180), which is located next to "Mega" Gallery of Arts, is a good shop for batik clothes and paintings. Good quality batik paintings are located in the back of the shop as well as upstairs. If you are interested in traditional Balinese jewelry, visit the gold shops along Jl. Hasanudin.

If you visit the suburb of Tohpati, you'll find an art cooperative supervised by the Department of Industry—**Sanggraha Kriya Asta**. Consisting of five buildings, each displaying particular crafts, this cooperative offers woodcarvings, garments, batik, silver, and paintings, and all at fixed prices. This is a good place to come for comparative pricing information.

NUSA DUA

Nusa Dua is Bali's resort and convention center. Here you will find several excellent hotels relatively isolated from the rest of the island. Both the Nusa Dua and Melia Bali Sol hotels have small shopping arcades where you will find a few excellent quality shops. At the Nusa Dua Hotel, for example, look for **Sinta Dewi Wood Carvings** for a large assortment of woodcarvings; **Silver Art** for jewelry and filigree figures; **Batik Danar Hadi** for fashionable batik clothes; **Dahlia Art Shop** for Balinese masks and colored carvings. The best quality shop here, however, is the **Indonesian Opal Center**. A branch of similar shops found in Jakarta (Borobudur and Jakarta Hilton hotels and the airport) and at the Pertamina Cottages in Bali, this shop offers excellent quality jewelry, silver, and antique kris. Their distinctive neck pieces, which integrate filigree and silver pieces, are very attractive.

The Melia Bali Sol hotel has a limited number of small shops that primarily cater to hotel guests. **Arts of Asia**, for example, has a small branch shop here selling textiles, leather bags, porcelain, wayang puppets, and gold and silver. **Apple**

Studios offers stylish clothing and accessories produced in Bali.
Opal Paradise has a mixture of jewelry, bags, and handicrafts.
Other shops include the **Sari Bali Boutique** and **Jade and
Silver Shop**. Several arts and crafts stalls selling everything
from Balinese paintings to woodcarvings, are found along the
ground floor of the hotel.

The Hyatt Regency Nusa Dua includes a shopping arcade
with small boutiques and an art gallery/museum exhibiting
examples of Balinese culture and history.

KUTA BEACH

What a wild, wild place! For some, Kuta Beach is a shopper's
paradise. For others, it's paradise lost, having succumbed to
bright lights, noise, congestion, tourist kitsch, and pestering
touts. Whatever your opinion, Kuta Beach at the least has the
largest concentration of shopping found anywhere on Bali. It's
non-stop shopping from 9am to 9pm. Shop after shop line the
main street—Legian Road—and a few adjacent streets selling
everything from T-shirts, used books, surf board covers, batik
patchwork quilts to jewelry, designer clothes, art, and antiques.
Here you'll find a real mixture from junk to trea-sures. Restaurants, bars, and guest houses are interspersed amongst the
many shops and are found along lanes and side streets.

Kuta Beach is an extremely crowded and congested place,
reminiscent of a honky-tonk strip development or a frontier
town run amok. It especially appeals to $7-a-day youthful world
travelers who are looking for an inexpensive fun time. And
many of the shops reflect the spending habits of Kuta Beach's
primary clientele—lots of cheap clothes and eats. Yet, Kuta also
draws other types of travelers and age groups to make this a
truly eclectic collection of visitors who enjoy Kuta's unique
atmosphere and inexpensive prices.

However, amongst the many eateries and T-shirt shops are
several shops offering good quality clothes, jewelry, and
antiques. In fact, during the past six years Legian Road has
blossomed with the arrival of several shops selling ethnographic
pieces from Kalimantan, Sulawesi, Lombok, Timor, and other
eastern islands. While many of the so-called antiques are
suspect, you will find some genuine antiques here.

Quality shops are not readily apparent in any one area of
Kuta Beach. You literally need to start at one end of Legian
Road and walk to the other end, including side trips into the
lanes and adjacent streets, in order to discover quality shops.
You'll most likely begin at Jl. Bukungsari which bounds Legian
Road. Along the way you are likely to become exhausted from

the long walk as well as irritated by transportation hawkers who pester you by repeatedly shouting that they have a very "special price" on rides along the street, which is usually five times the going rate! One thousand rupiah, or about US$.45, is plenty to pay for the journey along this street, which you will probably want to take advantage of for the return trip once you get to the end of the road and need to go back to where you started, which is three kilometers away!

You can easily spend a half day or more shopping along Legian Road and its adjacent streets and lanes. The street is most lively in the evening from 6pm to 9pm when everyone comes out to have a good time, eating and drinking in open-air restaurants and roaming the narrow, congested streets and lanes. And you'll do a lot of walking since Legian Road is very long—approximately three kilometers of shops on both sides of the street. This road eventually leads to Kuta Beach's great oasis—the Bali Oberoi Hotel—where you can escape from all the crowds, clutter, and noise.

If you are looking for arts and antiques, especially ethnographic items, you'll find numerous shops offering good selections of textiles, masks, carvings, beads, porcelain, kris, old silver, doors, boxes, baskets, chests, pottery, and furniture along Legian Road and the adjacent Jl. Tunjung Mekar: **Timor Arts Gallery**, **Thamrin Art**, **Mahakam**, **H. Sjamsuddin Art**, **Audy Art Shop**, **Kiki Antiques**, **Rofelan Art Shop**, **Asmat**, **Ujung Pandang Art**, and **Rudi Art Shop**. One of the most attractive shops is **Anang's Place**. Unfortunately, most items here are extremely overpriced—moreso than any other shop we found in Indonesia and reminiscent of New York City prices! You'll get better prices at other shops in Bali or even in Jakarta or Singapore. However, if you find something you love, you may decide to go ahead and pay the price. Many of the antique shops also sell textiles, both old and new.

Three of the best shops we've found along Legian Road, ones you should definitely visit, include the following:

- **"Nogo" Bali Ikat Centre**: Tel. 54335. This is a two-in-one shop. It's one of our favorite shops in Indonesia and a "must visit" on any trip to Bali. The front section of the shop displays fashionably designed ikat and silk clothes. The back part of the shop displays Iwan Sumichan's passion—ethnographic art from Irian Jaya, especially the Asmat. If you like this type of art, this shop may become your favorite. The shop has one of the best collections of such art we have found anywhere. Iwan regularly supplies dealers in Australia,

Europe, and North America with this art (shields, carved poles). Does an excellent job of packing and shipping. Very reasonable prices and very reliable.

- **Polos:** Tel. 51316. This is one of Bali's very best antique shops. Here you will find excellent quality furniture from Java and the island of Madura. While this is a small shop, be sure to see additional items in the back room and the back yard. Better still, get directions to visit their huge warehouse in Celuk near Batubulan. Many international dealers in search of quality antiques and furniture only buy at Polos when visiting Bali.

- **Jonathan Gallery:** 109 Legian Road, Tel. 54209. What a pleasant change from the helter-skelter shops that tend to dominate this street. If you are looking for inexpensive as well as good quality gold and silver jewelry, be sure to stop at this fine shop. You'll find a good selection of neckpieces, rings, bracelets, pins, and flatwear nicely displayed around primitive and folk art pieces. Many dealers come here to buy for their shops in Australia, Europe, and North America. The wholesale section is on the second floor.

Other good shops to look for are **Rama Collection** for leather bags using ikat designs; **Biak Biak** for uniquely designed clothes in cotton, silk, and rayon; **Gretha Leather** for handbooks and luggage; **Gecko** for nice leather coats, vests, shoes, and belts; **Ikar** for colorful and fashionable clothes and bed linens; and **Gallery Copper** for copper pieces that make nice gifts or home decorative items.

For handicrafts, one of the best shops is **Joger Handicraft Centre** (Jl. Raya Kuta, Tel. 53059) with its large selection and good prices. If you are interested in purchasing a large carved Balinese door, this is a good place to come. Since this shop is very experienced in shipping abroad, this may be a good place from which to ship your purchases.

SANUR

Compared to Kuta Beach, Sanur's shopping is much more limited and sedate. This relatively quiet, beach front resort area has two major hotels with nice shopping arcades—the Bali Hyatt and Bali Beach—as well as several shops that line the main street in Sanur, Jl. Tanjung Sari. Although the shops are limited in number, the quality of shopping here is generally better than in Kuta Beach. A few of the restaurants here tend to be some of the best in Bali.

The **Bali Hyatt Hotel** is one of Bali's loveliest hotels. A few small but excellent quality boutiques, craft, and jewelry shops are found on the ground floor just below the lobby. **Tilem Gallery**, for example, offers fine quality Balinese carvings by one of Bali's top carvers who also has a gallery shop in Mas. **Djody Art, Curio, and Antiques** has good quality silver and antiques. For stylish sportswear, visit **Taman Boutique**, **Sari Bali Boutique**, and **Lila Shop**.

The **Bali Beach Hotel** has the largest hotel shopping arcade on Bali, although it is still small by most standards. For excellent quality Balinese woodcarvings, visit both **Njana Tilem Gallery** and **Bali Indah**. For good quality silver, visit **Mahesa** and **Ardana**. **Djody** has a good selection of antiques, woodcarvings, and kris.

Jl. Tanjung Sari is the main beach-front road that connects most major hotels, restaurants, and shops in Sanur Beach. Running for approximately two kilometers, a one kilometer stretch between the Bali Hyatt Hotel and the Tanjung Sari Hotel is where you will find most of Sanur's shops. Both sides of this road have a smattering of good quality shops. We especially like **Nogo Bali Ikat Centre** for uniquely designed clothes; **Pappagallo Collection** for fashionable clothes; **Golden Kangaroo** for silver jewelry; **Eurasia Bali Gallery** for home decorative items; **Eden Home Furnishings** for cane furniture and accessories; **Ucok Antiques** for textiles, doors, and Batak carvings; **Sari Bumi** for uniquely designed pottery; **C.V. Tengalla** for ceramics; **Temptations** and **Bali Harum** for gifts and antiques; and **Felix's Collection** for interesting leather and ikat clothes, including T-shirts.

One of Bali's best furniture and handicraft shops is located in Sanur Beach, near both Jl. Tanjung Sari and the Bali Beach Hotel. If you are interested in good quality antique furniture, especially Madura chests, beds, head boards, tables, and chairs, as well as handicrafts, be sure to visit **Sekar Tanjung** at Jl. Pantai Br. Pekandelan (Tel. 88027). Both quality and prices are excellent at this large furniture refinishing shop. If you are interested in handicrafts, especially Balinese masks and doors, be sure to visit the second floor of this shophouse. Dealers who wish to export such products from Bali will be pleased to discover this shop. Across the street is a local shipping company that can quickly repack your purchases for your next flight or arrange for shipping abroad—**CV. Darma Sari International Cargo** (Tel. 87070, 88143, 88822).

If you visit the Bali Beach Hotel on Jl. Segara, just across the street is the **Beach Market I Sanur** which is filled with stalls selling beachwear, handicrafts, antiques, and tourist kitsch. One shop—**Lukman**—may look like a typical tourist shop, but it has some genuine antiques and old textiles amongst his handicrafts. If you are a serious antique buyer, Lukman will invite you to his home in Denpasar (Jl. Serma Made Pil 22) where he will show you his latest collection of antique jewelry, silver, kris, and textiles acquired from nearby islands. All items, of course, are for sale. Do be sure to bargain for everything.

UBUD

Plan to spend some time in this pleasant town—preferably 2-3 days. You won't be disappointed. It's inexpensive and you'll have a good time. Located approximately 8 miles north of Sanur Beach, Ubud is fast becoming a choice location for travelers—both budget and deluxe—who wish to get closer to the real Bali that largely disappeared years ago in Nusa Dua, Denpasar, Kuta Beach, and Sanur Beach. A small inland town that only recently acquired electricity (1976) and telephone lines (1987), Ubud is a well noted art center in Bali. Here you will find many of Bali's famous Balinese, Indonesian, and expatriate artists who have galleries displaying their distinctive paintings. This also is a center for inexpensive clothes, textiles, and antiques. It boasts a few good restaurants, too.

It's easy to shop in Ubud since this is a small town with most shops found along one main road, **Jl. Raya Ubud**. It's best to start at one end—preferably at the north end adjacent to the bridge and Murni's Warung—and walk this two kilometer stretch of road. If you start here, you may want to begin by visiting one of Ubud's best restaurants and shops. Murni's Warung is literally a small hole-in-the-wall restaurant overlooking a ravine, but it serves some of the best milkshakes in Indonesia! Next door is **Kunang Kunang I** (Tel. 95716), an upscale and stylish shop offering excellent quality textiles, pottery, purses, baby carriers, jewelry, clothes, wayang golek puppets, musical instruments, pillows, and furniture—the most fashionable boutique and gift shop in Ubud. Across the street and up a few shops is **Kunang Kunang II** an upscale shop selling antiques, jewelry, textiles, baskets, boxes, puppets, and clothes. The remainder of this street is lined with small shops selling arts, crafts, silver, jewelry, batik patchwork quilts, masks, and clothes shops. **Mirah Silver** has some nicely designed rings, earrings, necklaces, and pendants. **Mutiara Art Bali** produces distinctively designed batik shirts in cotton and rayon, many with ethnographic designs. The **Central Market**, a two-story building with numerous vendor stalls, is similar to many other central markets on Bali. You'll find everything from clothes, fans, and bags to jewelry here. Across the street from the Central Market you'll find several clothing, handicraft, and art shops. Look for **Lotus Studios**, which is located two doors from the Lotus Cafe, which offers textiles, hats, clothes, and paintings. Further along this road you will come to Ubud's two best art galleries, **Neka Gallery** and the **Bamboo Gallery**. Neka Gallery is adjacent to the Neka Museum which includes paintings from well known artists. The Bamboo Gallery represents the paintings of young promising artists. The remainder of this road has several art galleries displaying the paintings of local artists.

At this point, you might want to turn around and go back toward the Lotus Cafe. Be sure to turn left onto **Monkey Forest Street** which is lined with numerous arts, crafts, and clothing shops. Three of our favorite shops here include:

- **Jani's Place:** Tel. 95358. This is Ubud's best shop for ikat textiles. The second floor includes Mr. Jani's private textile collection. Downstairs includes newer pieces along with clothes and bags. Mr. Jani also operates the Garden View Cottages in Nyuh Kuning Village ($35 for a double, including breakfast). You'll enjoy talking with Mr. Jani who is justly proud of his textile collection and business.

- **Toko:** Tel. 95046. This upscale shop offers a nice selection of hots, clothes, textiles, belts, ceramics, carvings, and jewelry.

- **Gayatri Kids:** Jl. Monkey Forest 67. Offers a nice selection of children's clothes—dresses, shoes, swimwear, tops, coats.

The two best restaurants in town are **The Lotus Cafe** (Jl. Raya Ubud) and **Cafe Wayan** (Monkey Forest Street). Either one would be a good choice for breakfast, lunch, or dinner.

VILLAGES AND ROADS

You'll discover numerous workshops, shop houses, factories, and shops lining the roads between the major towns and villages. While many of these places offer similar products, occasionally you will find exceptional quality shops amongst the mediocre. If you are interested in furniture and antiques, be sure to visit the many shops lining Jl. Gianyar at the village of **Batubulan** just a few kilometers north of Sanur. We particularly like the unique selections available at **Puri Sakana** (Tel. 98205). This huge shop/warehouse is located on both sides of the road and includes an extensive collection of furniture and ethnographic pieces. Other good antique and furniture shops in this area include the two shops of **Bali Antiques, Antiques Kadek Nadhi, Puri Antiques, Mira Antiques**, and **Kembar Antiques**. Batu Bulan also is the center for stone carvers. We especially like the selections at **Made Kakul** (Tel. 98208) and **I Made Suasa**.

Most of the silver shops in the famous silver village of **Celuk** look the same and business here is highly competitive. They all seem to produce similar types of silver filigree jewelry and figures. Shop around, compare prices, and bargain hard in every shop you visit. Remember, many shops here are used to paying 20 to 35% commissions to tour guides and drivers for steering customers their way. One of the largest factory shops offering a good selection of silver jewelry, including gold and silver combinations, is **Rama Sitha**. A similar shop that also offers some handicrafts along with silver products is **Dewi-Murmi**. The best silver shop is **Melati Silver**. Also look for **Polis** (Tel. 51315 or 98601 for directions), one of Bali's best antique and furniture shops. This is where many foreign dealers come to make their selections.

Be sure to visit two galleries in the famous woodcarving village of **Mas**. The **Ida Bagus Tilem Gallery** produces and sells the works of Indonesia's premier wood carvers—Ida Bagus Njana and his son Tilem. This is a beautiful gallery consisting of a large compound with woodcarvers at work and a two-story shop-gallery. One section of the gallery is actually a museum with gorgeous carvings which, of course, are not for sale. While the carvings here are very expensive, they are all exquisite works of art. Tilem is now considered to be Bali's best carver. To own a carving from this place is to be a true connoisseur of Bali's finest woodcarving tradition. To a very large extent Ida Bagus Njana made Balinese carvings world famous for their graceful and elongated lines and carved in hibiscus wood. Tilem is well noted for his wonderful carved birds. Across the street is the **Tantra Gallery**, owned by the younger brother of Tilem. The quality of carvings here are also excellent. This large gallery actually consists of two shops, one selling woodcarvings and the other offering carved Balinese doors (carved on both sides), masks, paintings, ikat, and batik.

The area in and around the town of **Gianyar** has numerous

factory shops selling textiles and woodcarved banana trees, cactus, and garudas. You can easily spend a half day in this beautiful area browsing from one factory shop to another.

If you are interested in shopping at a large market for inexpensive arts and crafts, be sure to visit the **Sukawati Art Market** in the village of Sukawati. Here you will find an extremely crowded and congested two-story market with numerous stalls crammed with textiles, woodcarvings, jewelry, and T-shirts produced in home factories. This can be a fun market for those who enjoy bargain hunting and friendly haggling rather than for quality shopping. Be sure to carefully examine your purchases since some items may be seconds. Given the very dark and crowded conditions inside the market, you may need to take an item outside the market in order to carefully examine it in the light! Across the street from the Sukawati Art Market is the fresh market which also has numerous vendors selling locally produced baskets.

QUALITY SHOPPING

As we noted earlier, quality products are hard to find in Bali given the two types of buyers drawn to this island: the $7-a-day budget travelers and dealers. The first group spends little on shopping for items other than what they can wear—T-shirts, bags, costume jewelry, and cassettes. Dealers primarily look for inexpensive items they can resell abroad. Indeed, Bali is a dealer's heaven, especially for cheap silver jewelry, clothes, leather goods, and woodcarved masks, animals, banana trees, and flowers. Such items end up in numerous gift and handicraft shops around the world at five to 10 times the prices found in Bali. Consequently, Bali offers a good range of inexpensive clothes, jewelry, and woodcarvings to meet the needs of these two groups. Quality shoppers and collectors will probably do better shopping in Jakarta.

Nonetheless, in Bali you can find excellent quality products in the midst of all the tourist kitsch if you know where to go for quality. Some of Bali's best shops—several of which were described earlier—include the following:

ANTIQUES

Arts of Asia: Jl. Thamrin 27-37, Blok C.5, Tel. 23350
Kunang-Kunang II, Ubud, Tel. 95714
Polis, Jl. Legian, Kuta, Tel. 51316 (also in Celuk)
Puri Sakana: Jl. Gianyar, Batubulan, Tel. 98205

ETHNOGRAPHIC ART

"Nogo" Bali Ikat Center: Jl. Legian, Kuta, Tel. 54335
Timor Arts: Jl. Legian No. 423A, Kuta
Ujung Pandang Art: Jl. Legian, Kuta, 82762

FURNITURE

Sekar Tanjung: Jl. Pantai Br. Pekandelam, Sanur, Tel.
88027
Polis: Jl. Legian, Kuta, Tel. 51316 (also in Celuk)
Puri Sakana: Jl. Gianyar, Batubulan, Tel. 98205
Shops in Batubulan: Jl. Giangar

WOODCARVINGS

Ida Bagus Tilem: Mas, Tel. 95099
Tantra Gallery: Mas
Bali Souvenir Art Shop: Celuk

PAINTINGS

Bamboo Gallery: Jl. Raya Ubud, Ubud
Neka Gallery: Jl. Raya Ubud, Ubud
Agung Rai Gallery: Peliatan (village near Ubud)
Galleries and studios/homes of artists: in and around the
towns and villages of Ubud, Klungkung, Kamasan, and
Kerambitan

CLOTHES AND ACCESSORIES

"Nogo" Bali Ikat Centre: Jl. Legian, Kuta (Tel. 54335);
Jl. Tanjung Sari 173, Sanur (Tel. 88765)
Andree Collection: Jl. Legian, Kuta
Baik Baik: Jl. Legian, Kuta, Tel. 51622

BATIK

Popiler: Jl. Gianyar, Km. 5.7, Denpasar, Tel. 35162
Toko Winotosastro: Jl. Sanur, Tanjung Bungkak,
Denpasar
Batik Keris: Jl. Kartini 14
Batik Semar: Jl. Thamrin 33-35
Danar Hadi: Jl. Thamrin 6, Blok A6

TEXTILES

Arts of Asia: Jl. Thamrin 27-38, Blok C., Tel. 23350
Jani's Place: Monkey Forest Street, Ubud, Tel. 95358
Gianyar Town shops: 23 kilometers northeast of Denpasar
Antique and artifact shops in Kuta Beach: Jl. Legian and Jl. Tunjung Mekar

HOME DECORATING

Galerie Ikat: Jl. Legian, Kuta
Tropical Climax: Jl. Legian, Kuta, Tel. 51924
Eden Home Furnishings: Jl. Tanjung Sari, Sanur

SILVER AND JEWELRY

Indonesian Opal Centre: Nusa Dua Hotel shopping arcade, Nusa Dua
Jonathan: Jl. Legian 109, Tel. 54209
CV. Yusuf's Silver: Jl. Pantai Kuta, Kuta, Tel. 51106
Melati Silver: Celuk

HANDICRAFTS

Plaza Bali: By Pass I Gusti Ngurah Rai, Tuban, Denpasar (5 minutes from airport), Tel. 53301
"Mega" Gallery of Arts: Jl. Gianyar, Km. 5.7, Denpasar, Tel. 24592-25120
Joger Handicraft Centre: Jl. Raya Kuta, Kuta, Tel. 53059
Kunang Kunang: Jl. Raya Ubud, Ubud, Tel. 95716
Sanggraha Kriya Asta Handicrafts Centre: Tophati, Denpasar

STONECARVINGS

I Made Suasa: Batubulan, Gianyar
Made Kakul: Batubulan, Gianyar, Tel. 98208

ENJOYING YOUR STAY

There's plenty to see and do in Bali in addition to shopping. You can easily spend weeks lying on beaches, scuba diving, sailing, visiting temples and villages, observing art performances and ceremonies, learning to make arts and crafts, or touring the countryside and taking pictures. Of all places in Indonesia, Bali has the largest variety of things to see and do.

THINGS TO DO

Some of the most popular sightseeing attractions and things to do in Bali include:

- **Touring the island:** Many tour groups provide half or full-day tours of Bali's many regions. Alternatively, you can hire a car and driver to see the major highlights of the island. Most tours include time to shop since crafts are so important in Balinese life. Most will stop at major towns and villages, such as Celuk (silver), Sukawati (art and handicraft market), Mas (woodcarvings), and Ubud (paintings and crafts). You are also likely to visit a few of the major temples, such as Besakih, Pura Taman Ayun, and Tanah Lot, see the elephant cave (Goa Gajah) and monkey forest, stop at a palace, and view Lake Batur. You'll find many travel agencies located in Denpasar, Kuta, and Sanur. Most major hotels will have a tour desk, and other hotels can arrange group or private tours.

- **Temples:** Bali has nine major temples. The three most popular ones are the Pura Besakih, Pura Taman Ayun, and Tanah Lot. Pura Besakih, known as the mother temple, is Bali's holiest place. The trip here takes you through some spectacular countryside of terraced rice fields and mountains. Once at the base of the temple complex, you may want to ride on the back of a motorbike (Rp. 500) for the long trip to the temple gates. Otherwise, it's a long hot walk. Pura Taman Ayun is considered the most beautiful temple in Bali. Tanah Lot is an intriguing temple built on a small rock island which is connected to the main island during low tide. This is a popular place to watch spectacular sunsets. Try to arrive around sunset time when you should be able to get some wonderful photos.

- **Museums:** Bali has a few public and private museums throughout the island. The major one is the Bali Museum in Denpasar (Jl. Surapatwith its extensive collection of traditional Balinese art. The Puri Lukisan ("Palace of Paintings") museum in Ubud displays some of the best examples of modern Balinese paintings, drawings, and sculptures. Several galleries also have museum sections which display top quality art. While many pieces may not be for sale, others may; it's best to ask when you visit these museums. Njana Tilem Gallery in Mas, for example, has a museum of exquisite wood-carvings on the second floor. Neka Museum in Ubud displays many of Indonesia's famous artists.

- **Beaches:** Many visitors to Bali just want to lie on the beach and relax for a few days. The best beaches are found in the Nusa Dua, Kuta, and Sanur areas. If you like beaches, you might prefer staying at a beachfront hotel. However, lying on the beach does not necessarily take you away from shopping. In Sanur, for example, you will find a market (Beach Market I Sanur) fronting the beach next to the Bali Beach Hotel as well as many hawkers and masseuses approaching sun bathers. One word of caution: be very careful how long you stay on the beach and use a good sun screen product. Bali's equatorial sunlight can quickly give you a bad case of sun burn, even on overcast days.

- **Water sports:** Most of the major beach front hotels have a full range of water sports organized for guests. Outrigger sailboats are very popular with visitors and are readily available for rental along the beaches. You can also charter yachts and deep-sea fishing boats as well as go water skiing and wind-surfing. If you like scuba diving, the water around Bali is beautiful. In fact, you may want to stay at the Hotel Club Bualu in Nusa Dua, since this is the only hotel especially organized for scuba divers. They are fully equipped, including PADI instructors, to take care of all your scuba diving needs.

- **Performances and ceremonies:** Bali is alive with cultural activities. Everyday somewhere you will discover a colorful village ceremony, be it a cremation, wedding, or other rite of passage. Musical and dance performances are regularly staged at the major hotels as well as at the popular village of Batubulan. A major activity for tour groups, every morning at 9:30am an outstanding group of musicians, dancers, and actors perform the Barong and Kris dances in an open-air theater on the main road in Batubulan. While staged just for tourists, this performance is very well done and worth seeing. It's a great photo opportunity. You may want to arrive a half-hour early (9am) in order to get a good seat.

RESTAURANTS

Bali may impress visitors with its arts, crafts, culture, and landscapes, but it has yet to attract visitors with many good restaurants. Indeed, Bali is one of our least favorite places to dine in Indonesia. Nonetheless, we are increasingly finding a few good restaurants. Most dining takes place in open-air restaurants. Among our favorites are:

- **Amandari Resort Restaurant:** Amandari Resort, Ubud. Fabulous for both lunch and dinner. Reserve a day ahead since restaurant only seats 66 people. Great ambience at night.

- **The Dining Room** and **Pantai Jimbaran Restaurant:** Four Seasons Resort, Jimbaran. Two fine restaurants overlooking Jimbaran Bay.

- **Kul Kul:** Jl. Tanjung Sari, across from Penida View Hotel, Sanur, Tel. 88038. Elegant outdoor dining.

- **Telaga Naga Restaurant:** Jl. Tanjung Sari, across from Bali Hyatt Hotel, Sanur. Elegant outdoor dining. Chinese.

- **Tanjung Sari Hotel Restaurant:** Jl. Tanjung Sari, Sanur. Delightful rijsttafel in a romantic setting.

- **Spice Islander:** Bali Hyatt Hotel, Sanur. Elegant indoor dining.

- **Swastika:** Jl. Tanjung Sari, Sanur.

- **Lotus Cafe:** Jl. Ubud, Ubud. Wonderful surprise in this small town.

- **Cafe Wayan:** Monkey Street, Ubud. Very pleasant outdoor dining.

- **Poppies:** off Jl. Legian, Kuta, Tel. 51059. Breakfast, lunch, and dinner, 8am - 11pm.

- **Lenny's:** Jl. Legian, Kuta.

- **Indah Sari:** Jl. Legian, Kuta. Seafood and barbecue restaurant.

For what may be the best breakfast buffet in Bali, try the spread at the Bali Hyatt Hotel in Sanur.

ACCOMMODATIONS

While Bali has a full range of accommodations available, they are not available all of the time. Especially during the peak season (December-January and July-September), hotels and guest houses tend to be fully booked. If you plan to stay in a nice hotel, you should make reservations well in advance.

Accommodations are still a good buy in Bali, although prices are going up and deluxe hotels can be very expensive. However, you can still find lodging for as little as US$5.00 a night as well as plush hotels going for more than US$500 a night. In general, accommodations tend to be very good in Bali, with many hotels meeting international standards. Some of Bali's best hotels include the following:

Nusa Dua:

> **Amanusa:** Nusa Dua. Another fabulous Amanresort overlooking the Bali Golf and Country Club. Tel. 800-223-1588 (US)
> **Nusa Dua Beach Hotel:** Box 1028, Denpasar, Tel. 71210
> **Grand Hyatt Nusa Dua:** Tel. 71188
> **Hotel Club Buala:** Box 6, Nusa Dua, Tel. 71310
> **Putri Bali:** Box 1, Nusa Dua, Tel. 71020

Jimbaran:

> **Four Seasons Resort:** Jimbaran, Denpasar, 80361, Tel. 71280 (Bali). Tel. 800/332-3442 (US)

Kuta/Legian:

> **Bali Padma:** Jalan Padma No. 1, Legian, Kuta, Tel. 52111
> **Bali Oberoi:** Box 351, Denpasar 800, Tel. 51061
> **Pertamina Cottages:** Box 121, Denpasar, Tel. 51161

Manggis:

Amankila: Manggis. Another fabulous Amanresort
property with ocean views. Tel. 800-223-1588 (US).

Sanur:

Bali Hyatt Hotel: Box 392, Sanur, Tel. 88271
Tanjung Sari Hotel: Box 25, Denpasar, Tel. 88441
Bali Beach Hotel: Box 275, Denpasar, Tel. 88511

Ubud:

Amandari: Kedewatan, Ubud, Tel. 95333 (Bali). Tel.
800-223-1588 (US)
Kupu Kupu Barong: Jl. Kecubung 72, Denpasar, Tel.
95478

While you can easily spend US$200-500 a night or more on
these four and five-star hotels, you can also find nice accommodations in the $60 to $100 range, and even far below. Such
accommodations put you in closer contact with the real Bali.
Indeed, you'll find a great deal of moderately and inexpensively
priced accommodations in Bali. The least expensive hotels,
bungalows, and losmen will be found in Kuta Beach and Ubud.
For example, in Kuta, try the **Kartika Plaza**, **Barong Cottages**,
Poppies Cottages, or **Kuta Palace Hotel**; in Sanur, try **Alit's
Beach Bungalows** (Box 102, Denpasar) or **Segara Village**
(Box 91, Denpasar); and in Ubud, try **Tjampuhan** (Box 15,
Denpasar) or **Puri Saraswati Bungalows** (Ubud).

We highly recommend consulting Bill Dalton's ***Bali Handbook*** for details on these and other inexpensive accommodations.

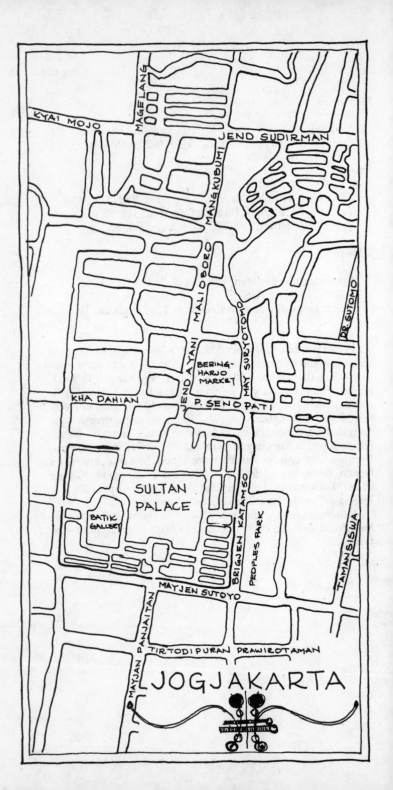

10

Jogjakarta

After Jakarta and Bali, Jogjakarta is a pleasant surprise. It's another example of the unique diversity of this fascinating country. This is a laid back city filled with some of the finest examples of traditional and modern Indonesian art.

Jogjakarta, called "Jogja" by most Indonesians and seasoned travelers, is the cradle of Javanese culture. At various times it served as the center for great Buddhist and Hindu kingdoms. During the 1940s it played a key role in the Indonesian Revolution. Today, Jogja maintains a special political and administrative relationship with Jakarta and a revered place in the minds of the Javanese. For many travelers, Jogja offers an excellent opportunity to experience the finest of Javanese culture and to shop for numerous unique items that best express this fascinating culture.

Located in Central Java approximately 370 miles from Jakarta, this city of over 500,000 people is the center for arts and crafts. Strategically located within a short driving distance of such noted historical temple complexes as Borobudur and Prambanan and the famous batik center of Solo (also called Surakarta and Sala), Jogjakarta is one of the more charming Javanese cities. It has a great deal to offer visitors in search of Indonesian treasures.

GETTING TO AND AROUND

Jogjakarta is easily accessible by air from most major cities on Java and from Bali and Sulawesi. The flight takes less than one hour. Jogja is also connected to the major cities on Java by rail and road. Although the 370 miles between Jakarta and Jogja may not seem far, the train trip from Jakarta to Jogja takes nearly 10 hours. The same trip by car or bus takes about 14 hours.

❑ Jogja is the cradle of Indonesian civilization. It's where culture and art come together in a unique setting.

❑ While you should have no problem finding accommodations in Jogja, don't expect to find the luxury hotels like those in Jakarta or Bali.

❑ Similar to Bali, many arts and crafts in Jogja are produced only for tourists. You must dig through a lot of junk to find good quality.

❑ Batik clothes and fabrics are widely available in small shops and home galleries.

❑ Jogja is well noted for its contemporary oil paintings. It's the center for Indonesia's most famous artists as well as budding young artists.

❑ Since Jogja's shopping is spread over a large area, plan to either rent a car with driver or hire a becak.

Once in Jogja, you will find the usual collection of worn becaks, bemos, colts, buses, and motorbikes plying the congested streets and lanes of the city. Since much of your shopping will be concentrated in the downtown section along Jl. Malioboro and adjacent streets, you may find the becak to be the easiest way to navigate this city. But beware of overcharging and commission-taking by the drivers. Becak drivers in Jogja tend to state outrageous prices to foreigners, sometimes feign misunderstanding when paying for ostensibly agreed-upon prices, and many are eager to take you shopping so they can get commissions from their favorite shops, which are often mediocre tourist shops. Alternatively, you can easily arrange for a car with driver through one of the local travel agents or by contacting the **Tourist Information Office** on Jl. Malioboro. This office also can provide you with maps, brochures, and information on hotels, restaurants, and cultural performances. It also has a small book section with literature relevant to Jogja and Central Java.

You should have no problem finding accommodations in Jogja. However, you will not find the luxury and first-class hotels you found in Jakarta and Bali. Although several new three and four-star hotels have been recently completed (**Hotel Santika, Aquila Prambanam, Phoniek Hotel, Central Jokja International Hotel**, and the **Jokja Palace Hotel**), The older **Ambarrukmo Palace Hotel**, although somewhat worn, is the major international luxury-class hotel in Jogja. It includes a shopping arcade and regularly puts on wayang and gamelan performances for its guests. Antique shops and galleries are located nearby. Even if you don't stay here, you should at least visit the hotel for the shopping and cultural performances. A few other hotels provide first-class accommodations, such as the **Hotel Garuda, Yogya International Hotel**, and **Sahid Garden Hotel**. Most accommodations in Jogja tend to be on the budget end—basic and inexpensive.

WHAT TO BUY

Since Jogja is the center for Javanese culture, the shopping here expresses the major traditional and contemporary arts of the Javanese. Hundreds of craftspeople and artists produce a dazzling array of items. This is the city where you find a fabulous range of traditional and contemporary **batik paintings** done by internationally renowned artists who display and sell their paintings from home galleries and shops, many of which are concentrated near the Sultan's Palace as well as along Jl. Tirtodipuran. The most famous such painters are represented at **Kuswadji K.**, **Amri Gallery**, and **Ardiyanto Batik**. A popular shop for both tourists and dealers is **Seno Batik Painting** located just off Jl. Tirtodipuran. Here, you can also spend a few days at a small studio learning how to make your own batik paintings and tulis cloth designs.

However, like so much of what you find in Bali, many arts and crafts in Jogja are produced only for tourists. Many are over-produced, look the same, and often appear tacky. As elsewhere in Indonesia, you must dig through a lot of junk in order to find exactly what you most want to purchase and take home. Most of what you buy again falls in the categories of home decorative or accessory items.

Batik clothes and fabrics are widely available in small shops and home galleries throughout Jogja. You can easily spend a day going from one shop and designer boutique/factory to another shopping for distinctive Jogja batik. The best batik is found at **Sapto Hudoyo Art Batik Gallery** (Jl. Solo, near the airport, Tel. 62443) and **Ardiyanto Batik** (Jl. Magelang Km. 5.8, Tel. 62777). Several batik shops are found along Jl. Tirtodipuran. **Batik Plentong** (Jl. Tirtodipuran 28, Tel. 62777), a long established batik factory, is especially popular with tourists which means they also are overpriced because they must give commissions to guides and drivers.

Wayang puppets, both leather (wayang kulit) and wood (wayang golek) are found in Jogja's many shops. Of all Indonesian cities, Jogja has the best selections for such puppets. The son of the most famous puppet maker—**Warnowaskito**—is found in the nearby village of Krantil. **Swasthigita** (Jl. Nga-dinegaran) is a popular studio and workshop that produces wayang kulit as well as musical instruments (another expensive tour bus stop). In addition, wayang performances are regularly held in Jogjakarta, with hotel performances conveniently scheduled for visitors.

Jogjakarta's antique shops offer a wide variety of Dutch, Chinese, Javanese, and Balinese **antiques and furniture** as well as **ethnographic/primitive art** produced by the Nias, Dayak, Batak, and Asmat peoples. Jogja's antique shops are well worth poking around in for items you will not find elsewhere in Indonesia. A few antique shops are found across the street from the Ambarrukmo Palace Hotel as well as along Jl. Tirtodipuran (the two best are **The Ancient Arts** and **Griya Kriyastra Nygraha**). Jogja's best antique and furniture dealer is **Yamin** (Jl. Wonosari, Ketandan, Banguntapan, Bantul, Tel. 75170) which can be contacted through the **Mahakam** shop at the Ambarrukmo Palace Hotel (Tel. 88488, ext. 737). For an exquisite display of antiques, furniture, and ethnographic art, be sure to visit the popular **Sapto Hudoyo Art Batik Gallery** (Jl. Solo, Km. 9 Meguwo, Tel. 62443) and their boutique in the departure lounge of the airport.

Jogja is well noted for its contemporary **oil paintings**. The family of Indonesia's world famous impressionistic artist, **Affandi**, maintains a gallery/museum of his works in Jogja. Several other noted artists, especially **Amri** and **Ardiyanto**, also display their works in Jogja's numerous galleries. This is the center of Indonesia's budding young artists, many of whom are associated with the Fine Arts Academy in Jogja. Many sell their latest creations from private studios.

Jogja is also well noted for its **silver work**. Handmade jewelry, tea sets, cigarette boxes, and items made in filigree are found in many art shops in Jogja as well as in the silver craft center of **Kotagede**, a village five kilometers southeast of the city. Two of the largest and most competitive shops, **Yogya Silver** and **Tom's Silver**, are found on the outskirts of Kota-gede.

You will find numerous **leather** shops selling a wide variety of leather goods, such as suitcases, briefcases, purses, bags, sandals, and belts. The light-tan colored leather has a rough and crude look to it and gives off a distinctive odor. A Jogjakarta specialty, you may wish to pass on these items. Other leather products are found along Jl. Malioboro in downtown Jogja. Some of the most attractive and unique leather products are found at the **Mahakam** shop in the shopping arcade of the Ambarrukmo Palace Hotel. **Kusuma** at Jl. Kauman 50 (just off

Jl. Malioboro) offers some of the best quality leather products in Jogja. Several leather shops, such as **Hadi Sukirno**, are found along Jl. Tamansari.

Theater **masks** used in Javanese performances make attractive wall decorations. The ones found in Jogja differ in style from the more popular ones found in Bali.

Pottery is also available near Jogjakarta. Fired and painted, the distinctive Jogja pottery has a Mexican look about it and much of it is produced in the form of brightly colored animals. Other earthenware pottery produced in the famous pottery village of **Kasongan**, located just a few kilometers south of Jogja, constitutes some of the most attractive and creative pottery available in Indonesia. Look for numerous money boxes shaped into many different types of animals. Several art and curio shops in Jogja sell this pottery, but a visit to the home factories in this creative and dynamic village is well worth while.

WHERE TO SHOP

Most of Jogja's shopping is centered among small shops and galleries found in downtown Jogja along Jl. Malioboro, Jl. Tirtodipuran, and streets adjacent to the Sultan's Palace. You'll also find numerous home galleries, a hotel shopping arcade (Ambarrukmo Palace Hotel), craft centers, and a few villages near Jogja specializing in the silver, pottery, and crafts.

Since Jogja's shopping is spread over a large area, you will need transportation to get around this city. Either rent a car with driver or take a becak. If you take a becak, be sure to negotiate a flat rate price by the hour, half-day, or day with your driver. If you plan to cover long distances, do not take a becak. The streets of Jogja appear flat, but they have a sufficient slope to exhaust any becak driver after two hours of peddling.

JL. MALIOBORO

Depending on where you stay, you may want to start your Jogja shopping adventure in the downtown area along Jl. Malioboro. The shopping area is located directly across the street from the Hotel Garuda. This is a lively area both day and night. Several small shops sell a wide range of average quality arts and crafts. You'll find some lovely batik designer clothes here along with batik yardage, tablecloths, wall hangings, and greeting cards. Directly across from the Hotel Garuda is the **Naga Art Shop** which offers several local art and craft products. For leather and silver products, visit **Toko Subur** and **Sinta**. Batik clothes are found at **Batik Keris** and **Terang Bulam**. Be sure to visit the second floor of Batik Keris where you will also find a good selection of handicrafts. At night this area becomes a huge market which is especially popular with Jogja's budget travelers. Brightly lit, colorful, crowded, and noisy, the area becomes a fascinating mixture of shopkeepers, sidewalk souvenir and fruit vendors, becak drivers, restaurants, warangs, beggars, and tourists. This is where the shopping action in Jogja is found at night. Vendors line both sides of the street selling an enormous variety of inexpensive arts, crafts, clothes, and tourist kitsch. You'll find everything from leather bags, T-shirts, sandals, and brassware to Balinese carvings and batik greeting cards. Jogja's famous portable restaurants, warangs, line both sides of the street for several blocks. However, you may want to pass on their inexpensive foods since most food stays uncovered for hours and dishes are rinsed in dirty water—a possible breeding ground for hepatitis. Be sure to bargain hard with all vendors since their first asking price is likely to be high—for tourists only! While you won't find many quality items along Jl. Malioboro, you should have an interesting time just browsing, people watching, and experiencing all the exotic sights and sounds—an evening of cheap street entertainment.

AMBARRUKMO PALACE HOTEL
AND CRAFT CENTRE

Another good place from which to start your Jogja shopping adventure is the Ambarrukmo Palace Hotel on Jl. Laksda Adisucipto. This is Jogja's leading first-class hotel. It also has Jogja's only hotel shopping arcade. Across the street from the hotel you'll find a few antique, arts, and crafts shops as well as the Jogjakarta Craft Centre. And just a short distance down the street is the famous Affandi Museum.

The shopping arcade at the **Ambarrukmo Palace Hotel** has several shops worth visiting for batik clothes, arts, crafts, jewelry, and leather products. Two of the best shops here are Mahakam for unique leather bags, textiles, and mats and Fine Arts for batik paintings. **Mahakam** (Tel. 88488, Ext. 737) is actually owned and operated by the wife of one of Jogja's leading antique and furniture dealers—Yamin Makawaru—who pasted away a few years ago. In fact, if you want to visit his two shophouses, which are filled with lovely antiques and furniture, you can make an appointment through this shop. The shop itself offers unique and fashionable leather and rattan bags, accessories, and mats from East Kalimantan. Many dealers from abroad purchase stock for resale from this shop. Mahakam also has some good quality ikat textiles and small Moko bronze drums from the island of Alor. The batik paintings at **Fine Arts** are a very different style from most you will see in Jogja. Other shops in this arcade also offer good quality products: **Kotu Keya** for batik and wayang puppets; **Ramayana Art and Craft** for Balinese woodcarvings, porcelain, silver, batik, wayang puppets, and dolls; **First Arts** for batik paintings; **Gayatri** for leather goods; **Prabangkara Art Gallery** for batik paintings; **Nuk Hedijanto** for batik; **Javana Jewelry** for Indonesian black opals, pearls, and gems; **Kotagede Srimoeljo** for silver jewelry; **Paramita** for batik clothes; **Old Star** for Balinese carvings, silver, and wayang puppets; and **Nasta Boutique** for nice batik clothes for both men and women.

The **antique, arts, and crafts shops** across the street from the hotel, and adjacent to the Jogjakarta Crafts Centre, offer a wide range of locally produced items. The best shop here is **Diamond Art Shop**. It's a small, cluttered, dark, and dusty shop that you may at first hesitate to enter. However, it yields some good quality antiques from Java and the outer islands for those who have the time and patience to poke through all the clutter to find a few treasures. Once in, you can hardly move without bumping into antiques, arts, and crafts that clutter the floor, walls, and rafters! The shop has a good selection of chests, woodcarvings, wayang puppets, porcelain, masks, textiles, bronzes, kris, stonecarvings, and ethnographic pieces. The other shops in this area primarily offer arts and crafts rather than antiques. Look for **Ancient Arts**, **Arjuna Art Shop**, **Art and Souvenir**, and **Batik Painting Studio**.

The once lively **Jogjakarta Craft Centre** has fallen on hard times, especially since few tour guides and drivers bring tourists here. The problem supposedly relates to commissions—since the Centre doesn't pay commissions to guides and drivers, it's boycotted by them. Hopefully it will not suffer the fate of the now defunct and abandoned government handicraft center on the road to the airport, which was largely killed by the commission game. You may have to go here on your own or do so in conjunction with a stop at the Ambarrukmo Palace Hotel. The Centre does sell some unique and interesting art and craft products. The first floor of the main two-story building offers a wide selection of wayang puppets, pottery, bags, bamboo products, Lombok containers, masks, and woodcarvings; the second floor is largely devoted to batik and silver. To the left of this building is a small art and craft shop offering batik paintings, wayang puppets, and batik clothes. To the right is a shop well worth patronizing—**Handicrafts Made By Disabled People**. Operated by a self-help charitable organization, you'll find numerous handicrafts here produced by Jogja's handicapped community: leather bags and sandals, greeting cards, embroidery, placements, and toys.

JL. TIRTODIPURAN

During the past ten years Jl. Tirtodipuran has emerged as Jogja's new shopping mecca. Here you will find the city's largest concentration of art studios and batik home industry shops strung along both sides of this narrow half kilometer street. More than 100 of Jogja's painters are represented in the many shops along this street. Some good quality antique and craft shops also are found here.

You can easily spend two to three hours browsing through all the interesting art and antique shops and discovering some unique batik and oil paintings produced by Jogja's many famous and budding young artists. The quality here ranges from tourist kitsch to excellent, cheap to expensive, depending on your tastes. Some of the batik art, for example, is very creative, demonstrating modern, abstract, and art deco motifs. Browsing through the many studios will give you a good sense of why Jogja is considered Indonesia's vibrant art center.

Batik Pentong (Jl. Tirtodipuran 28) is one of Jogja's most popular batik factories and shops. Here you can observe the traditional batik process—both hand and stamped on cotton and silk fabrics—as well as make purchases from a large selection of batik paintings, clothes, tablecloths, and toys. Most prices are fixed, although you may get a 10 percent discount on quantity purchases. Prices tend to be high because the shop works directly with tour guides and bus drivers.

Seno Batik Painting, which is located along a narrow lane just off Jl. Tirtodipuran, is the largest batik art studio in the area. It's a very popular shop with tourists and dealers alike. While you will find a large inventory from which to choose, don't expect to find unique quality art here. Most paintings are interesting and inexpensive, primarily mass produced for the tourist market and foreign dealers who are looking for colorful souvenir art. You'll undoubtedly find something of interest here. However, expect to get a 25 to 50% discount on your purchases here. This shop is one of the biggest practitioners of the commission game. Most becak drivers bring tourists here where they can collect commissions. You, of course, are paying the drivers indirectly by purchasing items at inflated prices. Whatever you do, don't pay the asking prices which are bit on the outrageous side. You can do better elsewhere.

Griya Kriyasta Nugraha (also known as Nug's Arts and

Crafts House) and **The Ancient Arts** are the two best shops for arts, crafts, and antiques. Riya Kriyasta Nugraha has a nice collection of pottery, wayang puppets, masks, gamelan instruments, ethnographic carvings, and leather bags. The Ancient Arts offers wood panels, wayang puppets, masks, woodcarvings, Madura chests, Sumba textiles, pottery, and kris.

Other shops to look for along Jl. Tirtodipuran include **Sutopo** for uniquely modern batik paintings; **Delly Art Shop and Antiques** for masks, wayang golek, kris, and ethnographic carvings; **Kartika Batik Painting** for similar types of paintings found at Seno Batik Painting; **Tulus Warsito** for unique style batik paintings produced by Warsito and his students; **Babo** for designer batik and leather clothes; **Yuli Gallery** ("no commissions" sign prominently displayed above the door way) for paintings, gamelan instruments, and a large selection of wayang puppets; **Dieng Art and Antiques** for porcelain, masks, wayang puppets, boxes, and lacquerware; **Winotosastro** for batik clothes and paintings; and **Madiyono** and **Harto** for antiques, carvings, masks, and wayang puppets.

❑ Jl. Tirtodipuran has emerged as Jogja's new shopping mecca with its large concentration of art studios and batik shops.

❑ Many shops give commissions to tour guides and becak drivers to bring tourists to their shops. These shops tend to be mediocre and overpriced by 50 to 80%.

❑ If you are interested in paintings, batik, and antiques, be sure to visit Ardiyanto Wijayakusuma Batik on Jl. Magelang Km. 5.8.

❑ Yamin is Jogja's best antique and furniture dealer.

THE SULTAN'S PALACE

Located at the center of the city, the Sultan's Palace is a major tourist attraction for learning about the history and culture of Jogjakarta. It's also a good place for shopping. Several streets surrounding the Sultan's Palace are lined with batik, art, craft, and leather shops.

One of Jogja's best batik art shops is **Kuswadji K.** (Jl. Alun-Alun Utara, Tel. 4995), located along a side street to the right of the front gate to the Palace and adjacent to Jl. Kauman. This is Jogja's oldest batik art gallery and shop which represents the city's top artists. In fact, this is where batik as a medium for painting first began with the works of Kuswadji K. We especially like the works of Totok H. Kuswadji. If you're looking for top quality and unique batik paintings, be sure to stop here early in your visit to Jogja.

Near the Palace is Jl. Kauman which has two of Jogja's better leather shops. **Kusuma** (Jl. Kauman 50) is one of Jogja's best leather shops for shoes, purses, bags, and belts. While it offers some attractive styles, the leather here is still somewhat crude; it lacks the smooth finishing touches you might expect from top quality leather. But it is some of the best leather you can find in Jogja. Along this same street you will find a leather bag shop—**Aris**.

Behind the Sultan's Palace is a large and rather traditional arts and crafts shop—**Tjokrosuharta**. Here you will find a good selection of silver, batik, musical instruments, kris, wayang puppets, head dresses, and batik canting supplies. Also behind the Palace, along Jl. **Lotowijayan**, are more than 10 batik shops selling batik paintings and clothes. Along nearby Jl. **Sompilan** you will find Jogja's popular Bird Market which sells all kinds of exotic birds and bird cages. A few batik shops are also found along this street. Nearby Jl. **Ngadisuryan** also has several batik shops.

If you are interested in good quality batik paintings, be sure to visit the shops along Jl. Panjaitan, near the south gate of the Sultan's Palace. Here you will find an excellent batik art gallery—**Trimurti** (Jl. Panjaitan 24). This gallery displays the works of three famous batik artists who produce some of the most unique designs in Jogja.

You'll also find several handicraft stalls located near the front gate of the Palace. Most offer inexpensive souvenirs for tourists. Don't expect to find much beyond the typical tourist kitsch offered to bus loads of souvenir seekers.

PRIVATE GALLERIES AND HOME SHOPS

Jogja has several outstanding private galleries and home shops that are found in different sections of the city. While some tour groups will visit a few of these places, you will probably have to find them on your own. Many are located along back streets of residential neighborhoods.

Jogja's best and most easily assessable gallery is the **Sapto Hudoyo Art Batik Gallery** (Tel. 87443). Located on Jl. Solo (Km. 9) near the airport, this is a "must visit" shophouse for any visitor to Jogja and one of the best shops in all of Indonesia. The shop rightfully advertises itself as the place *"where kings, presidents, and important people visit."* Everything here is beautifully displayed and service is exceptional—two characteristics largely absent to most Indonesian shops. Mr. Sapto Hudoyo is one of Indonesia's leading batik designers, antique collectors, and patrons of modern art. And this shop clearly displays his talents. Room after room is filled with beautifully designed batik and ikat materials and garments and a unique collection of arts and antiques from all over Indonesia—oil paintings, woodcarvings, wayang puppets, furniture, and masks. The shophouse is as much a museum and cultural experience as it is a retail shop. It's an art lover's and decorator's delight. Some tour groups have special arrangements to have dinner here. The unique batik shop in the airport departure lounge is a branch of this shop; it is operated by Sapto Hudoyo's talented wife who is usually present.

Yamin is Jogja's best antique and furniture dealer. If you want to visit the main shop on Jl. Wanosari, it's best to make an appointment through their Mahakam shop at the Ambarrukmo Palace Hotel (Tel. 88488, ext. 737). The main shop is filled with antique chests, tables, chairs, gables, ethnographic carvings from Borneo, old mats, bags, wayang puppets, pottery, masks, carved panels, Asmat shields, and textiles. The quality here is first-rate. The second shop, which is actually the owner's home, is filled with even more furniture, masks, and bags. Serious collectors and dealers who are looking for good quality antique Javanese furniture will love Yamin's shops.

Affandi Museum and art studio is located on Jl. Solo, just a few minutes walk from the Ambarrukmo Palace Hotel. This is the museum and art gallery of Indonesia's most famous abstract artist. While the artist Affandi is now deceased, his gallery is open to the public. Most paintings for sale in the adjacent studio are those of Affandi's daughter, Kartika.

The **Ardiyanto Wijayakusuma Batik** on Jl. Magelang (Tel. 62777) is the home studio and gallery of another internationally famous Jogja artist—Ardiyanto. While he has a shop in downtown Jogja and in the Hotel Santika, which primarily sells batik clothes and wall hangings, this home gallery mainly displays Ardiyanto's unique paintings and those of 50 other artists. His works are expensive but they represent the works of a master painter. This gallery also offers some antiques, clothes, pillows, and bedspreads. The lovely home compound is very quiet. Few tourists come here because guides and drivers generally avoid the place since it does not give commissions.

The **Amri Gallery** (Jl. Gampingan 67, Tel. 64525) is another world famous batik artist who maintains a home studio filled with unique paintings and designer clothes. Widely exhibited abroad, he produces very distinctive abstract paintings using bold splashes of bright colors. While primarily working in batik, Amri also produces some oils and watercolors. His art prices range from inexpensive US$60 to US$5,000 or more. The gallery also functions as a museum, which includes one of Imelda Marcos' paintings which she produced here in 1974. This gallery excels with excellent displays and good marketing.

You'll find numerous other famous and not-so-famous

artists and craftspeople with home galleries and shops found throughout Jogja and its outlying areas. The **Kabul Art Gallery**, for example, offers a large range of batik paintings that are especially popular amongst tourists and commissioned drivers!

FACTORIES

One of the real shopping treats in Jogjakarta is being able to shop at the various factories that produce the arts and crafts Jogja is so famous for. You can see the craftspeople at work and then purchase the finished products at the factory shop. This does not mean prices are necessarily any cheaper at the factory than in a regular shop. It's just more interesting and convenient: you get to buy what you see being made.

You'll find numerous factories throughout the Jogja area producing batik, silver, pottery, wayang puppets, musical instruments, and leather goods. Jogja's famous silver factories are concentrated in and around the village of **Kotagede**, which is actually a small town five kilometers southwest of Jogja. Just before reaching the main street of this village, you will find Jogja's two largest and most competitive silver factories—Yogya Silver-Works Centre and Tom's Silver. **Yogya Silver-Works Centre** was Jogja's most popular silver factory and shop until Tom's Silver opened nearby (900 meters) a couple of years ago. Now the two factories are in intense competition for tour groups and tourists. You'll have to visit both shops to decide which one is best for you. Be sure to bargain at both places. You'll find over 50 silver factories in the village of Kotagede.

Another popular village is **Kasongan** which is located near the 6.5 km. post on Bantul Road south of Jogja. Famous for producing unique earthenware pottery using animal motifs (fish, horses, dragons, birds), this highly entrepreneurial and increasingly wealthy village now exports its attractive products to Japan, Australia, and Thailand. More than seven households produce pottery as well as sell their products directly to visitors. This is one of the most interesting craft villages we have visited in all of Southeast Asia.

The village of **Krantil**, located near the 7.6 km post on Bantul Road south of Jogja, is home of the son of Indonesia's oldest and most famous mask and wayang golek puppet craftsmen—Warnowaskito, who passed away a few years ago. Everything is meticulously handcrafted at this home studio. While his son does not maintain a large inventory, because he produces the puppets and masks for special orders, you should be able to see him at work producing the traditional masks and puppets.

Swasthigita (Jl. Ngadinegaran 7/50) is a very large factory and shop that produces gamelan instruments and wayang kulit puppets. Popular with tour groups, this studio and workshop gives visitors a guided tour which enables you to see the many craftsmen making various instruments and leather puppets. Some tour groups are also treated to gamelan and wayang performances. At the end of the tour, you will enter the shop where you can purchase a large assortment of products: leather puppets, shields, placemats, lampshades, kris, wayang golek, masks, woodcarvings, and instruments.

A few factory/shops along Jl. Tamansari also produce leather wayang puppets. Two of the most popular are **Moeljosoe-hardjo** at Jl. Tamansari 37B (Tel. 2873) and **S. Nitiredjo** at Jl. Tamansari 37A.

If you visit Borobudur, you will see several shophouses along the road from Jogja to Borobudur that produce furniture, doors, and panels. Most shops do special orders, should you decide to use their services.

ADDITIONAL CITY SHOPPING

You will find numerous other shops spread throughout this bustling city. In general, expect to find small shops and vendor stalls near the major tourist attractions. In addition to shops near the Sultan's Palace, you will also find several shops selling batik clothes, paintings, and crafts along Jl. Cemara and Jl. Ngasem, next to the **Water Castle**. One of the best shops in this area for batik paintings is **Astuti** on Jl. Ngasem. Shops along Jl. Parangtritis, such as the **Galar Gallery** (#11), offer paintings, antiques, and jewelry.

If you depart Jogjakarta by air, be sure to arrive at the airport departure lounge earlier than you normally would. You'll be pleasantly surprised to discover a small but excellent quality boutique selling batik garments, Sumba textiles, Javanese carvings, jewelry, batik prints and paintings, and leather and straw bags. Indeed, this is one of the best shops in Jogja. Operated by the Sapto Hoedojo Art Gallery, this shop also puts on fashion shows for departing flights. It's great entertainment as well as good shopping here. Many men will appreciate this shop, because it is one of the very few that carries an attractive selection of large size batik shirts. This may well become your favorite shop in Jogja!

PRICEY BUS STOP SHOPS

On the road to Borobudur, Jl. Magelang, you will find a few art and craft shops that primarily cater to tour buses—**Art House, Art Silver**, and **Art Painting**. These are large shops which offer a wide selection of varying quality batik paintings, some of which are good quality. However, most of these shops charge high prices, because they must give large commissions to the tour guide leaders and bus drivers who have special arrangements for bringing tour groups to these shops. The sales people are real experts at their craft—very friendly and well organized. Art House, for example, is a favorite for Japanese tour groups and thus their salespeople will pamper you with the type of service normally expected by Japanese shoppers. Knowing this, you should be able to get a large discount on everything you purchase as long as you don't come here with a tour group. However, if you are with a tour group and your bus takes a "shopping break" here, beware that you may pay twice as much for many of the same items you can purchase in Jogja. While the salespeople may try to make you feel good by offering you a 20% discount, hold out for 50%, which they can give if you come here on your own. These shops do have good selections of batik paintings. However, many of the same paintings can be found in the shops and galleries in Jogja which obviously supply these "bus stop shops."

SHOPPING FOR QUALITY ON LIMITED TIME

If you have limited time for shopping in Jogja, we recommend that you focus your shopping on a few quality shops and major shopping areas where you are most likely to find the "best of the best." In fact, if you stop in Jogja but only have two or three hours between flights, you should visit the **Sapto Hoedojo Art Gallery** which is located only five minutes from the airport. This is Jogja's most outstanding shop and a "must" for any visitor to Jogja. You can easily visit this shop between flights as well as its smaller shop in the airport departure lounge.

While Jl. Malioboro is considered to be Jogja's major shopping center, you can do better elsewhere, especially if your shopping time is limited and you are looking for unique and quality items. The downtown area is filled with tourist shops and street vendors that sell similar average to low quality products. We recommend, instead, heading for the shopping arcade at the **Ambarrukmo Palace Hotel** as well as the many batik, art, and antique shops that line **Jl. Tirtodipuran**.

If you don't want to waste your time digging through all the tourist kitsch and encountering inflated "commission" prices, make sure you visit these places:

- **Sapto Hudoyo Art Batik Gallery:** Jl. Solo, Km. 9, Meguwo, Tel. 62443. Located only five minutes from the airport, this gorgeous shop displays excellent quality batik and antiques. As you will quickly discover, this also is the most entrepreneurial shop in Jogjakarta which constantly advertises and pays close attention to the details of customer service. You'll find just about everything here: batik clothes and yardage, silver, paintings, jewelry, and antiques. The biggest problem is knowing what is or is not for sale. Items for sale are interspersed with the private antiques of the owners. You'll have to ask or look for the "Not for Sale" signs. Unfortunately, all the really "good stuff" is not for sale. Nonetheless, this expansive and colorful shop is as much a cultural experience as it is shopper's paradise. Be sure to visit Mrs. Yani's boutique in the airport departure lounge. Lots of VIPs come here and, of course, they are dutifully photographed with the owners to impress visitors. Don't get too carried away with all the trappings of the savvy marketing. Prices tend to be very high for what is not always top quality. Tour groups can arrange private diners and performances here.

- **Ardiyanto Wijayakusuma Batik:** Jl. Magelang Km. 5.8, Tel. 62777. Known as "Ardiyanto," this home-based gallary, studio, and shop is a "must see" stop on any visit to Jogjakarto. It's one of our favorites in all of Indonesia. A real quality operation. The popular artist Ardiyanto operates a combination art gallery, antique shop, and batik boutique in this expansive residence. You'll find some very interesting paintings here done by Ardiyanto and 50 other artists he represents in the gallery. Since Ardiyanto's wife runs one of the largest batik factories in Indonesia, you may want to examine their product line for export purposes. Also has a small shop in the Hotel Santika and across the street from the Garuda Hotel in downtown Jogja.

- **Yamin:** Jl. Wonosari, Ketandan, Banguntapan, Bantul, Tel. 75170 (but probably best to make your initial contact through the Mahakam shop at the Ambarrukmo Palace Hotel, Tel. 66488, ext. 7160). This is Jokjakarta's best shop and warehouse for antique Javanese furniture and collectibles. Many international dealers buy directly from the warehouse. The quality is excellent and prices are still reasonable. If you have any interest in furniture, make sure you visit Yamin.

- **Amri Gallery:** Gampingan 5, Tel. 64525. This is the gallery/boutique of one of Indonesia's most famous abstract painters, the internationally renowned Amri. The gallery displays a good selection of his paintings, and the adjacent boutique includes several of his unique clothing designs. Amri's paintings are very expensive—for serious collectors only! Closed on Mondays.

- **Griya Kriyasta Nugraha** (also known as Nug's Arts and Crafts House). Jl. Tirtodipuran 65, Tel. 72467. One of Jogja's best antique shops. Includes Javanese wedding figures, wayang puppets, old batik, masks, and pots. Also has a separate furniture shop. Ask the owner, Ambar, to see his "collection" at home. Altogether, he operates four shops. Previously associated with Jogja's premier antique dealer—Yamin.

- **The Ancient Arts:** Jl. Tirtodipuran 51. Located directly across the street from Griya Kriyasta Nugraha on Jl. Tirtodipuran. This is one of those dark and dusty antique shops that can yield lots of fine treasures. Here, you'll find excellent quality textiles, pots, masks, wayang puppets, Javanese wedding figures, chests, and kris. Since nothing is displayed well, you must dig around in the various rooms in search of something that grabs your interest.

- **Kuswadji K:** Jl. Alun-Alun Utara, Tel. 4995 (located near Sultan's Palace, next to Jl. Kauman). One of Jogja's oldest batik art shops. Produces traditional batik paintings. While this is a small and unpretentious shop, you may find some nice quality batik paintings here produced by major painters. Since this gallery is not on the bus and becak drivers' tour route, you get good quality at good prices.

- **Borneo Boutique:** Jl. Tirtodipuran 49, Tel. 75983. Specializes in ikat textiles and carvings from the Dayak of Borneo. Nicely displayed in three rooms. Includes Sumba textiles, carvings figures and bowls, spears, baskets, and masks. Includes both new and old items. Fixed prices.

- **Kabul Art Gallery:** Jl. Timoho 29A, Gendeng GL4/17A, Tel. 66669. Watch your wallet! We hesitate to recommend this shop, but since you are likely to end up here anyway, and a little education into pricing practices and bargaining can't hurt you, here goes. This is the art gallery of the former becak driver who became a talented batik artist, Wiji Hartono. You'll find lots of lovely batik paintings here, but the prices are outrageously high. It's due to the touristy "bus and becak stop" nature of the shop. Try to come here on your own and ask for a discount that should reflect the true value of these paintings. In fact, a 70% discount is not unreasonable; 80% would be just right. If they ask US$1000 for a painting, do not pay more than US$300. If you're really good with your bargaining skills, as outlined in Chapter 5, you should walk away with an ostensibly US$1000 painting for US$250! Unfortunately, the tour bus crowd gets "taken" here as well as at other similar art emporiums. Nonetheless, this gallery does have a nice selection of paintings. Just know what you're doing here.

ON TO SOLO

If time permits, you may want to visit the city of Solo which is located approximately 60 kilometers east of Jogjakarta. Also known as Surakarta and Sala, it once served as the capital of the Mataram kingdom (1745). Today it remains a noted cultural center and Indonesia's major batik production center with a population of over 500,000.

While only 60 kilometers from Jogjakarta, the drive between Jogja and Solo may take up to two hours, depending on the traffic situation. The picturesque countryside of rice, sugarcane, and tobacco fields is laced with a continuous traffic jam of people, horsecarts, bicycles, becaks, and pollution belching buses and motorcycles. If you plan to visit Solo, expect to spend a good part of your day getting to and from this place. With additional time for shopping and sightseeing, a trip to Solo should be planned as a full-day event.

Solo is a quaint yet bustling city which looks similar to Jogjakarta minus its many tourists. Its wide streets, lined with fences, walls, and gates, are occupied by the usual bewildering maze of becaks, motorcycles, cars, and horsecarts as well as double-decker buses. In many respects, the city has more character and charm than Jogja but it still has a typical worn and makeshift look to it. Its attractiveness is centered around its major historical attractions.

While most tourists visit Solo to see the two sultan's palaces—**Mangkunegaran Palace** and **Kraton Kasuhunan** —many also discover Solo's shopping attractions. These primarily consist of an antique market, batik factories, a central market, and a few arts, crafts, and antique shops.

If you travel to Solo on your own, you may want to stop at the **Tourist Information Centre** which is located on the main street, Jl. Brigjen Slamet Riyadi. Sponsored by the Surakarta Municipality Tourism Office, this Centre can provide you with a useful map of the city as well as brochures on batik factories and hotels. It distributes what should be a useful guide to handicrafts, hotels, and restaurants in the Solo area. However, the English is somewhat unintelligible since someone without a command of the English language either wrote it or translated it from Indonesian! The Centre also has a showroom with samples of batik produced by Solo's leading batik manufacturers—Danar Hadi and Batik Keris. You can also hire a private guide here. A few freelance guides may approach you while you are gathering information at the counter.

ANTIQUE MARKET

Solo's famous antique market—**Pasar Triwindu**—is bigger than the more popular Jl. Surabaya antique market in Jakarta. It's the only one of its kind in Central Java and the largest in Indonesia. Located off of Jl. Diponegoro, this is a fun place to shop if you enjoy flea markets and junk shops. You'll find nearly 100 small stalls selling a large range of antiques, arts, crafts, and junk. Most shops repeat the same products: lamps, tables, kris, porcelain, walking canes, wayang puppets, masks, beads, coins, brassware, ethnographic carvings, bottles, scales, irons, tools, dishes, clocks, jewelry, Madura chests, and even meat grinders! The second half of this market is devoted to shops selling used appliances and spare parts for cars, bicycles, and motorcycles, a fascinating commentary on the fact that this is not a throw-away society. You may find some genuine antiques here, especially old batik fabric, furniture, bottles, and clocks. However, you should know your antiques before making any serious purchases since you can easily buy "new" antiques at "old" antique prices in this market. Indeed, you will find many copies of antiques here. Fortunately, the copies are poor quality and thus easy to detect. Quality items are hard to find in the midst of all the junk, but you may find a treasure or two if you have the time and patience to dig through the cluttered messes. In the end, you may find the market of more interest as a cultural experience than as a great shopping experience. Be sure to bargain for everything in this market, and expect deep discounts of 40% or more.

CENTRAL MARKET

The Central Market, or **Pasar Klewer**, is located just outside the walls of the Kraton Surakarta along Jl. Coyudau. Solo's largest market, it is also reputed to be Indonesia's largest batik market. The two-story building is crammed with vendors selling batik clothes and yardage as well as shoes, sandals, and bags. You will also find the traditional handwoven but not so fashionable material called lurik here. The batik vendors are primarily found on the second floor. Keep in mind that since most of the batik found here is produced for the local market, the designs may not be particularly appealing to your tastes. Nonetheless, you will find a good range of traditional designs at good prices. Be sure to bargain here as you would in any Indonesian market. Photo buffs will find this colorful market an excellent photo opportunity.

BATIK FACTORIES/SHOPS

As Indonesia's batik center, Solo has numerous batik factories and shops open to the public. The three major batik producers—Batik Keris, Danar Hadi, and Batik Semar—have shops in the city. If you've already visited Jakarta, Bali, or Jogjakarta, you may have visited one of their branch shops.

While each of these shops produces very attractive brochures on their products, we're not impressed with the styles, colors, selections, and sizes available at their batik factories and shops in Solo, especially those found at Batik Keris and Danar Hadi. Their more stylish garments seem to be in Jakarta. Many colors are too blended for the fashion tastes of Western tourists. All three factory/shops mostly stock small and medium size ready-made garments. While appropriate for local buyers and Japanese tourists, the absence of large sizes effectively eliminates any shopping by larger sized tourists. This is a persistent problem throughout Indonesia, but it is especially pronounced in Solo, the center for batik production! Until shops learn to produce better styles and larger sizes, we'll pass on making any batik purchases except in a few shops in Jakarta that are more oriented to foreign markets and tastes. However, you may want to buy some lovely batik yardage. Since most visitors have limited time in Solo, a four to seven day waiting period for tailored garments is impractical. You'll have take the material with you to have it made into garments or home decorative items elsewhere. In the meantime, if you have not observed the batik process, factories in Solo are good places to observe how batik is produced.

Batik Semar, however, is well worth visiting. Located at 148 Jl. R. Mas Said (Tel. 2938, 5590, or 6173), this large three-story factory and showroom has an excellent selection of quality batik fabrics, clothes, stuffed toys, neckties, bags, and pillows as well as numerous attractive handicrafts, such as ceramics, baskets, bags, fans, and slippers. Be sure to go to the third floor where you will find the best quality fabrics—silk, hand batik, and ikat. If you have time to visit only one batik factory and showroom, we highly recommend Batik Semar.

ART AND ANTIQUE SHOPS

Real art and antique lovers will want to head for a few shops found along Jl. Jend. Urip Sumoharjo, Jl. Kepatihan, and Jl. Imam Bonjol. Solo's oldest and most reliable antique shop—**Sing Pellet**—is found on Jl. Jend. Urip Sumoharjo (Mesen 117/113), one of the city's major shopping streets. Operating in Solo for nearly 50 years, this shop offers a good collection of old bells, masks, chests, textiles, wayang puppets, spears, swords, bronzeware, knives, kris, porcelain, vases, jars, shields, and musical instruments. The owner's son, Willy Moertojo Widodo, operates another art and antique shop at Jl. Kepatihan 31—**Pellet Kepatihan** (also known as Toko Barang2 Kuno). This shop offers porcelain, jewelry, vases, lamps, furniture, canons, knives, coins, and old cigarette lighters. Another good art and antique shop worth visiting is **Nila Artshop** at Jl. Iman Bonjol No. 81, located just around the corner from the Kusuma Sahid Prince Hotel. A small shop, it has a nice collection of good quality wayang puppets, masks, Madura chests, kris, baskets, spears, and old batik fabrics. You will also find a small souvenir and art shop on the grounds of the **Mangkunegaran Palace** offering wayang kulit puppets, masks, photos, and new kris for tourists.

ENJOYING YOUR STAY

The Jogjakarta-Solo area is a rich historical, cultural, and artistic area that has much to offer visitors who are interested in learning more about Indonesia and the Javanese. You can easily spend a week here sightseeing, shopping, and enjoying the performing arts. You can even learn to play musical instruments and produce batik paintings and fabrics in several of Jogja's studios and factories. This is truly an arts and crafts paradise.

THE SITES

Several tour companies provide half and full-day tours to several interesting sites in and around Jogjakarta and Solo. You may prefer to rent a car and driver to visit these same places. Some of the most popular sightseeing attractions include:

- **Borobudur:** Located about 42 kilometers northwest of Jogja, this is Indonesia's most famous and grandest Buddhist monument built during the eighth and ninth centuries. Considered by many observers as one of the great wonders of the world, this huge restored step-pyramid complex measures about 380 feet on each side and has 504 Buddha statues and 2500 carved relief panels. The newly constructed visitors park has many shops selling all types of souvenirs. Be prepared to be pestered by numerous vendors who approach you with books, postcards, hats, tops, umbrellas, and clothes. Located nearby are two additional temples worth visiting—**Pawon Temple** and **Mendet Temple**. These temples, too, are surrounded by souvenir shops and aggressive vendors.

- **Prambanan:** Located 17 kilometers from Jogjakarta on the road to Solo, this famous Hindu temple complex was constructed during the 7th century. The newly constructed visitors park has similar vendors and vendor stalls as found at Borobudur. Other temples in this vicinity include **Bany Nibo Temple**, **Sewu Temple**, **Plaosan Temple**, **Kalasan Temple**, **Sari Temple**, **Sambi Sari Temple**, and **Gebang Temple**.

- **The Sultan's Palace:** The Sultan's Palace, or Kraton Ngayogyakarta Hadiningrat, is the city's major attraction. Located at the center of the city at the southern end of Jl. Ahmid Yani, this one square kilometer complex houses nearly 25,000 residents, many of whom produce arts and crafts. Informative tours explain the history and present use of the palace.

- **Sono Budoyo Museum:** This is the best of Jogja's museums. Located on the square in front of the Sultan's Palace, it includes an interesting collection of arts and crafts from Java and Bali.

- **Water Castle:** Located to the southwest of the Sultan's Palace in Tamansari, the Water Castle at one time served as a recreational area for the royal family. You can still see its two bathing pools and walk through the underground passageways. Several shops sell batik and souvenirs, and many batik artists live along Tamansari's narrow pathways.

- **Affandi Museum:** Located near the Ambarrukmo Palace Hotel on Jl. Solo, this museum is devoted to the works of Indonesia's most famous abstract painter. An exhibition hall displays a permanent collection of Affandi's works.

- **Sasono Wirotmo:** The former house of Javanese hero Prince Diponegoro, this museum displays many of his possessions.

- **Cultural performances:** You should also visit the **Academy of Fine Arts** on Jl. Gampingan and attend wayang, gamelan, and Javanese dance performances held at the **Agastya Art Institute** (Jl. Gedong Kiwo MD III/237), **Arjuna Plaza Hotel** (Jl. Mangkubumi 48), or the **Ambarrukmo Palace Hotel**. Contact the **Tourist Information Center** on Jl. Malioboro for details or contact these places directly for information on performance times. These cultural activities will give you an excellent overview of the central Javanese culture which is so well represented in all of the shops, factories, and galleries you will visit in Jogja.

- **Solo sites:** The **Mangkunegaran Palace** and **Kraton Kasuhunan** are Solo's two major tourist attractions.

Both palaces include excellent museums with extensive collections of antiques, arts, crafts, and memorabilia. The museum at the Kraton Kasuhunan is one of the best in Central Java.

ACCOMMODATIONS

Both Jogjakarta and Solo have a few first-class hotels, but most accommodations are appropriate for budget travelers—basic and inexpensive. You won't find deluxe-style accommodations as you do in Jakarta and Bali. Jogjakarta's best hotels include:

- **Ambarrukmo Palace Hotel:** Located on Jl. Laksda Adisucipto (Tel. 88488), this is Jogja's best hotel. Located outside the city center, it includes a shopping arcade and three restaurants. Look for special gamelan and wayang performances.

- **Hotel Garuda:** Located on Jl. Malioboro, this grand old hotel is centrally located for downtown shopping. Great location for observing all the street activities and shopping at night in front of the hotel. Includes a gamelan orchestra in the hotel lobby.

- **New hotels:** Several new third and fourth class hotels have been recently completed: **Hotel Santika, Aquila Prambanam, Phoniek Hotel, Central Jokja International Hotel**, and the **Jokja Palace Hotel.**

- **Yogya International Hotel:** One of Jogja's better hotels. Includes a hotel shop.

- **Guest Houses:** Jogja has long been one of Indonesia's guest house meccas. You can still find inexpensive accommodations from $3 to $25 per night. One of the best areas to explore is **Jl. Prawirotaman**, which is lined with numerous guest houses. Better still, it is actually an extension of one of Jogja's major shopping streets for arts, antiques, and crafts—Jl. Tirtodipuran.

- **Solo accommodations:** Although most visitors stay in Jogja and only visit Solo as part of a day tour, should you decide to stay in Solo, consider the **Kusuma Sahid Prince Hotel** on Jl. Sugiyopranoto 22 (Tel. 6356) with its lovely landscaped gardens and excellent restaurant. Another, although less attractive, possibility is the **Mangkunegaran Palace Hotel** which is located next to the palace. Solo also has numerous inexpensive guest houses.

RESTAURANTS

Jogja is especially famous for its street food vendors. The largest concentration is found along Jl. Malioboro. However, you may or may not want to sample these street foods since neither refrigeration nor hygiene are evident as foods stay uncovered all day and dishes get rinsed—not washed—in dirty water. You might, instead, try some of Jogja's good restaurants. Some of the best and safest include:

- **Sintawang Restaurant:** Jl. Magelang 9. Jogja's best seafood and Chinese restaurant.

- **Pasta Perak:** Jl. Tentura Rakyat Mataran 8. Serves excellent Javanese cuisine. Try their rijstaffel.

- **Bale Kambang Restaurant:** The Ambarrukmo Palace Hotel, Jl. Laksda Adisucipto. Buffet style dining with Indonesian food.

- **French Grill:** Arjuna Plaza Hotel, Jl. Mangkubumi 48. Good French food.

- **Palm House Restaurant:** Jl. Prawirotaman, in the heart of the guest house area. Excellent Indonesian, Chinese, and Western food at inexpensive prices.

- **Solo restaurants:** One of the best places for breakfast, lunch, or dinner is the **Kasuma Sahid** at the Kasuma Sahid Prince Hotel (Jl. Sugiyopranoto 22).

11

The Other Indonesias

J akarta, Bali, and Jogjakarta are the primary destinations for 90% of Indonesia's visitors. The tourist infrastructure in these areas is relatively well developed to make your visit convenient and comfortable. If you confine your visit to these three areas, you will experience some of the very best traveling and shopping Indonesia has to offer.

Another Indonesia awaits more adventuresome travelers and shoppers. For many visitors, this other Indonesia is a more satisfying yet arduous journey. Consisting of nearly 90 million people dispensed over thousands of islands, this other Indonesia is where you will find the production centers for Indonesia's famous ethnographic arts and textiles. While you occasionally get glimpses of this other Indonesia in a few antique, art, and craft shops on Java and Bali, there is no substitute for going to these places if you want to experience the peoples and cultures. If you are on a tight budget or neither have the time nor motivation to adventure beyond the creature-comforts of Jakarta, Bali, and Jogja, then head for the ethnographic shops in these cities. Here, you will discover some interesting textiles and ethnographic pieces from the outer islands.

But be forewarned that the shopping in the outer islands is not nearly as good as the shopping you find in Jakarta, Bali, and

Jogja. The really "good stuff" is found in the major shops of those three cities.

But there is no substitute for packing your bags and taking off to discover this truly exotic other Indonesia. What you will quickly find are very different cultures producing arts and crafts which have little relationship to the Javanese and Balinese. Java and Bali indeed represent the refined (*halus*) arts and crafts. The other Indonesia appears cruder (*kasar*) with its more primitive styles.

APPROPRIATE STRATEGIES

If you venture beyond Java and Bali, be prepared to adjust your shopping approaches to best fit the situations found in the outer islands:

1. **Fly to the major centers:** We recommend flying between locations for both convenience and comfort. Taking anything other than a cruise ship or car between cities and towns may be foolish. The boats and buses are extremely cheap, but they can be miserable. You will actually get more than what you paid for. If you want to punish yourself, take a bus for four hours in the heat, humidity, and hills of Sumatra or Sulawesi. You will feel every pothole along the way, and you will most likely share your tiny beat-up seat with fruits, vegetables, and the local animals on the way to the market. This is fun for about 45 minutes and then the novelty wears off quickly. Remember the word "miserable!" You'll quickly discover that the outer islands have a transportation infrastructure, which should not be confused with a tourist infrastructure.

2. **Hire a car with driver:** The most convenient way to get around in the outer islands is by private car. Arrange for this at your hotel. A few tour operators, such as Pacto, do have organized as well as private tours. You can arrange many of these through the head offices in Jakarta or through a local travel agent once you arrive. We find it's not necessary to pre-book arrangements in Jakarta. You should have no problem organizing your tour once you arrive at your destination.

3. **Stay at good hotels:** The best hotels in many cities and towns outside Java and Bali look like worn motels or old YMCAs. Staffs are not well trained, and maintenance is a foreign concept. If you opt for a cheap hotel, you may quickly learn that there is a big, big difference between first and second-class. On the other hand, you will find some nice clean, yet basic, accommodations in these areas. But don't expect to find Jakarta's Grand Hyatt and Borobudur or Bali's Four Seasons Resort and Amandari in these areas.

4. **Be prepared to spend money:** The outer islands are not cheap, but neither do they need to be expensive. The most expensive areas are Kalimantan and Irian Jaya. The cost of traveling in these areas may be 25% more than on Java, Bali, Sumatra, and Sulawesi, depending on how you plan to travel.

5. **Watch out for overpricing:** Except for the entrepreneurial Batak in northern Sumatra, the business people in the outer islands do not seem to price according to the concepts of supply and demand. Many ask outrageous prices, won't bargain, and may try to cheat you. This most often occurs in what appear to be tourist shops. You often will do better in quality shops located near major hotels—or in Jakarta, Bali, and Jogja!

6. **Ask questions:** Many of these areas lack good maps and literature to assist you in traveling and shopping on your own. Don't be afraid to ask questions about where to best shop for particular items. Indonesians will try to help, although they often give inaccurate information. If you ask enough times, you'll be successful!

GETTING THERE

Traveling and shopping outside Java and Bali is relatively convenient. Garuda and several domestic airlines regularly fly to the major cities as well as some of the more remote areas. The "Visit Indonesia Decade Pass" is an excellent way to organize this shopping adventure. Airports in the larger cities are relatively modern and well organized and many have shops offering good quality and selections of arts and crafts. Be sure to survey the airport shops before going into town.

Indonesia's airports tend to be organized very similarly to each other. Upon arrival you will find information, hotel, and taxi counters from which to get maps, brochures, hotel reservations, and a car into town. Once you arrive at your hotel, contact the front desk for information on shopping and transportation. Within a few hours you should be able to cover most of the city and surrounding area and then head off to your next destination. Overall, we have found shopping in such exotic places to be very convenient as long as we follow the same plan of action— airport to hotel to private car to shops and back to the hotel and airport and out to our next city. If you decide to do this on the cheap—using becaks, bemos, and buses, and staying in second and third-class hotels or losmen— you will be vulnerable to all the negatives of traveling to these areas—wasting valuable time, getting ripped off more than once, feeling uncomfortable, and being frustrated at getting lost and unable to communicate clearly.

WHAT TO BUY

What you will shop for in the outer islands depends on where you go. In general, you will find a large variety of **textiles** particular to each region and ethnic group. In fact, the outer islands of Sumatra, Sulawesi, Lombok, Sumba, and Sumbawa have some of the most unique and exciting textiles found anywhere in Indonesia.

Many antique and curio shops also offer a large variety of **ethnographic arts and crafts**, most of which are relatively new creations. The latter range from impressive house gables, staffs, and woodcarved containers and figures from the Batak in Sumatra to war shields, spears, and drums from the Asmat in Irian Jaya. In between Indonesia's far west and far east you will find masks, war shields, baby carriers, beads, head bands, wood ancestral figures, antiques, containers, staffs, woodcarvings, baskets, and wood panels from the Dayak in Kalimantan, the Toraja and Buginese in Sulawesi, and the Atoni in Timor.

SUMATRA

Sumatra, the world's fifth largest island, is one of the most diverse and fascinating cultural areas. A beautiful island of mountains, volcanos, lakes, gorges, and mangrove swamps, Sumatra is in the midst of a development take-off which could well transform the cultures and life styles of its 30 million inhabitants. The arts and crafts produced by the various ethnic groups make wonderful additions to almost any textile and primitive art collection and can be used as decorative home furnishings. This is the region of the Batak, Achenese, Minang-kabau, Nias, transplanted Javanese, and the migrant Kubu and Sakai tribes. Most maintain very well developed traditional cultures while adjusting well to the electricity, roads, radios, and televisions of the modern world.

MEDAN

A journey into Sumatra best starts in Medan, Indonesia's third largest city on the northeast coast of Sumatra. A bustling and becak belching city of over 2 million, it is the major gateway to the northern half of Sumatra. From here you can journey to Aceh to the north, Lake Toba and Nias Island to the east, and connect with Padang and Bukittinggi to the southwest and Palembang in the south. All of these areas offer interesting traveling and shopping experiences.

Medan is not a particularly attractive city, although it does have a few shopping surprises. While it is no one's favorite city, it does have a few things to offer before heading into the hinterland. Before leaving this city, be sure to visit the antique, art, and curio shops along **Jl. Jend A Yani** in downtown Medan. This is the main shopping area. However, you will need to dig through these shops. Most have the typical tourist junk, but many have unique quality items tucked between, behind, above, and below the junk. While many of these shops carry Balinese and Javanese arts and crafts, some also have some Batak, Nias, Dayak, and Toraja pieces worth examining. You'll have to look carefully in each of these shops, especially above your head, since most are very cluttered. Three of our favorite shops here are **Toko Julida** (#33), **Rufino's** (#64), and **Borobudur Art and Antique** (#32). Other art, antique, and curio shops worth visiting along this street are **Toko Bali Arts and Souvenir Shop**, Toto Asli, **A.B.C. Art Shop**, and **Toko Selatan**.

While exploring Jl. Jend A Yani, stop at the Tip Top Restaurant for its ice cream and Padang food. You should also check a few of the major hotel shops. Altogether you should be able to shop Medan in two to three hours. You may or may not want to stay here, depending on your other travel plans for Sumatra. If you do plan to stay over, one of the best hotels in town is the **Tiara Medan** (Jl. Cut Mutiah, Tel. 516000). Their coffee shop serves an excellent buffet.

LAKE TOBA

From Medan most travelers head directly to the **Lake Toba area**, the home of the fascinating and very entrepreneurial Toba Batak. The best and most comfortable way to get there is by car, a four to seven hour drive, depending on whether you take the low or high road to Lake Toba.

Once you arrive at Lake Toba, you have a choice of staying in the resort town of Parapat or on Samosir Island. We recommend **Parapat**, because it is more convenient for shopping. One of the best hotel is the Parapat Hotel which is located adjacent to the major shopping section in Parapat—**Jl. Haranggaol**. Both sides of this street are lined with antique, art, and curio shops run by aggressive female merchants who speak English and who are delightful to haggle with. While many of the shops have a great deal of typical tourist junk, a few shops offer good quality Batak antiques and house panels. However, the quality pieces are quickly disappearing and may be gone by the time you visit Parapat. The prices are excellent—if you bargain hard and with a smile. Several shops at the end of this street have good selections of woodcarvings, containers, and staffs.

Samosir Island, which is actually larger than all of Singapore, is the home of the Toba Batak, once a fierce headhunting group now Christianized and preying on tourists. You can stay at several inexpensive losmen and guest houses in the major villages. It's a good place to relax. If you go here to shop, you will be assaulted by numerous open-air stalls primarily selling identical handicrafts. Most are woodcarvings recently made for tourists. The horn containers are often said to be old, but don't believe it. Most likely they were recently made and drug through the mud to look old. Be sure to bargain hard with these female vendors. Do comparative shopping since many stalls sell the same items. Initial asking prices tend to be very high. You can get 70% discounts on many items. Surprisingly, you may find some worthwhile woodcarvings in the midst of the junk!

The major villages to visit and shop are **Ambarita, Tuk Tuk**, and **Tomok**. You can take a ferry or rent a speed boat from Parapat to visit these villages on the shore of the island. By speed boat you should be able to go to the island, visit the major sites, shop all three villages, and return to Parapat in about four hours. Our shopping preference is still the shops in Parapat along Jl. Haranggaol.

After completing your stay at Lake Toba, it is best to return to Medan by car. If you plan to head west for Nias Island or southwest for Padang and Bukittinggi, you will be at the mercy of a most uncomfortable bus ride. Back in Medan you can catch a flight to Aceh, Nias, and Padang, or any other major city in southern Sumatra.

Aceh in the north is an interesting cultural region, best noted for its orthodox Muslim culture. Shopping here focuses on textiles, daggers, filigree jewelry, and antiques.

Nias Island is a culturally rich area famous for its wood and stone carvings, posts, panels, containers, war shields, and carved figures. However, it's difficult to get here comfortably other than by cruise ship. The trip by regular boat from Sibolga or Padang is some-what arduous. You can fly to Nias from Medan. The best place to stay is the port of entry—Teluk Dalam—from which to visit the villages by bus. You may need more time than it's worth to visit and shop here.

PADANG

Padang, the gateway to western Sumatra, is a commercial city most visitors pass through on their way elsewhere in Sumatra, especially to nearby Bukittinggi. It's an extremely hot and humid coastal city that is noted for its neatness, orderliness, and cleanliness as well as for its unique Minangkabau archi-tecture—three-tiered sway back roofs—and culture. In contrast to other cities in Indonesia, the streets in Padang actually have curbs and sidewalks. No becaks are found here, but horsecarts along with city buses, oplets, and bemos are a frequent sight.

If you have a few hours for this city, Padang does offer some interesting shopping, however limited. Most shops of interest to visitors carry woodcarvings, bamboo handicrafts, songket textiles, rattan items, and gold and silver jewelry. Topping our list for the tackiest-item-you-can-buy-in-Indonesia are Padang's large dead stuffed frogs that have been gutted, puffed up, and eye sockets wired with red and blue electric lights. They come in different poses including frogs playing bongo drums, fiddles, and flutes. They seem to be everywhere, and they are truly tacky. You'll have to see these to believe them. Many a frog have died for what must be some equally tacky tourists!

While you may discover some interesting souvenirs in Padang, you will find few quality items that will integrate well into your home and wardrobe. After all, this is the shopping backwaters of Indonesia. Few local products appeal to tourists. They may admire the intricate traditional patterns and hand skills used in executing local textiles, embroidered goods, jewelry, and clothes, but few tourists will walk away with purchases. The colors and designs of the beautiful songket, for example, are too ethnic and traditional for foreigners who have difficulty knowing what to do with such items. Clothes also have a decided ethnic look and primarily come in small sizes. Many handicrafts are too fragile to pack in a suitcase. And then there are those tacky frogs! In contrast to what you see in Jakarta and Bali—or even in Kuala Lumpur and Bangkok—producers in Padang, as well as in most of Sumatra, have yet to change the colors, styles, and designs of their products in response to international tastes. In the meantime, the shops in Padang offer many interesting handcrafted items that have limited appeal to visitors who actually get excited about shopping in Jakarta, Bali, and Jogjakarta. Little of this excitement will get transferred to Padang and the rest of Sumatra.

If you have a few hours to shop in Padang, we recommend heading for the city's best arts and crafts shop—**Sartika Art Shop**. In fact, this may be the only shopping stop you need to make in Padang, especially if you are quickly passing through this city. Located at Jl. Sudirman 5 (Tel. 22101), this shop has the largest collection of arts, crafts, and antiques in Padang. In the two rooms downstairs you will find ethnographic carvings from northern Sumatra (Nias and Batak) and the Mentawai Islands, songket, silungkang (a local cotton and silk fabric), hand embroidered items, wayang puppets, lacquerware, Bukittinggi chests, model Minangkabau houses, knives, rattan baskets, porcelain, woodcarvings, and brassware. The dusty second floor includes Mentawai carvings, anchors, sago bowls, and arrows. While this shop has a few real antiques, most items that appear to be antiques are recently made for tourists. The owner knows antiques from copies and should point out to you what is real versus fake.

Other shops offering arts, crafts, textiles, and souvenirs include the **Abu Nawas (Panay) Souvenir Shop** (Jl. Imam Bonjol 5IV, Tel. 21259), **Silungkang (Antique) Souvenir Shop** (Complek Atom Shopping Centre No. 6A, Tel. 26426), and **Ambun Sari** (Jl. Permindo No. 42A).

Padang also has a modern shopping center called the **Duta Plaza**. Popular with local residents, it's filled with shops selling local consumer goods—toys, clothes, shoes, and electronics. It includes a small **Batik Samar** shop as well as a **Ramanda** department store and supermarket. You'll find numerous vendors on the first floor selling all types of inexpensive market goods, from shoes to famous name brand socks, which are obvious copies from Bally and Gucci.

One reason most visitors quickly pass through Padang is that they don't find a great deal to do here. You'll be hard pressed to find much to see and do other than walk the streets and watch the people. Indeed, you can easily visit two shops and the museum in two to three hours and then continue on to other more interesting destinations, such as Bukittinggi. The city does have an interesting museum—**Adityawarman Museum**—which is located on the corner of Jl. Diponegoro and Jl. Gereja. You may want to drive around the city to see the interesting Minangkabau architecture and observe the seawall. A few tour companies, such as **Setia Tours and Travel** (Jl. Bundo Kandung No. 35, Tel. 25466), provide half-day city tours.

If you plan to stay over in Padang, the two best hotels are the Muara Hotel and Mariani International Hotel. Both are within walking distance of the museum (Musium Adityawarman). The **Muara Hotel**, a Natour hotel, is used by many tour groups. The **Mariani International Hotel** (Jl. Bundo Kandung 35, Tel. 25466-25410) is one of the more unique hotel experiences in Indonesia, one you are not likely to forget for some time. The owner, the charming and assertive Mrs. Mariani, enjoys meeting her guests and making them feel at home. The furnishings are uniquely Mrs. Mariani, who has a preference for the bright and flashy. Always entrepreneurial, she will even rent you her room should you wish a German suite and the price is right! The hotel is truly a decorator's surprise as it gives new meaning to what might best be termed an "Oriental Baroque" style. Serves good food in a homey atmosphere. You will also find numerous inexpensive accommodations in Padang's hotels and guest houses.

Padang is famous throughout Indonesia for its unique spicy foods served in mini-buffet style. You'll find numerous restaurants throughout this city serving this local cuisine. Two good ones are **Simpang Raya** at Jl. Prof. Yamin 125. and **Roda Baru** at Jl. Pasar Raya 6. For Chinese food, try **King's** at Jl. Pondock 86.

BUKITTINGGI

Located two hours north of Padang by road, Bukittinggi is a pleasant city nestled in cool hills 930 meters about sea level. This is truly Minangkabau country with its distinctive architecture and lifestyle.

Bukittinggi is a more interesting city than Padang, with many more opportunities for shopping and sightseeing. Yet, you don't need a great deal of time here to cover the basics. One or two days may be sufficient. When you shop here, you will have a chance to visit some interesting craft villages as well as observe the weaving and embroidery processes that this area is so famous for. Some shops in Bukittinggi commission textiles and embroidery from villages in the surrounding area. Others offer the same types of arts, crafts, and souvenirs produced locally as well as imported from other parts of Sumatra, Java, and Bali.

The trip by road from Padang to Bukittinggi will take you through a few interesting craft villages where you can observe weavers, furniture makers, woodcarvers, and silver smiths. In Padang Panjang, look for **Yus Jamal** (Simp Pd. Siket Koto Baru) for traditional weaving. This shop has a songket loom which it demonstrates for visitors. They sell a large variety of songket and traditional handcrafted items such as slippers, hats, and dresses. The shop also offers those tacky electrified frogs posed as flute players and brooms. Everything is produced in traditional designs which you may not find appealing to your own tastes.

The interesting and entrepreneurial village of **Pandai Sikat** is noted for producing furniture, woodcarvings, and textiles. Several workshops line the main road that pass through this village. The furniture and woodcarving shops will do custom work to your specifications. Most have photos of items they have produced and can replicate such as carved doors, book stands, beds, house panels, and chests. One of the largest shops here is **Limbago**. Also look for **Satu Karya** and **Cahn Umar**. **Mis Chandra** and **H. Nurmalia** both produce songket; they have working looms in the shop where you can observe the traditional weaving process. This village also has a department shore which is actually a very colorful traditional Minangkabau house with a small workshop next door with 14 looms used for producing songket. The store sells songket cloth, bags, and purses produced by the local cooperative. It also has the only computer in the village!

Another highly entrepreneurial village, **Kota Gadang**, is famous for producing traditional costumes, accessories, silver, and embroidery. The community center building—**Kerajinan Amai Setia Souvenir Centre**—is operated by the Women's Needlecraft Association. This shop offers a good selection of silver filigree jewelry, lace, dolls, handbags, shawls, and embroidered goods. While in this village, you can visit the houses that produce the items found in this shop.

The city of **Bukittinggi** has a few shops worth visiting. Most are found in the downtown area along Jl. Minangkabau and Jl. A. Yani and along Jl. Cindurmato and Jl. Supratman. One of the biggest and best shops is **Aisha Chalik** at Jl. Cindurmato No. 94 (Tel. 21156). This shop specializes in all types of Sumatran and Indonesian textiles: batik, songket, embroidery, kristic, and tapis (Lampung). The shop even offers kits for making embroidered dresses and blouses. If you only have time to visit one shop to see the textiles produced in Western Sumatra, be sure to visit this shop. Next door you will find a very small shop offering embroidered goods—**Nina Souvenir Shop**.

Jl. Minangkabau, which is adjacent to the Central Market, has several art, craft, and souvenir shops that tend to offer similar products: textiles, brassware, rattan bags, masks, model Minangkabau houses, lamps, gongs, kris, musical instruments, and those tacky frogs. You may find an antique or two amongst all the textiles and souvenirs. Look for such shops as **H. Moechtar Is.** (No. 90), **Tiga Putra** (No. 14), **Crystal Art, Tigaputra, Ber Ingin** (No. 64) and **H. Nurani**. Just around the corner from Jl. Minangkabau is **Nefa Art and Antique** at Jl. Jenjang Minang No. 6 which offers textiles, wayang puppets, silver kris, primitive carvings, musical instruments, and brassware. On nearby Jl. A. Yani, look for **Aladdin Art and Antique Shop** (No. 14), which offers a good selection of kris, lacquer, coins, porcelain, wayang puppets, textiles, primitive woodcarvings, old songket, and silver; and **Toko Antik** (No. 2), which sells wayang puppets, primitive woodcarvings, kris, porcelain, textiles, musical instruments, and masks.

The nearby **Central Market** is worth visiting. Go to the second floor where you will find several handicraft stalls which are part of the **Pasar Wisata**, a cooperative project sponsored by the Trade and Promotion Center of Handicraft Industries. These well organized stalls offer a wide selection of similar handcrafted items produced in the Bukittinggi area: songket, embroidery, silver, model Minangkabau houses, and rattan products. You will also find a demonstration area here where you can see young people making rattan items. If you have limited time and want to purchase handicrafts, this is a good one-stop-shopping place to visit.

Two shops along **Jl. Supratman** are also well worth visiting, although somewhat difficult to find since they are located in a quiet residential area. **Ambun Suri** (No. 21) is a department store offering a good selection of embroidery, songket, kristic, purses, shoes, and ready-made clothes in traditional styles and colors. One of the real treats in visiting this shop is to observe the embroidery being produced by 30 young women with foot powered sewing machines. They are real artists who quickly turn out some lovely designs. You can easily miss this workshop since it is located on the second floor. Ask to see it. **Widuri** (No. 7A) also offers hand embroidered items, kristic, songket, bags, and slippers. Most items here are commissioned in nearby villages.

Bukittinggi especially appeals to visitors who enjoy local culture, architecture, and beautiful mountainous landscapes. The dis-tinctive sway-back roofs of Minangkabau buildings and small town atmosphere give this city a quaint and relaxing atmos-phere. Many visitors enjoy stopping at the museum where they can learn more about the Minangkabau culture as well as the famous Nagarai Canyon. Located on the southeast corner of the city, the canyon is most beautiful when visited early in morning as the fog and mist cover the canyon valley.

One of the best hotels in Bukittinggi is the **Denai Hotel** (Jl. Rivai 26, Tel. 21466). Other good hotels include the **Minang Hotel** (Jl. Panorama 20, Tel. 21120) and **Dymens Hotel** (Jl. Hawawi, Tel. 21015). You will also find several inexpensive hotels along Jl. A. Yani and Jl. Benteng.

Bukittinggi is a city of small restaurants that primarily serve spicy Padang food. Some of the better restaurants include the **Roda Group Restaurant** (Pasar Atas, Blok C-155), **Hotel Restoran Selamat** (Jl. A. Yani 19), and **The Mona Lisa** (Jl. A. Yani 58).

PALEMBANG

If you venture into southern Sumatra, you will be entering Indonesia's oil rich and swampy area famous for songket textiles, transplanted Javanese, and wild jungle animals (tigers and wild boars). **Jambi, Palembang**, and **Telukbetung** are particularly famous textile centers. However, the best place to shop is Palembang, a famous historical city which serves as a major commercial center in Sumatra and one of Indonesia's most important oil ports.

Boasting a population of nearly 800,000, Palembang is a large and sprawling commercial center located along the Musi River just 80 kilometers upstream from the sea. Like so many worn and makeshift "up-country" cities, Palembang is not particularly attractive. It's noisy, hot, humid, and congested— more a cultural experience than an attractive and interesting destination. While it has some interesting shopping, it's not sufficiently interesting to make a special trip here just for shopping. If you do visit Palembang, you will want to visit a few factories and shops.

Palembang is especially famous for producing and exporting songket material, red lacquerware, and rattan products. While in Palembang, you can visit a few factories that produce such products as well as sell them directly to visitors.

Palembang's best shopping center for visitors is the **Pulau Mas Plaza** which is adjacent to one of the city's best hotels—

King Hotel (Jl. Kol. Atmo). Take the escalator to the second floor where you will find three shops offering a wide variety of textiles and handicrafts. **Songket House** offers songket, ikat, and lacquerware produced in Palembang; **Istana Songket Arts Gallery** also has songket and ikat as well as shell lamps—a locally produced version of the popular Filipino craft. **Istana Art and Fashion** is essentially a Danar Hadi batik shop offering similar garments you will find in the Danar Hadi batik shops on Java.

While you will find several small shopping centers in downtown Palembang, most cater to the consumer needs of local residents—especially clothes and electronic goods. Most are also very crowded, noisy, and congested, offering little of interest to international shoppers. Most street shops along Jl. Sudirman, the main commercial street, also primarily offer local consumer goods. However, one shop in particular may be worth visiting. **Sriwijaya** (Jl. AKBP. HM. Amin No. 43) offers a good selection of handcrafted items—lacquerware, chests, small silver and gold containers, lamps, and stools. You may have difficulty finding this shop since the sign in front says **Mir Senen Gallery** which is also the name of a branch shop on Jl. Jend. Sudirman No. 616. It also has a branch shop in the airport departure lounge where you can purchase lacquerware, songket, pottery, ceramics, and wayang puppets.

If you are interested in observing the production of local textiles—songket—you should visit **Serengam Setia** (Jl. Serengam I No. 230, 32 Ilir Rt. 9, Tel. 20820). The first floor has a demonstration of the songket weaving process. The second floor includes a small shop which sells songket products—sarongs, slippers, and wall decorations—as well as lacquer-ware and ceramics.

Palembang's famous red lacquerware is found at **Mekar Jaya** (Jl. Selamet Riyadi No. 45A, 11 Ilir Rt. 11). The small shop offers a wide variety of lacquer products—vases, cabinets, chests, garden stools, bowls, and boxes—as well as some textiles and porcelain. The quality here is very good and the prices are much cheaper than you will find in the shops of Jakarta, many of which buy directly from this factory. If you are interested in observing the lacquer application process, ask to visit the factory which is located directly behind the shop. Following a narrow walkway, you will come to three buildings where you can see workmen applying different layers of colors on the various products.

The best place to see and buy Palembang's famous rattan products is at **Mia and Zuhra Rattan Handicraft** (Jl. Cut Nyak Dien No. 16, Rt. 36 - 30 Ilir). This is another factory/

shop where you can observe craftspeople stripping the rattan and weaving it into a variety of forms. The shop offers a large variety of products—bags, purses, magazine racks, lampshades, and boxes—which it sells in Indonesia as well as abroad.

Palembang also has a large colorful **market** located along the Musi River and adjacent to the Ampera Bridge. While it offers few items of interest to international travelers, it is a good photo opportunity and cultural experience. Most vendors and stalls sell fresh produce or local consumer goods. This market also functions as the transportation hub for both riverboats and the many pollution belching oplets or mini-buses that dominate the streets of Palembang.

You won't find a great deal to do in Palembang aside from visiting the two local museums, viewing the riverfront, and stopping at the city's two traditional houses, the Limas House (one on Jl. Mayor Ruslan and the other on Jl. Pulo). In fact, most visitors quickly pass through this city on their way elsewhere in Sumatra or to Java. You can easily shop the city within five hours. While oplets are the cheapest way to get around the city, you may find them confusing, inconvenient, and uncomfortable. It's best to rent a car and driver through your hotel or one of the local travel agencies if you wish to visit the factories and shops we've outlined.

One of the best hotels in Palembang is the **King Hotel** on Jl. Kol. Atamo. It's ideally located in relation to downtown shopping and restaurants. Other hotels worth considering are the **Sanjaya Hotel** (Jl. Kapten A. Rivai, Tel. 24299) and the **Swarna Dwipa** (Jl. Tasik 2, Tel. 28322).

Some of Palembang's better restaurants include the **King Palace** (3rd floor of the Palau Mas Plaza on Jl. Kol. Atmo), **Kuda Mas** (Golden Horse) (Jl. Veteran 5486F), **Mandala** (Jl. Veteran 86-88), and **Citra** (Jl. Kol. Atmo 582) for Indonesian, European, and Chinese food; and **Pagi Sore** (J. Jend. Sudirman 96), **Samudra** (Jl. Perintis Kermerdekaan 27A), and **Har** (Jl. TP. Rustam Effendi 2/4) for Indonesian food.

KALIMANTAN

Kalimantan is different from most other islands. This is a large island, the size of Alaska, sparsely populated with nearly 8 million people and covered with dense jungle. Kalimantan is actually the southern and eastern section of the world's third largest island—Borneo. Most of the major towns are found at the mouth of rivers along the western (Pontianak), southern (Banjarmasin), and eastern (Balikpapan) coasts. The Dayak, formerly a fierce headhunting tribe and now the object of tourists' curiosity, populate small villages along the many rivers and lakes that cut through this mountainous and swampy jungle island. Today, Kalimantan is best noted as the major production center for Indonesia's rubber, oil, timber, and gemstones.

You should have no problem getting air connections to the major cities on Kalimantan. However, once in Kalimantan, the major means of transportation are boats which stop at towns and villages along the rivers. You will find roads, but these do not go far beyond the major cities. As a result, your trip to Kalimantan will be more adventuresome than your travels to other major Indonesian islands.

Most of the cities and towns in Kalimantan have only rudimentary tourist facilities. Being essentially frontier towns, most are worn, makeshift, dilapidating, and uninteresting river towns. Many look as if they came directly out of a James Conrad novel. Kalimantan is not a major tourist destination nor does it have many attractions to draw tourists, other than the tribal Dayaks. The eastern coast, around Balikpapan and Samarinda, is a major oil exploration area. Here, you will find the better hotels, restaurants, and shops catering to expatriate oil riggers and businessmen. This also is the area where you can most easily visit Dayak villages by chartering a boat to take you up the Mahakam River. Whatever you do, you may find Kalimantan overpriced for what you get. The overpricing is more due to the presence of the oil community and a local entrepreneurial mentality than to the need to import consumer goods—the local excuse for overcharging.

Most visitors primarily journey to Kalimantan to see the **Dayak** culture and shop for Dayak arts and crafts. The Dayak tribesmen were once famous for headhunting. Today, they no longer hunt heads and only some remain primitive tribesmen in the remote interior. Many Dayak now live in villages and towns where they farm or they work as laborers in the oil and timber towns.

Consisting of nearly 200 different tribes, the Dayaks are famous for producing ceremonial masks, war shields, blow guns, tobacco pouches, baby carriers, carved figures and utensils, baskets, bark cloth, scabbards, and a variety of items made from bamboo, rattan, and beads. Basketry and bead work are two of the major Dayak specialties.

You will also find Chinese and Dutch antiques in the major towns on Kalimantan. The Chinese and Dutch were the initial foreign settlers who established the major coastal towns.

Kalimantan is also noted for textiles and gemstones. Unique

ikat textiles are found in and around the major cities as well as in the Dayak villages. Precious and semi-precious stones, such as amethysts, agates, and sapphires, are abundant in Banjarmasin, Indonesia's gemstone center. The nearby town of Martepura is the center for diamonds in Indonesia.

Any trip to Kalimantan must be planned in relation to Kalimantan's geography and transportation systems. If you only want to visit the shops in major cities, then you can easily do Kalimantan in a few days by scheduling flights to each of the cities. In fact, one day in each of the three major cities may be enough. These are not attractive cities and towns one wishes to linger in for long. Many shops in these cities sell Dayak handicrafts, antiques, and textiles. However, if you are adventuresome and desire to buy directly from Dayak craftsmen in the villages, you must set aside a few days to travel up river.

Each of the three major cities offers river trips into Dayak villages along the rivers. You can take the long riverboats that stop at every little town and village along the way to pick up and discharge passengers, produce, and motorbikes. Alternatively, you can charter a speedboat to take the same trip in one-seventh the time and in greater comfort.

Aside from being cheap, the problem with the riverboat is that it is slow, boring, and uncomfortable—a seemingly romantic but highly overrated means of travel. Like many of the buses in Indonesia, the boat novelty may wear off after the first few hours and stops along the river at small, nondescript towns and villages. In addition, you will have to stay overnight in a small town or village, an experience you may never forget! Accommodations are at best rudimentary, mosquitos may be thick, and you may have to share some space with a rat. Furthermore, many of the Dayak villages are disappointing. You travel hours in the heat and humidity to find you have come to a tourist trap consisting of a few handicrafts of questionable quality which are also overpriced.

Nonetheless, one of these river trips can become a unique travel and shopping adventure. We only caution you to the fact that such trips are not as romantic as they may appear in other accounts. Be prepared to experience some of the most unsanitary conditions of your trip. The rivers are one big sewer, and you may be shocked at the extent of trash and garbage you see everywhere. The idea of staying in a Dayak longhouse seems exotic and romantic, but it may be less appealing after you see one. You undoubtedly will have some interesting "war stories" resulting from such a trip.

Pontianak on the east coast is primarily a Chinese trading city and a noted rubber center. The beaches to the north of

Pontianak are some of the best in all of Kalimantan. There is little of interest in this city of 250,000. Many visitors use Pontianak as the staging area for river trips into Dayak villages along the Kapuas River, Indonesia's largest river. If you are truly adventuresome, you can travel up the Kapuas River from Pontianak, cross the jungle, and continue to Samarinda on the east coast by way of the Mahakam River. However, this is not recommended unless you are skilled at jungle survival and have a great deal of time on your hands.

Banjarmasin in the south is a noted orthodox Muslim area. Located near the mouth of the Barito River, Banjarmasin is built over a swamp and bog. Canals with water taxis are the major streets in this city. From Banjarmasin you should go to Mandomai if you wish to begin a trip up river to visit the Dayak villages. If you prefer shopping for your Dayak handicrafts in Banjarmasin, go to the shops on **Jl. Simpang Sudimampir**. Banjamasin is best noted for its semi-precious stones. Indeed, it is Indonesia's gem center for agates, sapphires, and amethysts. Much of the jewelry you find in Jakarta comes from this area. The nearby town of **Martapua** is Indonesia's largest diamond producing area.

Balikpapan on the east coast is Kalimantan's frontier oil town. Of all cities on Kalimantan, this one has the best facilities for international travelers—a deluxe hotel, travel agents, discos, and tourist shops. You will find several antique and Dayak handicraft shops here. In fact, the deluxe **Hotel Benakutai** has a small but good shop selling a few Dayak handicrafts. Several other shops are located along **Jl. Garuda**. If you wish to visit Dayak villages, you must travel up the Mahakam River. This means first traveling by road or plane to the bustling river town of Samarinda, 200 kilometers north of Balikpapan, and departing from there or proceeding on to the small town of Tenggarong, where the road ends.

Samarinda is primarily a trading town and port for exporting lumber processed in the lumber mills along the Mahakam River. There are five antique and handicraft shops in Samarinda offering a variety of Dayak goods. Most, however, are overpriced, the selections are limited, and the shopkeepers are somewhat lethargic. But it's still worth visiting these shops before embarking on your river adventure. If you compare prices among these shops, you should get some idea as to what you can expect to pay should you not make purchases in the Dayak villages.

We don't particularly recommend this trip if you only have a few days to explore the area. It will take you a full day by speedboat to get to your first Dayak village, and you may have to take a small canoe part of the way, depending on the water level of the river and lake. You may find the popular lakeshore village, **Tanjung Isuy**, disappointing. After traveling so many hours in the heat and humidity, you enter a tourist trap with a government-sponsored longhouse and dancers waiting for you to pay them to perform. The handicrafts are your typical tourist knickknacks, although you may find a memorable artifact or two here. The village itself is another dumpy river town—worn, ugly, and unsanitary. You can stay overnight at the longhouse, but if you came by speedboat or canoe, you may want to stay at the nearby town—Muara Muntai.

Muara Muntai has one basic losman where two people can share a hot room for $12 a night. Like the rest of the people in this town, you also can bathe in the sewer water pumped from the sewage-laden river into the bathing facility at this losmen—a bathroom with a water filled oil barrel. The most interesting thing about Muara Muntai is its elevated wood walkway which makes walking easy and also covers all the garbage strewn throughout this town.

This first day on the Mahakam River may be enough to see the wisdom of shopping in Balikpapan and heading on to another island. If you are having a good time—many of our readers have—you may wish to push forward to other Dayak villages along the Mahakam River. During certain times of the year, when the water level is low, you will have to go into these villages by motorized canoe. For the time and money you must invest on this little adventure, you may be disappointed with the shopping. Please do not take this trip if you think this is the way to shop for Dayak handicrafts. It is not. This is the trip to test your patience, perseverance, physical stamina, sanity, and humor. If you take a slow boat and find you are unhappy on the second day with this trip, remember it takes two more days to get back to Tenggarong or Samarinda! On the other hand, you may find this becomes one of your most exciting Adentures in Indonesia.

SULAWESI

The island of Sulawesi is one of the lovelier areas in Indonesia. It offers great sightseeing and some shopping. The **Toraja people**, who live in the beautiful central mountain region, are well worth visiting. They produce a number of handicrafts of interest to many visitors. Better still, the area has not been overrun by tourists. Indeed, fewer than 30,000 tourists visit Toraja Land each year.

You can easily get to Sulawesi by flying into Ujung Pandang (formerly Makassar) in the south or to Manado in the north. Regular flights connect through various cities on Java. Unless you want to do scuba diving and see the wonderful reef near Manado, we recommend going by way of Ujung Pandang. There is more to see and do in this area, and there are some good shopping opportunities in this city.

Most visitors begin their journey into the fascinating Toraja Land area from **Ujung Pandang**. One of the few Christian areas in Indonesia, Toraja Land is famous for its house and granary architecture, burial sites, effigies (*tau tau*), and sacrificial rituals. Life and death are inextricably linked in the daily lives and rituals of the Toraja as well as represented in their handicrafts. The key element in Toraja culture is the buffalo which is prominently displayed on house and granary panels and at burial sites. You travel to Toraja Land to view this fascinating culture of a people who seem to live in an exotic paradise.

Most visitors to Toraja Land enter by road. You can go by regular bus, tour bus, van, or car. The trip takes about 9 hours from Ujung Pandang. Along the way you will see interesting Buginese architecture in the coastal and plain areas and then begin a long ascent into the beautiful mountains of Toraja Land. The mountain roads offer some of the best scenic views in all of Asia.

Rantepao is the major town in Toraja Land. Rather than enter by road, you can fly into this town. A few flights each week go into Rantepao from Manado and Ujung Pandang. You will most likely stay in one of the pleasant bungalows within a 10 kilometer radius of Rantepao.

Toraja Land has several arts and crafts primarily designed for tourists as well as some traditional woodcarvings. Funeral effigies are particularly striking as are carved house and granary panels with the ubiquitous Toraja buffalo head. Woodcarvings and models of Toraja houses and granaries, using the buffalo and boat motifs, are found in a few shops in Rantepao and surrounding villages. Distinctly carved panels, using traditional black, white, yellow, and brown colors, are found throughout Toraja Land. You also will find bamboo containers, textiles, baskets, porcelain, and occasionally antiques in this area.

If you begin your Sulawesi adventure in **Ujung Pandang**, shopping there will be quick and easy. Most antique, handicraft, and jewelry shops are found along **Jl. Sombu Opu**, one block east of the pleasant waterfront Golden Makassar Hotel. Within three hours you should be able to cover all of the shops of interest to you. You will find several jewelry shops along this street selling famous local filigree silver jewelry. Several of the shops sell Toraja handicrafts, but you may prefer to wait until you shop in Toraja Land before making purchases here. The selections and prices are better in Toraja Land, and chances are you will have to return to Ujung Pandang before departing Sulawesi. Some of the handicraft and antique shops also have a few good ethnographic art pieces from Irian Jaya, Kalimantan, and Sumatra, but you will have to dig for these. A few antique shops carry Chinese porcelain as well as Dutch and Makassar antiques and old coins. This is not a great place to shop, but some shops have a few surprises.

When shopping in Toraja Land, you can make purchases in **Rantepao** and villages within a 30 kilometer radius of this town. Just off the unique traffic circle at the center of Rantepao along **Jl. Pahlawan** you will find several handicraft and antique shops, as well as a few stalls in the adjacent town market, selling a variety of Toraja handicrafts, woodcarvings, textiles, old coins, baskets, knives, pottery, and antiques. Most are tourist shops, but you will find a few worthwhile pieces if you slowly dig through these shops and stalls.

The other major shopping area is in the **surrounding villages**. You will find tourist shops, stalls, and hawkers at all of the burial sites and major villages open to tourists. Again, most of the items in the areas are made for tourists, although you may find a few unique textiles and carved pieces. Be sure to bargain everywhere you shop.

Don't go to Sulawesi just for shopping. If you do, you may be disappointed. There are many things to buy in Ujung Pandang and Toraja Land, but it is the fascinating cultural experience related to the woodcarvings, textiles, and handicrafts that make this one of the highlights of Indonesia.

Ujung Pandang has a few worthwhile sites to visit, such as **Fort Rotterdam**, the **Diponegoro Tomb**, and the **Clara Bundt Orchid Garden and Shell Collection**. One of the best places to stay, and enjoy the city at the same time, is the oceanfront **Golden Makassar Hotel**. Get a room facing the water so you can see the ships plying the water and view the gorgeous sunset. The town itself is a bit dirty, the becak drivers are somewhat aggressive, and the city has one of the larger more aggressive concentrations of beggars in Indonesia who hang out in front of the local department store next to the Golden Makassar Hotel. Since this department store is geared to the local population, you may wish to skip it as well as the beggars by heading for the other side of the street where you will be walking toward the better shops.

The real treat in Sulawesi is the trip to **Toraja Land**, an area of farmers who cultivate wet-rice and raise livestock. The water buffalo plays a central role in all of the local customs and rituals. Here, you will become immersed in a truly exotic culture which has adapted well to modernization. Traditional architecture, a unique caste system, and local culture and rituals continue to this day. A Christianized people, the Toraja continue to practice their animistic traditions in which the world of the dead occupies the central role in the rituals and animal sacrifices. Noted as pork eaters and alcohol drinkers, they have little in common with their lowland Islamic Bugis neighbors. Once you leave the Buginese coastal and plain areas, you enter into a totally different world which will forever impress you as unique, exotic, and delightful. Best of all, the climate in this area is much cooler and less humid than in other parts of Indonesia. Evenings are often cool and require a jacket or sweater—a pleasant departure from the heat and humidity of Ujung Pandang and elsewhere.

IRIAN JAYA

Irian Jaya is the least developed and most primitive and exotic area of Indonesia. Occupying the western half of the world's second largest island (Papua New Guinea occupies the eastern half), this is one of the world's most primitive areas. Covered with dense jungle, rugged mountains with some snowcapped peaks, and mangrove swamps, this is a truly adventuresome area. Here you will find Stone Age tribes, oil riggers, mines, logging camps, transmigrants, missionaries, anthropologists, bird smugglers, and revolutionaries. Over 200 languages are spoken amongst the 245 relatively isolated tribal peoples of Irian Jaya.

Irian Jaya also is the area made famous in the United States with the still unexplained disappearance of Michael Rockefeller in the 1960s and whose adventures and memories amongst the Asmat in southern Irian Jaya are enshrined in the New York Metropolitan Museum of Art. To see this exhibit as well as other fine collections of Irian Jayan art in the national museums of Indonesia, the Netherlands, and even New Zealand is enough to make many a curious museum goer itching to visit those areas where such talented craftsmen continue to produce intriguing primitive artifacts that also make interesting home decorative items in many eclectic Western homes.

While it is not difficult to get to Jayapura, once you are there you may have difficulty traveling within Irian Jaya. Recognizing the difficulty of traveling to remote areas, limited tourist facilities, and sensitive to local ethnic groups, the Indonesian government limits the number of visitors who are permitted to travel outside Jayapura. If you plan to visit other areas of Jayapura, you will need special permission from the Indonesian police to enter the interior. This permission is normally granted upon applying for a police pass in Jayapura. Consequently, if you plan to visit more of Irian Jaya than just Jayapura, set aside a sufficient block of time to visit this intriguing place since you may encounter scheduling problems.

We don't recommend this trip if you are going primarily to shop. Go for the adventure and hopefully do some unique shopping at the same time. If takes a great deal of time to get there, it can be expensive, it is difficult to get from one location to another, and much of the fascinating arts and crafts produced by the Asmat on the southern coast can be found elsewhere in Indonesia. In fact, you will most likely have difficulty getting permission to visit the Asmat area which is centered around the southern coastal town of Agats. You might be better off flying into Jayapura, the capital of Irian Jaya, and shop there for a day or two and then catch the Wednesday morning flight to the neighboring country of Papua New Guinea. There you can take the famous Sepik River tour and shop to your heart's content in the villages along this fascinating river while cruising down the river in air-conditioned comfort on the Melanesian Discover or Sepik Spirit. The trouble is that there is only one flight a week—Wednesday, Flight PX049—departing from Jayapura for Vanimo, Wewak, Mt. Hagen, and Port Moresby in Papua New Guinea. Furthermore, it can be difficult trying to re-enter Irian Jaya from Papua New Guinea. You may have to proceed on to Australia and forget about returning to Indonesia. The Wednesday return flight (PX048) is very unpre-dictable—depending on whether the Indonesians permit the Air Niugini plane to land. The continuing border problems between Indonesia and Papua New Guinea make one of the world's most fascinating and exotic shopping trips also one of the most difficult to plan because of local politics.

If you plan to include Irian Jaya on your Indonesian shopping and travel itinerary, you can take a regularly scheduled domestic airline into the island of Biak—off the north coast—or into Jayapura, the provincial capital. Keep in mind that Irian Jaya is a long way from Jakarta, Bali, or Ujung Pandang. As part of your international and domestic air ticketing, you may want to include Irian Jaya at either the beginning or end of your trip. If, for example, you take a regularly scheduled Garuda Indonesia flight from Los Angeles or Honolulu, include Irian Jaya at the beginning of your trip since the plane will stop in Biak enroute to Bali and Jakarta. In Biak you can catch a direct flight into Jayapura. You can also go to Irian Jaya by ship.

Two words of caution before you get too involved in planning your trip to Irian Jaya. First, you may need a special permit to visit the interior of Irian Jaya. Granting such permission depends on the prevailing political climate in the interior as well as the present number of tourists using very limited travel facilities. There is no certainty you will receive a permit. However, many visitors have no problem getting into Biak, Wamena, Sorong, Timika, and Meranke—the five largest towns outside Jayapura. Getting into such places as Agats, the center for Asmat woodcarvings on the southern coast, however, is a different matter altogether. Chances are you will have difficulty getting a permit to go into this area since it does not offer tourist facilities nor regular flights. In other words, you may or may not get permission to travel into many parts of the interior. Getting a permit prior to arriving in Indonesia is nearly impossible given the complexities of the Indonesia bureaucracy. So your best bet is to hope you will get permission once you arrive in Biak or Jayapura. Check with the local police station in either city before venturing into the interior.

Our second word of caution concerns combining a trip to Irian Jaya with a trip to the neighboring country of Papua New Guinea. If you plan to leave Irian Jaya on the Wednesday flight for Papua New Guinea, be sure you have a regular Indonesia visa. You can enter and exit Indonesia without a visa as long as you both enter and exit through one of the official entry/exit cities. Since Jayapura is not one of these cities, you need a visa —obtained prior to entering the country—to enter or exit here. You will be in deep trouble if you enter Indonesia through another city without a visa and then try to exit at Jayapura. You will be detained and have to travel all the way back to Jakarta and then try to arrange a flight from Singapore into Papua New Guinea. Not only will this be inconvenient, it will be a very expensive way to go!

Most of the cities and towns in Irian Jaya are worn and makeshift, typical of upcountry, frontier administrative and trading communities. With roads primarily confined to towns in the immediate vicinity, you must travel by air to visit the towns and from there trek into the villages. The domestic airlines fly into the major towns of Sorong, Monokawri, Wamena, Nibire, Timika, Meranke, Tanah Merah, Oksibil, Bokodini, Ilugu, and Enarotali. In addition, missionaries and mining companies regularly fly into these and other interior towns and villages. If you are truly adventuresome and enterprising, you can arrange to fly with the missionaries or private companies. You can arrange a missionary flight through the missionary offices at Sentari Airport in Jayapura. Remem-ber, these are small planes flown by bush pilots who rely on sight take-offs and landings. The trip may very well be one of the most hair-raising you ever experience. There is nothing but dense jungle, mud, rivers, and mountains below! And when you reach your destination, don't expect much in terms of food and accommodations. This is rugged frontier country—if you can get permission to enter.

Wherever you go in Irian Jaya, don't expect first-class accommodations. Except in the city of Jayapura, which has one international class hotel and a few acceptable restaurants for those unwilling to risk the local dining establishments, it's best to plan to rough it in Irian Jaya. Bali and Jakarta are not more than 8 hours away, and they may be welcome sights after a few days in Irian Jaya.

Irian Jaya is primarily a center for acquiring primitive arts and crafts produced by its many tribes. While not as prolific as the tribal groups in neighboring Papua New Guinea—especially the Sepik River and Trobriand Island peoples—the Asmat in Irian Jaya have long been a source for some of the world's most intriguing primitive art.

Much of the old and unique primitive art in Irian Jaya is gone. So don't expect to travel to Irian Jaya to collect rare pieces. The good and valuable stuff left with the Dutch colonialists or found its way into museums, European auction houses, or private collections during the past 80 years. Good quality antique pieces are best found in the shops of Holland or at a Sothesby auction in London. What you will find today in Irian Jaya as well as elsewhere in Indonesia are primarily copies or replicas of a continuing artistic tradition. The Asmat on the southern coast of Irian Jaya—around the town of Agats—are the most noted artists and craftsmen of Irian Jaya. Under the sponsorship of the Indonesian government and the United Nations, they are producing a great deal of handicrafts for the tourist market. You will find their work in many of the antique, art, and craft shops in the major cities on Java, Bali, and Sulawesi. They produce a unique style of rust, black, and white carved panels, masks, baskets, war shields, spears, drums, canoe paddles, and woodcarvings. While production is largely stimulated by the tourist market, nonetheless, the quality of the work is quite good, with many carvings produced by some of Agats' master craftsmen. Other tribes and peoples on Irian Jaya produce a large variety of similar arts and crafts.

BIAK

Biak is one of Indonesia's major gateway cities. All flights originating in the United States (Los Angeles or Honolulu) make Biak their first stop in Indonesia in transit to Bali and Jakarta. Biak is also the gateway city to Irian Jaya and East Indonesia. From here you can get connecting flights into the major towns in Irian Jaya—Jayapura, Timika, and Sorong—as well as to Ambon in the Moluccas.

Famous for its international airport, port facilities, and air force base as well as a noted smuggling center for exotic birds, Biak also played an important role in World War II. Here is where nearly 10,000 Japanese soldiers died in the face of advancing Allied troops in 1944. Indeed, Biak is an important center for Japanese visitors who come here several times each year to pay homage to the fallen brothers.

A beautiful coral and limestone island with picturesque shorelines and villages, and a landscape still pocked by bombs and abandoned and burnt out vehicles of World War II, Biak is not on the beaten tourist path. Indeed, few tourists venture outside the airport in transit to the more popular tourist destinations of Bali and Jakarta. Except for its picturesque beaches and famous World War II sites, Biak has little to offer visitors. On the other hand, this is an interesting island and it offers shopping opportunities for those who have a few hours or a day or two to explore this island.

If, for example, you fly directly from the U.S. on Garuda Indonesia, your first stop will be in Biak. If you are flying directly on to Bali or Jakarta on this same flight, you will have approximately a one hour refueling layover. During that time you are given a choice of either staying on the plane or visiting the transit lounge. The airline does not tell you about the services and shopping opportunities awaiting you in the airport terminal. Our advice: visit the transit lounge where you will have an opportunity to exchange money, shop, and watch a dance performance. If you want to take some pictures of the performance, be sure to take your camera.

The new airport terminal is nicely located overlooking the ocean. Be sure to go upstairs in the transit lounge and walk along the overhead walk way where you will pass by an information booth and a money exchanger on the left. At the end of the corridor you will come to three shops on your left. If you go down the stairs, you will see another shop adjacent to a sitting area where you can watch the welcoming dance performance.

The three shops upstairs sell a variety of Indonesian hand-crafted items. Most, however, are imported from other islands such as Bali, Sulawesi, and Java. The small bookshop does sell a few unique drums made in Biak. The other shops offer batik, jewelry, Balinese carvings, leather bags masks, belts, and bags—all items you will find in abundance in Bali, Jogjakarta, and Jakarta. The shop downstairs primarily sells woodcarvings, penis gourds, and jewelry produced by the Asmat in Irian Jaya. You can also buy audiocassettes of Irian Jayan music. Purchase these from the dance troop that is performing here on the first floor. You have a choice of three different tapes which sell for US$7 each.

Keep in mind that the airport shops and dance performance only operate when the international flight lands in Biak, which at present is for one hour, Monday, Wednesday, and Friday, from 5:30am to 6:30am. As soon as the plane leaves, these shops and performers shut down. Consequently, if you plan to stay in Biak for a day or two, be sure to do your shopping at the airport as soon as you arrive on your inbound flight. If you wait until you leave, these shops will be closed. The only shop open will be a small souvenir shop in the departure lounge which has a very small selection of batik and carvings.

If you plan to stay in Biak for a day or two, we recommend that you first tour the island by car. You will have an opportunity to visit its two major sites—the Japanese Caves and beaches—and the town of Biak. Along the way to the caves and beaches, you can visit one of Biak's master woodcarvers—**Mr. Micha Ronsumbre** in the village of Swapodibo. Also known as the Inobobo Biak group of carvings, Mr. Ronsumbre comes from a family of famous Biak carvers. You can see a few of his attractive works in the departure lounge of the airport. You will find him and his workshop along Jl. Bosnik, on the road between the Japanese Caves and Bosnik Beach. You can't miss it since it you will see a big sign saying "Swapodibo" in front of the outdoor work area on the left hand side of the road. If no one is working in this area, go to the house on the right and ask for Mr. Micha. He has some inventory to show visitors. However, his real strength is in doing commissions to the specifications of his clients. If you want to have a unique piece carved for yourself, talk to him about your design preferences and pricing and shipping arrangements. At present he charges by the square centimeter—Rp. 35 to 40 per square centimeter carved. Since Mr. Micha does speak English, you should be able to communi-cate with him.

Most of the shopping of interest to international travelers is concentrated in the downtown area. Here you will find a few art and craft shops along the streets as well as in the old market area. Most of these shops are crammed with items made in

Irian Jaya as well as a few items from Sulawesi. Look for Asmat woodcarvings, porcelain, bags, shells, beads, penis gourds, bows and arrows, shells, drums, grass skirts, and axes. Most of the shops will bargain and give up to 30% discount on most items.

The old market area has five arts and crafts shops catering to international visitors. Located near each other, shops such as **Pusaka Art Shop** and **Anugrah Shop** are filled with similar items primarily imported from Irian Jaya. Along nearby Jl. Erlangga, look for **Antika Art Shop** which sells a limited selection of Asmat carvings and Chinese porcelain along with bags, beads, penis gourds, axes, and shells. One of the best shops in Biak is the **Cleopatra Art Shop** adjacent to the Cleopatra Restoran and the Sentosa Tosiga Tours and Travel on Jl. A. Yani, just behind the Titawaka Hotel.

A few hours in Biak may be sufficient for most travelers who wish to shop and sightsee. If you are proceeding on to Jayapura from a flight that originated in the U.S., you will have plenty of time—eight hours—to do everything you need to in Biak.

Biak is a very picturesque island of coral and limestone formations. In addition to visiting the shops at the airport and in Biak, you may want to tour the island. You will find several lovely beaches, such as Bosnik Beach and Koorem Beach. **Bosnik Beach** is a coral beach with some historical significance. Here you will see abandoned World War II amphibious craft rusting on the beach and look out toward the island that served as an American base for capturing Biak from the Japanese in 1944. The beach and surrounding area are still pocked from the intensive shellings and bombings of the island. This is not a good beach for swimming. **Koorem Beach**, located on the other side of the island about two hours from Bosnik Beach, is best for swimming.

Biak's major tourist attraction is the **Japanese Caves** that served as both a hideout and death chamber for nearly 10,000 Japanese soldiers during World War II. The soldiers hid in the caves until they were discovered by the Allies who intensively bombed the site as well as poured aviation fuel into the caves and ignited them. They remain as one of the great holocausts of the Pacific War. Today these caves are an important memorial for the Japanese who come here to pay respects to their fallen friends and relatives. You can visit these caves and a nearby building housing relics (machine guns, helmets, bottles, dishes, hand grenade, radios) that remind you that indeed Biak played an important role in the outcome of World War II. All that is left are these caves, a pock marked landscape, and a few rusting relics of the Japanese occupation and subsequent battles with the Allied Forces.

Since there are few tourists that visit Biak, you will not find many organized tour services and upscale hotels to accommodate you. It is best to rent a car and driver to see the island. One of the best travel agencies for touring the island is **Sentosa Tosiga Tours and Travel** (Jalan A. Yani 36, Tel. 21398 or 21956). You can contact them through the tourist information desk on the second floor of the airport or through the money changer who is also found in the same area.

If you plan to stay overnight in Biak or want a hotel room for a few hours between flights, your best choices for hotels will be the Titawaka Hotel or the Hotel Irian. The **Titawaka Hotel** is located just behind the Sentosa Tosiga Tours and Travel office and the Cleopatra Restoran and art shop; it also has a second location in downtown Biak. The **Hotel Irian** is located across from the airport. Please keep in mind that these are very basic hotels which lack such amenities as hot water.

JAYAPURA

Located on the northeast corner of Irian Jaya, Jayapura is the largest city on the mainland section of this island. Boasting a population of over 200,000, Jayapura is nestled around a picturesque harbor surrounded by steep hills and a lush tropical coastal area. Famous in World War II as General MacArthur's Pacific headquarters, a key city in the struggle for Indonesian independence against Dutch colonial rule, a major center for Christian missionary activity, and a strategic administrative and military area for governing Indonesia's richest and most remote territory, Jayapura is an important city for Indonesia's past, present, and future.

Jayapura is relatively spread out, consisting of a city proper and several suburbs that stretch along a 50 kilometer area from the Sentani Airport to beyond the city. This is a very picturesque area of lush tropical vegetation, beautiful hills and mountains, scenic lake and ocean views, and friendly people. Just outside the airport you can visit MacArthur Hill, the former headquarters of General Douglas MacArthur, who commanded the Pacific War from one of the most scenic and impenetrable spots in Irian Jaya.

The 45 minute drive from Sentani Airport to Jayapura will give you a good introduction to Jayapura. It's a scenic drive along the shores of Lake Sentani, through small towns, and over winding hills that lead into the bustling city of Jayapura. You will see few private cars here—mostly motorcycles, government vehicles, and crowded minivans that serve as public transportation. You will see and smell smoke everywhere as locals keep fires burning to dispose of trash and unwanted vegetation. Combined smoke from fires with the noxious fumes of vehicles give the tropical air of this city a decided Third World odor.

Like so many other upcountry Indonesian towns and cities, Jayapura is not a particularly attractive city. Its main saving grace is its picturesque location on the ocean with a backdrop of steep hills. Aging one and two-story wooden commercial and residential buildings topped with ubiquitous rusting tin roofs line Jayapura's many crowded and narrow streets. The beach at Yos Sudarso Bay in the nearby suburb of Hamadi still houses remnants of World War II. Rusting assault vehicles and Sherman tanks, now serving as trash recepticals, testify to the fact that Jayapura saw some significant action in World War II.

This is a bustling city. Beginning early in the morning until late at night—and except for the traditional afternoon closing hours between 12 noon 4pm—downtown Jayapura is alive with people.

One of the best hotels in town is the Matoa Hotel which is located in the heart of the city along Jl. Jen. A. Yani. From here you can walk to most of the shopping places in the downtown area.

Like Biak, Jayapura is no shoppers' paradise. Most department stores, shops, and markets are geared toward providing basic consumer goods to the local population. However, it does offer a few surprises for those interested in tribal arts and crafts

Jayapura's two main shopping streets are Jl. Jen. A. Yani and Jl. Percetakan located in the central business district. Parallel to one another, both streets can be walked and shopped in less than two hours. We found nothing in the markets, department stores, and shops worthwhile recommending for visitors. These shopping places, especially the long and winding market, are of greatest interest as a cultural experience for observing local residents hawking goods and haggling over prices. The sanitation standards here may quickly turn you off from experiencing similar cultural events in other Indonesian cities. Our best purchase was a bag full of bananas. You will find several department stores in downtown Jayapura, but most of these places sell general consumer goods of interest primarily to local residents. The best time to shop is in the evening when you can observe the interesting nightlife on Jayapura's crowded streets and in the night market and around the town square.

Assuming your shopping interests in Jayapura include tribal arts and crafts, we only found one shop in downtown Jayapura offering such items. The **Matoa Hotel** (Jl. Jen. A. Yani) has a small room just off the main lobby that has numerous excellent quality carved boards and figures. Indeed, we could not find comparative quality Asmat carvings elsewhere in Indonesia. While the prices here may seem high by local standards, they will seem cheap once you see comparative quality carvings—if you can find them—in Bali or Jakarta. The shop will give discounts—20% if you bargain hard.

Most shopping for tribal artifacts in concentrated in the **market at Hamadi Beach**. A rather dirty, smelly, and disorganized market located about 5 kilometers from downtown Jayapura, it houses nine tribal artifact shops that sell a wide range of products: shields, carvings, bags, grass skirts, bows and arrows, spears, penis gourds, drums, axes, bracelets, and baskets. The shops are located next to as well as across the street from each other and go by such names as Madinah, Wamena, Harapan, Cahaya Rahmat, Hasil Budaya, Agats Raya, and Jaya Wijaya. Be sure to bargain hard here. You will find prices in these shops to be one-third to one-half what you will pay for similar items found in the shops of Bali, Jogjakarta, and Jakarta. A US$50 shield here, for example, will sell for US$100 to US$200 elsewhere in Indonesia. If you are looking for old tribal artifacts, you won't find them in these shops. Most of these artifacts have been produced recently. Again, the "good stuff" has gone to quality shops in Bali, Jogjakarta, and Jakarta.

If you are interested in purchasing some unique batik, be sure to visit Jayapura's only batik factory—**Batik Project**. Located one kilometer off the road to the airport—turn right at the sign just after the prison and cemetery but before coming to the Expo site and provincial museum on the left—the Batik Project is sponsored by the United Nations and a foundation. Here you will find a batik factory and shop. What is particularly unique about Batik Project are the local designs using primitive motifs. The shop, which is located on the ground floor of the administrative office building, has a wide selection of ready-made clothes and fabrics. The clothes are produced under the label "Batik JDF." The clothes and fabrics are only available at this factory shop as well as at the foundation office in downtown Jayapura. No other shops in Indonesia carry this brand. We found the motifs and colors to be some of the most attractive of any batik we found in Indonesia. Most of the shirts range in price from Rp. 25,000 to Rp. 35,000. While they do carry some large sizes, most shirts come in small and medium sizes. If you arrive at the administrative building when no one is around, just be patient. The shop may look closed but someone has a key to open it. If you ask for assistance and are persistent, someone will get the key and open the shop. Once inside the shop, you will find there is a back room filled with additional stock. While this room was not lit during our visit—

the light bulb was ostensibly burned out—with the assistance of our flashlight we were able to find some very attractive items.

You will also find two shops at the **airport** selling tribal artifacts. One shop is attached to the restaurant at the entrance of the airport; the second shop is found in the departure lounge. Both shops offer a limited selection of tribal drums, carvings, spears, bags, and penis gourds. However, be forwarded that you will pay about twice as much in these airport shops for the same items found in the market at Hamadi Beach.

There's not a great deal to do in Jayapura itself other than watch people, visit historical World War II sites, and enjoy the beaches. If you stay here a couple of days, you will have time to visit the major attractions: Hamadi Beach, Bestiji (Base G), Lake Sentani, and the provincial museum. Located five kilometers east of downtown Jayapura, **Hamadi Beach** was a major Allied defense area during World War II. Here you can see the remnants of the Pacific War as rusting Sherman tanks and armored personnel carriers line this picturesque beach. **Bestiji**, or Base G, served as General Douglas MacArthur's headquarters after Allied troops seized this area from the Japanese in 1944. A journey to the park and monument at the top of this hilltop command post is rewarded with a lovely panoramic view of the valley. Picturesque **Lake Sentani** is located between the airport and Jayapura. The lake is noted for its unique fishermen and women who live along the shore in stilted houses. The provincial museum, **Museum Negeri Irian Jaya** (Jl. Raya Waena Km. 17,8), has a limited collection of historical and cultural artifacts representative of Irian Jaya's many different ethnic and linguistic groups.

You can rent a car and driver to see these areas or contact a local tour group. One of the best is **Setia Tours and Travel** (Jl. Koti 72, Jayapura, Tel. 22180). Most daily tours cost US$30-60 per person and include hotel pickups and lunch. The tours depart with a minimum of two persons.

Jayapura is also an excellent gateway city into the interior of Irian Jaya. From Jayapura you can arrange tours to visit interior towns and and tribal villages that represent the "real" New Guinea. One of the most popular destinations is the **Baliem Valley** where you can visit the once fierce Dani tribespeople. You fly from Jayapura into the small town of Wamena and then continue on by land into the Baliem Valley. If you are interested in culture and tribal societies, this is one of the most interesting adventures in Indonesia. While you can arrange for guides to take you into the Baliem Valley once you arrive in Wamena, you may want to contact a tour company in Jayapura to arrange a complete tour. Two of the most reliable companies are **Setia Tours & Travel** (J. Koti 72, Jayapura, Tel. 22180) and **Natrabu Tours & Travel** (Jl. Batukarang No. 1, Jayapura, Tel. 22689). These all inclusive tours range in price from US$300 to US$600. Since most Baliem Valley tours take from four to eight days to complete, be sure to budget your time accordingly for your Irian Jaya adventure.

Accommodations in Jayapura tend to be very basic with the major hotels found in the downtown area and Jl. Jen. A. Yani and Jl. Percetakan. The city's best hotel is the Matoa on Jl. Jen. A. Yani. Other hotels include the Hotel Dafonsoro, Irian Plaza Hotel, Triton Hotel, and the Nimbai Hotel.

You may have difficulty finding many good restaurants in Jayapura and few have air-conditioning. The most popular ones are also found along the major downtown streets: Jaya Grill, Hawaii, and Restaurant Nirwana. However, don't expect anything fancy in these establishments.

THE OTHER ISLANDS

The other major areas to visit in Indonesia lie between Bali and Irian Jaya—the Lesser Sundas and the Moluccas. Consisting of thousands of small islands populated by a diverse mixture of ethnic and linguistic groups, these are the least well traveled areas of Indonesia. While most of these islands lack basic tourist facilities, they can be easily reached by plane or ship and offer some shopping opportunities.

THE LESSER SUNDAS

The Lesser Sunda Islands consist of a series of islands within 500 miles east of Bali. The major islands are Lombok, Sumbawa, Komoko, Flores, Alor, Timor, Roti, Sawu, and Sumba. **Lombok** is very similar in geography and culture to Bali and is increasingly becoming a popular destination for tourists from neighboring Bali. **Komodo**, essentially unpopulated, is the popular island for seeing the world's most unique large prehistoric dragon-lizards. **Flores** is one of the most beautiful Indonesian islands outside Bali and Java. **Sumba** is one of the most important islands for unique ikat textiles. **Timor** remains a politically controversial island, but it also offers some unique ikat textiles and woodcarvings.

Venturing into the Lesser Sunda Islands takes some time and patience. Two domestic airlines have regularly scheduled flights into these islands: Merpati and Bouraq. Regular ships and passenger ferries connect the various islands. Once you arrive on these islands, most have surfaced roads and regular transportation, including taxis. You will find adequate accommodations, but not the luxury and first-class accommodations associated with Bali and Jakarta.

The Lesser Sunda Islands produce several items of interest to travelers. Many will be found in the antique shops of Kuta Beach in Bali. Textiles are by far the most popular item found on several of these islands. Each island has its own distinctive textile motifs and colors. The dramatic ikat textiles from Sumba are especially prized by world collectors as are those from Flores, Sawu, Roti, Ndao, Sumbawa, Lombok, and Timor. The Sumba textiles include bold human and animal figures as well as trees, ships, and an occasional bicycle. You also will find unique bronze drums (mokos) on the neighboring islands of Alor and Pantar, woodcarvings and antique ivory on Timor, and Chinese porcelain and antiques on Sumba and Lombok.

THE MOLUCCAS

The Moluccas or Spice Islands are located further east and north of the Lesser Sundas and west of Irian Jaya. Divided into northern and southern sectors, the Moluccas consist of such islands as Tenate, Tidore, Moti, Mare, Makian, Ceram, Ambon, Halmahera, Leti, Bucan, Obi, Sula, and Tanimbar. The domestic airlines Merpati and Bouraq regularly fly into these islands, and you can find ships and passenger ferries to take you there also. You can take such public transportation to do this trip on your own. Alternatively, you can visit the Moluccas in luxury by joining the new "Spice Island" Expedition Cruises, complete with international telephone service, telex, videos, and scuba diving equipment. The 5 to 15-day cruises can be arranged by contacting P.T. Lumba Permai, Jl. S Parman 78 (3rd Floor), Jakarta, Tel. 593401 or 593402.

The Molucca Islands are even less well traveled by tourists than the Lesser Sundas. They have very limited tourist facilities. Furthermore, they offer little in terms of shopping. Several islands produce various shell crafts. You will find unique woodcarvings on the islands of Leti and Tanimbar.

Textiles are found on each of the Molucca Islands. The tribes on **Ceram**, for example, make numerous woven crafts, especially red, blue, and while colored ikat sarongs in geometric patterns. **Tanimbar**, for example, produces unique indigo blue loin cloth with geometric designs which have been historically traded among other islands in the South Moluccas and Timor.

ENJOYING YOUR STAY

Indonesia offers a kaleidoscope of travel and shopping experiences. The scenery is often breath-taking; the food is excellent; service can be outstanding; the flora and fauna are simply incredible; the beaches and scuba diving are some of the world's best; the pace of life is usually relaxing; and the history and culture are rich. Take time to absorb many aspects of this country while you shop. Above all, relax at Lake Toba; tour the museums and visit Beautiful Indonesia in Miniature Park in Jakarta; enjoy the beaches and temples in Bali; visit wildlife preserves and parks on Java; attend wayang puppet and barong dance performances in Jakarta or Jogjakarta; observe the fascinating culture in Toraja Land; and glimpse at the many cultures on Irian Jaya.

Largely undiscovered by international travelers, Indonesia is a multi-faceted country which offers a great deal to travelers and shoppers who know where to go and how to get what they want. Take it easy, and let the Indonesians show you what it is to live in such a incredibly diverse, beautiful, and culturally expressive environment. If you shop and travel exotic Indonesia the way we do, you'll return here again and again to enjoy its many peoples, pleasures, and products!

Index

More Treasures and Pleasures

The following "Impact Guides" can be ordered directly from the publisher. Complete the following form (or list the titles), include your name and address, enclose payment, and send your order to:

IMPACT PUBLICATIONS
9104-N Manassas Drive
Manassas Park, VA 22111 (USA)
Tel. 703/361-7300
Fax 703/335-9486

All prices are in U.S. dollars. Orders from individuals should be prepaid by check, moneyorder, or Visa, MasterCard, or American Express number. If your order must be shipped outside the U.S., please include an additional US$1.50 per title for surface mail or the appropriate air mail rate for books weighting 24 ounces each. We accept telephone orders (credit cards). Orders are shipped within 48 hours.

Qty.	TITLES	Price	TOTAL
__	Shopping and Traveling in Exotic Asia (5 countries)	$16.95	_____
__	Shopping in Exciting Australia and Papua New Guinea	$13.95	_____
__	Shopping the Exotic South Pacific	$16.95	_____
__	Treasures and Pleasures of the Caribbean	$16.95	_____
__	Treasures and Pleasures of Hong Kong	$14.95	_____
__	Treasures and Pleasures of Indonesia	$14.95	_____
__	Treasures and Pleasures of Singapore and Malaysia	$14.95	_____
__	Treasures and Pleasures of Thailand	$14.95	_____

Available in mid-1996:

__ Treasures and Pleasures of India	$14.95	_____
__ Treasures and Pleasures of Italy	$14.95	_____
__ Treasures and Pleasures of Morocco	$14.95	_____
__ Treasures and Pleasures of Paris and the French Riviera	$14.95	_____
__ Treasures and Pleasures of the Philippines	$14.95	_____

SUBTOTAL $ _____

Virginia residents add 4.5% sales tax $ _____

Shipping/handling ($4.00 for the first title and $1.00 for each additional book) $ _____

Additional amount if shipping abroad $ _____

TOTAL ENCLOSED------------- $ _____

SHIP TO:

Name _____

Address _____

_____

_____

PAYMENT METHOD:

❏   I enclose check/moneyorder for $ _____ made payable to IMPACT PUBLICATIONS.

❏   Please charge $ _____ to my credit card:

   ❏ Visa   ❏ MasterCard   ❏ American Express

   Card # _____

   Expiration date: _____

   Signature _____